John Wimber

JOHN WIMBER

His Influence and Legacy

EDITED BY
DAVID PYTCHES

eagle

Guildford, Surrey

British Library Cataloguing in Publication Data. A catalogue record for this book is available from the British Library.

Published by Eagle, an imprint of Inter Publishing Service (IPS) Ltd, St Nicholas House, 14 The Mount, Guildford, Surrey GU2 5HN.

Typeset by Eagle
Printed by Cox & Wyman
ISBN No: 0 86347 277 X

Contents

PREFACE

This book is a compilation from several contributors each focusing mainly on one particular area of John Wimber's life or teaching. It contains many fascinating personal reflections from mature Christian people and significant leaders of our generation, who knew him personally or whose ministries have been beneficially impacted by him. We have not sought to 'gag' our writers in any way, wanting John's character to have the integrity of fallibility; the book attempts to show some of the 'upside' and the 'downside' of John's ministry. One or two contributors may appear in some places to contradict each other – even as James 'appeared' to contradict Paul; but together, I believe, the chapters build up a fair picture of the ministry of an ordinary man whom God used in an extraordinary way; both within the Vineyard and across the wider church in so many parts of the world.

At this time, when a great part of the church is still grieving his passing, it seems fitting to have a book such as this to mark, for our generation, some of the good biblical things John rediscovered for us: the particular treasures he has left to the church in his 'will', as it were. They are culled from personal experiences and memories of conferences, from his books and many tapes, from his inspired gift for imparting knowledge and his public modelling of its application, and also from some writers' own reflections in putting his teaching into practice in the local church. This book does not pretend to be a biography, though an 'official' biography may yet appear, but it does include a great number

of interesting biographical insights, which will help the
reader to understand the man and see where John was
coming from in his ministry and also to underscore his
legacy to us.

David Pytches
April 1998

1

A MAN CALLED JOHN

DAVID PYTCHES

*David Pytches (b. 1931) was on the staff of St Ebbe's,
Oxford and in charge of St Patrick's, Wallington, Surrey
before going to South America with his wife Mary in 1959.
He was consecrated a bishop in 1969 and elected Bishop of
the Anglican Diocese of Chile, Bolivia and Peru in 1972.
He was vicar of St Andrew's, Chorleywood from
1977–96. He has written numerous books – the latest,*
Leadership for New Life *(Hodders), and overseen the*
New Wine Christian Family Conferences *at the Royal Bath
& West Showground since they were started in 1989.*

The *Daily Telegraph* obituary column (25:11:97)
described John Wimber as an evangelist. True! I
remember him telling how that in the early years after
his conversion, in the mode of his spiritual mentor,
Gunner Payne, God used him to lead many hundreds
to Christ. He just loved it. Evangelism was fundamental to all John's ministry, but he became much more
than an evangelist – he was an apostle, a prophet, a pastor and a teacher beside. And these gifts were used to
inspire the church worldwide. It is reported thatRobert
Schuller, renowned pastor of the Crystal Cathedral and
worldwide tele-evangelist, called John 'one of the
twelve most influential Christian leaders of the last two
decades'. Peter Wagner, pioneer of the School of
Church Growth at Fuller Theological Seminary and
prodigious producer of books, has written that 'John

was one of those extremely rare people who will be
remembered as a molder of an entire generation'. Jim
Packer, revered theologian and extensive writer,
described him as 'one of the outstanding leaders of our
time'. Rick Warren, inspiring practical visionary known
for planting and growing one of the most remarkable
churches of the decade, referred to John as 'a man who
truly loved Jesus more than anything else. I always
enjoyed our conversations because that love for Christ
caused an uncommon passion in his life that was con-
tagious.'

A respected doctor of science once assured me that
in his academic world the influence of another scientist
would not necessarily be measured by the number of
books that the scientist himself had written, but by the
number of times he had been named or quoted in books
written by others – whether in disapproval or approval.
On such a rule of thumb, John Wimber's influence must
surely be rated as considerable – especially if 'air-time'
is included.

Others have been raised up specifically to impact the
minister in the pulpit, but John Wimber had a unique
way of reaching the man in the pew also. There were
few Christian leaders who could expect a gathering of
between two to five thousand in so many of the major
cities across the world that included such a large number of leaders of all Christian denominations.

Where did this man come from?
John was born, an only child, in Peoria, Illinois, the
American Midwest, on February 25th 1934. His father
left home soon after and he was brought up in a one-
parent family. 'I had barely emerged from my mother's
womb when my father abandoned both mom and me.
This, along with the fact that I had no brothers and sisters, explains why I was so withdrawn as a child spending long hours alone . . .' John wrote. It was years later,

towards the end of his life that, for the first time, he met two half-brothers, his father's offspring from a second marriage.

His maternal grandfather was a significant influence during his early boyhood. John used to watch him training horses to trot in a particular stylish mode by yoking an experienced horse with a younger one. He became so impressed with his grandfather's training techniques, that he used the model later as a method for training laity.

There was no religious influence in his early life. He described himself as a fourth-generation pagan: 'I didn't even know God had a book out!' he used to say. 'I do not think I had ever met a Christian – if I did he never blew his cover!'

He was raised in a deprived environment

He could recall the familiar neighbourhood streets of badly constructed homes. He also watched them all being pulled down for redevelopment before he left the area. His mother remarried after a few years, when they had moved to California; the state which, except for a short break in Las Vegas, was to become his home for the rest of his life.

His stepfather was a good man but never filled the void left by his father. Feelings of rejection and abandonment were not helped when in his early twenties he finally met up again with his natural father. His hopes that a meaningful loving father/son relationship might still develop were disappointed.

One of John's major interests as a lonely teenager was his music and he had a fine voice. We heard an early record of his tenor singing in a review of his life at the funeral memorial in Anaheim, California, and it displayed delightful talent. He could play a wide range of instruments (over twenty), including piano, strings and wind; his favourite being the saxophone. Another talent

was the teaching, writing, directing, orchestrating and
recording of music.

Into the world of jazz

While still a teenager, John became involved in the local
jazz clubs, playing his first professional music gig at the
Dixie Castle, Orange County, California in 1949 when
he was only fifteen, and in 1953 he won first prize at the
Lighthouse International Jazz Festival. He was soon
earning a living providing musical back-up for numerous Hollywood films. In 1962, he brought a music
group together which called itself 'The Righteous
Brothers' that reached the top of the charts a couple of
times.

Marriage and young family

John had married Carol in 1955; a non-practising
Roman Catholic. She was the eldest child of a local
medical practitioner with three sisters and a brother.
John and Carol lived in Westminster, California. By the
time they had three children – two boys and a girl –
their marriage deteriorated until tragically they separated. It was 1961 when John decided to move out to
Las Vegas, two hundred and fifty miles away in
Nevada, a neon-lit gambling centre. He went there to
look into the possibility of a sixty-day no-fault divorce.
While there he shared with a friend in the band the
despair he felt over his marriage to Carol. The friend
encouraged him to go out into the desert and watch the
sunrise. 'It's great! – A really cool way to "groove in" to
a religious experience,' he said. 'You should try it!' John
had to confess he had never been particularly interested in sunrises before but he decided to give it a go.
Motoring out to the desert very early the next morning
he found himself weeping uncontrollably. He felt he
was being overwhelmed by Someone or Something
without the vaguest idea who or what? Then choosing

a suitable spot he pulled up in his car and got out. Agonizing to the starry heavens he cried: 'If there is anyone out there, please help me!' He thought he was alone but, suddenly sensing he might have been seen, he felt embarrassed and began to kick the cacti at his feet. 'I'm talking to the dark. I'm going crazy,' he said to himself. 'I'd better commit myself into a hospital!' Then, remembering his mother's advice about having clean clothes in case of accident and being unexpectedly taken to hospital, he thought he had better get back first and change – besides there were some drugs he would need to hide also.

Carol says 'Come and get me?'

Once back in the hotel, John was amazed to find a message from Carol asking him to phone her. He was even more amazed, on doing so, to hear her say: 'Come and get me, John. I want to try one more time to make our marriage work.' Only hours before John had been crying out to the heavens – and now this! – there had to be some connection. He must have been in touch with the supernatural! 'Hot Dog!' he cried, looking up to heaven once again, 'you got her to change her mind!' She had seemed so insistent about a divorce that he knew only some force bigger than she could have made her do this. John believed he had discovered Something greater than himself though he still did not have a clue who this could be. What he did not know at the time was that Carol had also been praying to the God of her childhood asking for help. Through some insight from her past slight knowledge of the Bible she sensed an evil force was trying to destroy their marriage. Once John had put down the phone he drove at top speed to collect Carol and the children and take them back to Las Vegas. He told her he was in touch with the supernatural! She asked what he meant, and when he explained, she told him it was called 'prayer'.

Old friends: new life

In November 1962, one of John's old friends suddenly
appeared in Las Vegas, looking for them. This was Dick
Heying, who had at one time been a stand-in drummer
for their band. But Dick and his wife Lynn had very
recently become Christians. They had travelled quite a
distance from LA. They had taken some gin with them
in the car as a gift for John who they knew was a heavy
drinker (not to mention his five packs of cigarettes a
day and the drugs).

To reinforce themselves against a sudden unfore-
seen drop in temperature, they opened the bottle en
route. The journey got colder and colder and the gin in
the bottle got lower and lower. By the time they arrived
their state was not quite as they had intended.
Obviously something wonderful had happened to them
but they were hardly coherent in sharing the good
news. Their breath was reeking of spirits. John, in no
way put off by their evident intoxication, was highly
intrigued. He interrogated them closely. Afterwards
Dick felt very ashamed at their inebriated state; their
greatest desire had simply been to share their new-
found faith with their old friends. He prayed for another opportunity to speak.

'King James' Virgin'

Both John and Carol now found they had an insatiable
thirst for a deeper knowledge of God. Having searched
the usual shops in vain, they finally discovered where
they could buy Bibles in Las Vegas. John wanted to be
sure he got a genuine one. A man in a bar told them to
ask for the 'King James Virgin'! The girl at the Bible
shop smiled and sold them King James Versions which
they both began reading but found difficult to understand.

Las Vegas was not good for family life and they
returned to Orange County where Carol soon became

pregnant with their fourth child – a son. In their search for a suitable spiritual environment and a school for their children, they went to the Catholic church in the area where Carol had been brought up. John started taking instruction in the Catholic faith and Carol began going to confession regularly. They renewed their wedding vows with the church's blessing since their first marriage, conducted by a Baptist pastor, picked at random from a telephone guide, was not considered valid by the Catholic priest. This was the first occasion when John had ever been inside a Christian church building.

All the while they felt themselves to be drawing closer to God, though John began having difficulties with his priest. He found out later that the priest was simultaneously going through some problems of his own. Impatient with John's persistent questions he had brought the period of instruction to an abrupt conclusion.

First experience of church

Dick Heying, now so much nearer the Wimbers in their new home, began dropping by casually to talk to John. Lynn would be frequently on the phone with Carol. The Heyings wanted to talk about their faith and the Wimbers were only too keen to listen. The Heyings begged the Wimbers to visit their church. John shared his impressions at a public meeting later which was taped – he admitted he might have been exaggerating a little but he was making a point. Men he took to be 'bouncers', with flowers in their lapels, showed the Wimbers to the very front seats and one of them handed John a 'menu' with a big smile and a loud greeting. John studied the 'menu' uncomprehendingly. 'What does it say, dad?' asked one of the boys. 'Hell, I don't know, son,' replied John, never previously having been confronted by such pious terminology. He needed to dispose of his cigarette but could find no ashtrays in the pews. Then he was troubled by the musicians – to John's professional ear they were awful. And a man in the seat behind John joined them loudly in one of the congregational psalms in a voice a long way off the notes – about six inches off, John thought!

Next there was the preacher's voice. It seemed strangely 'throttled'. In answer to John's questions afterwards Dick explained that they all sounded like that. Dick believed they were trained to speak that way in seminary. Finally there was an 'altar call'. In spite of his unfamiliarity with religious language and ecclesiastical furnishings John knew an altar when he saw one – he'd been to the cinema and seen the altar-bound heroine surrounded with flames of fire leaping up around her just waiting to be rescued! When the 'call' came John was still searching for the altar as people came forward and knelt at the rails right in front of him. 'Most of my problems,' John explained later, 'were due to the fact that I had not yet learned to speak Christian-ese.' When the service finally closed, John could not wait to get out.

Dick caught up with him. 'How did you like it John?'

John: That was weird!

Dick: I was about to ask you to come again tonight?

John: How often do you have to do this?

Dick: We come every time they open the doors. We love it. This is our church.

It certainly gave John something to think about.

Meeting a spare-time evangelist

In 1963, Dick introduced John to Lawrence Gunner Payne, an evangelist in his spare time, who was currently having weekly meetings for Bible study with a group of about twenty-five people.

The Wimbers were keen to find someone who could answer their questions, but John was too embarrassed about showing his ignorance of the Bible before such a large group.

By April 1963, John and Carol had started attending a new, but smaller, group. It had been specially planned for this to meet on Tuesdays. John was still not sure he wanted to go to it so he declined. He had a good excuse. Being a musician who was out playing into the early hours of every morning, he only had one night off weekly from his work and that was on a Monday. Half an hour later he got a call back saying they had changed the night to Monday. John now had no excuse, but he was also bowled over by their readiness to switch their diaries around so unselfishly just for him.

Once there John found he had a problem. He was not really interested in discussing Jesus. He wanted to know about God. He felt talk about Jesus was getting off track. Carol was quite clear about why she was there. She just wanted to know 'Who is Jesus Christ?' For three or four months these meetings were held weekly and frequently went on well past midnight. Week in and week out they hammered Gunner with their questions while at home they were now reading modern versions of the Bible in earnest. John was increasingly impressed by Gunner's character; he appeared so sound, complete and uncorrupted. Nothing seemed to matter to him but living for God and the peace of God seemed to pervade his life. Gunner's witness was more important to John than his words. The way he lived embodied the gospel he preached. John was hungry to know his secret.

Carol leads the way

Walking into the kitchen one morning, after they had been attending the Bible study group for a few weeks, John heard Carol declaring that she had found the answer. 'Jesus is the Son of God,' she said. 'Yeah! And Chicago is in Illinois. So what?' John replied, still

uncomprehending. 'But that changes every thing,' said
Carol. 'It means there is something we need to do.' But
still she could not fathom what it was.

They kept up with the Bible studies, now sometimes
driving there hours early just to be in the area – surely
God must live there, they felt. They would call in on
Gunner at his welding workshop. 'What do we need to
do?' they begged him. 'Nothing yet!' he would say. 'It's
too soon. You're not ready yet. Premature births don't
produce healthy children. Apples fall when they are
ripe.'

Thought I was a good guy

It was the relevance of the cross and the need for a liv-
ing relationship with Jesus that changed John radically.
'The cross made this kind of change in me at a home
Bible study group in 1963,' he wrote later.

> I remember that evening as though it were last
> night. I did not arrive having planned to turn to
> Christ . . . I had learned a lot *about* Christ and the
> cross – I could have passed an elementary exam on
> the atonement. But I didn't understand that I was a
> sinner. I thought I was a good guy. Oh, I knew I had
> messed up here and there, but I didn't realise how
> serious my condition was.

During that same meeting Carol suddenly announced
to Gunner that she thought it was time to do something
about the things they had been talking about. Then,
aghast, John watched her going down on her knees to
the floor weeping. She began telling God how sorry she
was for all her sins. It suddenly dawned on John that
God was Someone one could really talk to about these
things. In a flash he understood and, like Carol, he
ended up on the floor crying out to God for forgiveness.
At the same time he was thinking, 'I hope this works,

because I am making a complete fool of myself.' It
brought to John's mind a man he had seen years before
when he had gone into Los Angeles to borrow some
money off a 'druggy' friend. Waiting in the plaza he
spied a man parading between a sandwich placard. It
bore the words 'A fool for Christ's sake!' on the one side
and 'Whose fool are you?' on the other. John had
thought it the most stupid thing he had seen in his life.
Now he was beginning to realise what it meant 'The
message of the cross is foolishness to those who are per-
ishing' (1 Cor 1:18). 'That night at the cross I believed in
Jesus,' wrote John. 'I have been a fool for Christ ever
since.' Something revolutionary had been going on
inside John – he was certainly changing.

Parable of the pearl

It was while sitting at the feet of Gunner Payne that
John first heard the parable of the Pearl of Great Price.
Gunner was explaining about the need to be willing to
sacrifice everything in life for God's Kingdom. 'The
kingdom of heaven is like a merchant looking for fine
pearls. When he found one of great value, he went
away and sold everything he had and bought it' (Matt
13:45–46). This suddenly caught John's attention. 'Hold
on!' he said. 'Are you saying that in order to become a
Christian somebody might have to give up everything
he has?'

'Well what do you think it means?' Gunner replied.

'I'm not sure,' said John. 'It sounds like it might
mean that. But – well, I know a guy who is a musician.
He does not know how to do anything except play
music. I mean this guy can't even tie up his own
shoelaces. Are you saying he might have to give up his
music career in order to become Christian? How else
could he make a living?'

'Your friend would have to work that out for himself,' said Gunner, who understood perfectly well that

they were talking about John. 'But in my opinion, he has to be ready to give up his career because it is a possibility.' As he said that John was thinking, 'No way!' He was on the threshold of musical success. The group he was with had records in the Top Ten. 'This is crazy. I'm finally a success. And I am about to make a *lot* of money. *No way* am I going to give it all up now,' thought John.

During the next few days he felt miserable, cursing and swearing around the house. So far he had liked all that he had learned from the Bible and was inwardly saying 'Yes! Yes! Yes!' all the way, but now this . . . he had run into a real problem. 'To think that I might have to give up everything, even my career, to go on with God,' he grumbled. It was hell. Within three weeks he was on the floor crying out to God repenting. 'I knew I had found the Pearl of Great Price. And I was so glad to have it. I just did not care anymore what God might ask in return for it.' Over the next few weeks, with the help of God, he began to liquidate his assets. He prayed 'OK, Lord, you can have my career,' and it was as though two giant hands came out of heaven to prize fingers open as a voice said 'Thank you!' and took it.

John decided to get a regular job.

Goodbye 'Righteous Brothers'

To the great chagrin of the Righteous Brothers John announced his decision to leave them. He told me once that he would not necessarily suggest that others following Christ should take the same course of action, but it was something he felt God clearly wanted from him. The course of his life was beginning to move in a completely new direction though for while he could not see clearly where God was leading him. 'Suddenly,' he wrote, 'I was in the real world where *alarm clocks* go off, where people get up and go to work in *broad daylight*. I had never done this. In a matter of weeks I was working in a factory, clocking in and learning how to relate to normal people.'

It so happened that one day he was assigned to clean some oil drums and was out at the back of the factory. The work was hot, filthy and smelly – the most menial job one could be asked to do. John was down inside one of the oil drums when he heard a car drive up. A voice he recognised called out: 'Where's John Wimber's office?' Reluctantly John clambered out of his filthy drum. He really did not want to meet an old friend from the music business right then. 'In his hand was a contract I had signed that was worth a lot of money. In order for him to fulfil it, I had to relinquish my part of it.' The man stood staring at John who looked an absolute mess with grease all over his hands, clothes, face and hair. Finally, looking puzzled, he said, 'What *are* you doing here?' 'I looked at him and back at myself,' said John, 'and I could see myself as he must have seen me.

Right at that moment I did not particularly feel like I had the Pearl of Great Price and I could not think of a single thing to say. After a long silence I said lamely "God did this to me." His eyes narrowed with a look of resolve, as if to say "He's never going to do that to me".' John felt ashamed. Obviously this must have seemed utter folly to his friend, but at that moment he could not think of a single persuasive explanation for why God should seemingly be leading him that way. He watched his friend drive off and realised that sometimes there is no way of explaining obedience and sacrifice to God to those who know nothing of the Pearl. His friend could see no value at all in the humiliating way God seemed to be leading John – stripping him of his lofty position in the music world and teaching him simple obedience.

It appeared natural for John to follow the model of 'Gunner' Payne and start evangelising and he did this very effectively; indeed he and Carol began leading

many to Christ. They were soon into personal evangelism in a big way. They sensed the 'presence' of God on
their ministry. But John said later, 'We did not realise
that the presence and the power were the same thing.'

Although John was 'baptised in the Holy Spirit' in
1964, he was not baptised in water until 1978 due to his
Christian upbringing in the Quaker Church which
interpreted the sacraments spiritually and did not minister baptism or the Lord's Supper in any physical
sense.

Full time ahead

By 1970 John was leading eleven Bible study groups a
week. By the next year he was taken on the staff of the
Yorba Linda Friends Church where his brother-in-law,
Bob Fulton, was on staff already as a youth pastor.
Thirsty to increase his understanding of Scripture, John
also began studying theology at the Azusa Pacific
University, a Pentecostal foundation, where he earned a
degree in Biblical Studies. During his time with the
'Friends', John saw this church grow from 200 to 800,
becoming the largest church of their denomination – so
much so that they had to build a new facility. But then
it seemed it could grow no bigger. John realised that
family powerblocks were controlling the church. They
were resisting growth because they saw that if it
became any bigger their power to control would significantly diminish. One good lady even accused John of
'ruining her church'. He knew what she meant. John
was frustrated with himself too. He had been in this
church for nearly thirteen years. He was conforming to
a degree where his conscience felt uncomfortable. 'I
was institutionalising myself,' he said. He 'was preaching the party line.'

Peter Wagner, a disciple of Donald Mcgavran, and a
former missionary in Bolivia, had arrived at Fuller
Seminary (in 1971) to teach on evangelism and church

growth, and in 1974 John signed up for the course. Peter soon recognised John's gift as an evangelist, his talent for clear analysis and his practical comprehension of the principles of church growth, so he invited John to become a founding director of the new School of Church Growth. This was to be in what has since been re-named the Charles E. Fuller Institute of Evangelism and Church Growth.

John also became a church consultant, which involved him in travelling extensively across the American continent and meeting many different church leaders from many different denominations. During his three and half years doing this John reckoned that he had met with some 40,000 pastors coming from twenty-seven different denominations and nine para-church organisations. But he was beginning to feel an increasing sense of physical stress (the onset of his heart problem) and spiritual barrenness.

The church consultant has a paradigm shift

The experience on the teaching staff at Fuller and amongst the different denominations had brought John into stimulating and fruitful contact with some deep thinking and widely read Christians. He was introduced to George Eldon Ladd's writings on the Kingdom of God when he saw that the heart of the gospel lay in the Kingdom of God. 'Power for effective evangelism and discipleship relates directly to our understanding and experiencing the Kingdom today.' Many who came on the courses at Fuller were very dedicated and experienced missionaries. Their reports on 'signs and wonders' in the Third World, together with Eldon Ladd's teaching, directed John's thoughts towards the Holy Spirit and divine healing.

He discovered Francis McNutt's book, *Healing*. He said: 'I carried the book around for months, reading it at a time when I didn't believe in healing. I'd been

trained as a cessationist regarding spiritual gifts, with
the notion that God "didn't do that" today.' He became
especially interested in the relationship between healing and church growth overseas. He sensed his world-
view was changing. Hitherto he had seen life through a
rational materialistic Western world-view. He realised
that he was undergoing a paradigm shift in his
approach to the Bible and theology. He was beginning
to understand life supra-rationally. John also found he
was developing a love for the whole church; denominations no longer mattered to him. He was encounter-
ing more and more evangelical anomalies. He once
described his amazement when he met a beer-drinking
Lutheran priest who led a barmaid to Christ in a pub! In
John's book Lutheran priests were not supposed to be
able to do that – let alone a beer-drinking one! He came
to love Richard Baxter's maxim: 'In necessary things,
unity; in doubtful things, liberty; in all things charity.'
How often he would remind his future hearers 'Your
brother is not your enemy. Your brother is your brother – is your brother!'

Quaker rejects

During this time, John and his family had still remained
members of their Quaker church. Then his wife Carol,
her sister Penny and her husband Bob Fulton and nearly forty others, all became 'baptised in the Holy Spirit'.
According to John, Carol had been particularly hostile
to anything of the sort; especially divine healing. This
was possibly due to being the child of a doctor. She
described the result of her new Holy Spirit experience
graphically as a 'personality meltdown' and soon after
she had a dream from which she awoke speaking in
tongues! She went through some weeks of deep repentance with a lot of weeping, believing she had grieved
the Lord by her previous attitude – prejudice and resistance to the Holy Spirit. Others of her friends were

going through similar experiences. Their Quaker church became increasingly uneasy about this and eventually asked them to leave. They did this regretfully and began meeting in a private home to worship God – some thirty of them. Carol, who had always said she would not want John to lead a church again, was becoming convinced that God wanted John to be their pastor. She let him know that if he ever felt God calling him back into pastoring a local church she would support him, but John brushed off the idea. He would never want to pastor another church; churches were too hard on their pastors.

Desperate in Detroit

One winter's night in 1977, when John was flying into Detroit, he was crying out to God in desperation. He felt spiritually bankrupt and physically sick – the latter were early symptoms of the heart troubles that were to hamper him for the rest of his life. He had missed the first plane and was flying in late. When he arrived it was snowing hard and there was no one to meet him. He booked into the Metropolitan Hotel at the airport. Feeling so ill and exhausted, he knelt at his bedside and opened his Bible to read it 'for himself'. 'Don't get me wrong,' he said, 'I was reading the Bible all the time preparing one talk after another but I realised it was a long time since I had read it "for myself".' He turned to Psalm 61 (a psalm which was to become a favourite and was read at his graveside); it started, 'Hear my cry, O God; listen to my prayer. From the ends of the earth I call to you, I call as my heart grows faint; lead me to the rock that is higher than I.' The psalm reflected exactly his desperate condition. Still crying out to God he fell asleep. He later awoke and crawled into bed. During the night he sensed that God was speaking into his heart and he heard the Lord say: 'John, I've seen *your* ministry. Now I want to show you *mine*.' He began to weep with relief and thanksgiving. *Lord that's all I ever wanted*,' he said. He did not understand till later that this experience marked a turning point in his relationship with God.

God was 'on his case'

John was speaking on the subject of 'spiritual gifts' at a church conference near home soon after and the pastor told him there was a female in the church who had a prophecy for him. John had already noticed the rather plump little lady he referred to, and felt the last thing he would want was a prophecy from her. But the pastor insisted that she really did hear from God, and he should meet her, so they planned a meeting outside in the grounds. She arrived at the appointed time and started weeping – she went on and on and on. Feeling perplexed and even annoyed, after about a half hour John eventually stopped her and said: 'When are you going to give me the prophecy? – I thought you had a word from the Lord for me!' 'That's it,' she said, 'God is weeping over you!' And saying that, she was gone.

Later she came to him again with another word: 'God wants to know when you are going to use your authority?'

'What does that mean?' asked John.

'I don't know what it means,' she said, 'I just get the messages!'

Wimber felt that God, for some good reason, was certainly 'on his case'. Following this, he reckoned God spoke to him in nineteen different ways about his future ministry. Peter Wagner casually suggested to him one day that he ought to think about starting a church which modelled what he was beginning to teach about – the connection between evangelism and signs and wonders. Soon after, a Lutheran pastor in a Church Growth seminary in New York, came up to John saying he was very embarrassed but he felt that the message

God had given him was for John. He had written it down on a folded piece of paper. This he then gave him. Opened up it read, simply: 'Go home!' John finally got the message and resigned from his job at Fuller's.

John's new flock

He took over the little flock of ejected Quakers. To begin with he could not understand why they spent so much time just singing tender worship songs, but then he began to discern the new thing God was doing and entered into it with all his heart. He even wrote some songs himself and joined the music group playing his synthesiser keyboard, a practice he was to continue for several years to come. This group had officially linked with another denomination for a short time, but John could not forget what he sensed the Lord had told him about his priority as a leader being to bless what God was doing. The group soon developed its own particular values and ethos. Needing the freedom to do just that it became an independent congregation calling itself now the Vineyard Christian Fellowship.

Searching for premises

As the VCF grew numerically the search was kept up for new premises to rent. They settled for a time at the Canyon High School in the Anaheim Hills for their Sunday worship. In spite of an early commitment to plant churches out into other areas (over eighty planted out from this original fellowship in the first twenty years), this centre also eventually became too small. They moved again to larger rented accommodation until they finally acquired their own property where they are now.

The vast complex at La Palma, Anaheim Hills, which became their new home, had been built originally for a company dealing in the production of high-tech aero equipment. After several internal re-developments, including a worship centre with seating for over three thousand, there were still numerous large halls for lecture rooms and classrooms and plenty of office space, storerooms, and a separate business department for producing 'Vineyard Ministries International' music tapes. Numerous new composers were encouraged through the opportunities John gave them from this 'platform'. The interiors of the building were well equipped but decorated very simply – nothing ornate except for a few appropriate banners. The only exception was a most beautiful gift to the church by the artist, of a remarkable life-size sculpture – a bronze statue of Christ washing the disciples' feet, which greeted visitors inside, on their way to the worship sanctuary.

Mercy ministries

Another huge facility alongside the main building served as a warehouse for storing foodstuffs. They were latterly distributing thousands of dollars' worth of food to the poor on a regular basis, amounting to a million meals a year for the destitute. There was still plenty of floor space in this other building for a Christian bookshop and a Christian school for children.

From the beginning, John tried to be faithful to his commitment to try and discern and to do whatever he sensed God was doing, and do all he could to bless that, rather than making his own plans and asking God to bless them. He underlined those verses, 'Except the LORD build the house they labour in vain that build it' and 'Every plant that the Father has not planted will be rooted out'!

Laid back Californian style

When they met together, their Californian style was very much 'laid back'. The first thing that struck me, as a visitor to the Canyon High School, was the informality of their dress. 'Casual' would be an understatement.

This approach was carried over also into the conduct of worship. The music leader, in tee-shirt, shorts and trainers, would stand up with his guitar before the mike on a raised platform, and invite folks to sing along and worship the Lord. And there was John Wimber on the synthesiser and Dick Heying, now on the drums behind him! (I used to wonder what Dick must have felt to see those thousands before them and to recognise that he had been a small link in the chain that brought these crowds together?) The music that followed matched their culture and was, in spite of all appearances, superbly professional. Everyone soon entered into it, and seemed truly lost in wonder, love and praise; this singing would continue unabated for about forty to forty-five minutes. The stunning impact of this was profound and unforgettable! Then there would be brief notices and a report, a testimony, a prophecy or the dedication of babies. This was followed by a further forty-five minutes of teaching from John.

Liberated preacher

John read widely and always listened carefully. He was proud of his large library packed with Bible commentaries and knew where every book should be on the shelves, systematically numbered and categorised, John had a clear mind for easy analysis and a very retentive memory for facts. This made him a fascinating speaker or conversationalist and, wherever he was, people within earshot would fall silent to listen in rapt attention. His pulpit practice was to expound passages of Scripture with plenty of illustration (often very personal). He majored on the central meaning of the Word. He would stress that 'the main thing was the plain thing and the plain thing was the main thing'. John could relate a story brilliantly and could make it very humorous so that the crowds were frequently crying with laughter – a very cathartic experience. When he sensed he had expounded for long enough he would simply break off and pick up from there the next time. Each talk was recorded.

Over the twenty years with the Anaheim VCF John worked through thirty-seven books of the Bible, verse by verse, besides preaching through many major series on subjects such as the Kingdom of God, the cross, worship, prayer, discipleship, holiness, prophecy, healing, deliverance, equipping the saints, giving, leadership, church-planting, temptation, trials and suffering, and mercy ministry to the poor etc. The informal service would end with a short blessing and any that felt they needed prayer were invited to come forward, and then trained team-members would take them off quietly and minister to them. While others might leave to go home many would stay around for drinks and doughnuts, chatting or waiting for friends needing prayer

'Corporate renewal'

In early 1980 the Vineyard had an experience of the Holy Spirit which John Gunstone referred to as one of 'corporate renewal'. On the evening of Mother's Day, a young man named Lonnie Frisbee gave his testimony. He was one of God's irregulars and had been an early convert of the 1960s Jesus movement, where he became one of the leaders working with Chuck Smith. He followed this testimony by asking a number of young people to come forward.

Then he simply called the Holy Spirit down upon them in the name of Jesus. Some 400 of them fell about crying, groaning and speaking in tongues. Neither John nor the congregation had ever experienced anything like that before. Though John sensed it was good, it was so unusual that he was concerned lest they could be being deceived in any way. He had a duty to protect his flock if this was not God. Staying up all night reading through the history of revivals and praying, John finally cried out 'Lord, if this is you, please tell me?' Within moments the phone rang at John's side. A friend from Denver, Colorado, was calling. 'John,' he said, 'I'm sorry I am calling so early but I have something very strange to pass on to you. I don't know what it means, but God wants me to tell you simply, "It's Me, John!" ' That was all, but that was all John needed to know. He would not be alarmed by outward manifestations again.

Disappointed and almost disillusioned over healing

Leading up to this 'Pentecost', John had been disappointed about the very limited physical healing they were experiencing in the fellowship. A verse, John 14:12, impacted John powerfully where Jesus had said: 'I tell you the truth, anyone who has faith in me will do what I have been doing . . .' His new understanding of this verse was a life-changing moment for John. He began to preach sermons on healing – his people had been praying for the sick from the time John had adopted the group as their pastor, but no one was seeing any significant results.

When after some ten months someone was actually healed, John could hardly believe it. A member of the VCF had asked John to visit his home and pray for his wife. John went with a sinking heart to find the woman in bed with a heavy fever. Very diffidently he laid his hands on her head and then turned to the husband to explain why people are not often healed. As he did so he realised the husband was not listening but looking past John's shoulder and grinning. On turning round, John was astonished to see the woman was already up out of bed and looking perfectly healthy. 'What's happened?' asked John. 'I'm well!' she said. 'Would you like to stay for some coffee?' John politely declined and left excitedly. 'I could not believe it,' he said later. 'She was well!' He needed time to think about this alone. Once away in the car he was suddenly overwhelmed by what had happened. 'We've got one!' he yelled at the top of his voice.

This was the beginning of a whole new dimension in John's ministry. On the way home John saw a vision of a huge honeycomb – it was high up in the sky and dripping honey. All sorts of people were gathered round it – some simply catching it and eating it. Some were taking some and sharing it with their families and friends. Others were watching fascinated. Others were standing by scoffing. He felt God was saying to him: 'John, that's my mercy. For some it's a blessing and for others it's not, but there is plenty for everyone. The problem is not with the supply – the problem is with the people.' John was sure that healings could be expected as signs of the Kingdom of God. By the time of his death it was estimated that a million sets of John's teaching tapes on healing and the Kingdom of God had been distributed, with probably double that number duplicated and shared around the world. I myself sent one set (from a case-full given me by John) to a friend in Chile. He listened to them with another Chilean friend of his. Having heard them, the latter went off and planted a Vineyard Fellowship, and ended up planting another four.

First heard about Wimber

I first heard about John Wimber in 1980, through Eddie Gibbs, a former missionary and friend from Chile, and it was agreed that he would sound John out for me about coming to the UK. I had been praying for some time that God would show us the next step for St Andrew's though I really had little idea of what it could be. My particular concern was the use of the gifts of the Spirit in the life of the local church. I became especially enthusiastic about having John after I knew that David

Watson, the vicar of St Michael-le-Belfry in York, had also met him during his visit to Fuller Seminary, California, in 1981. David wrote after that visit to say that 'his ministry would never be the same again!' David Watson was such a respected leader of 'the renewal' in the UK that this certainly helped confirm for me the rightness of having approached John (of whom I had only heard and never met) about coming. David also invited John to St Michael-le-Belfry. 'Good!' I thought to myself – 'we can go shares on John's travelling expenses.' John duly arrived at St Andrew's with a team of some twenty-nine others to teach on 'Equipping the Saints for the Work of the Ministry' on the weekend of Pentecost, 1981. I immediately warmed to John, as nearly everyone did who met him.

Embarrassing misunderstanding

But I was almost in shock. There seemed to have been some terrible misunderstanding. How were we ever going to cover the cost of so many air fares? I thought I ought to explain my problem to John as soon as possible. 'But who has said anything about your paying for all this. We believe God has sent us. All we ask is that if God blesses you in any way as a result of our visit then you give it away. "Freely you have received – freely give"! Remember?' I accepted the conditions with relief though I had no idea quite what wonderful blessing we were about to receive.

Another little incident at the very beginning impacted me profoundly. We were sitting in the church lounge for a team briefing before the first meeting. John was walking to and fro, perhaps a little nervously, giving some advice about differences of culture. He went on, 'I think in deference to our British host church we might moderate the ministry somewhat this weekend.' Suddenly I heard him say: 'Wait a minute. I just want to backtrack on that last statement. That was not the Lord

– that was me! You do just whatever you feel the Lord
is telling you to do!' I thought: 'This man is certainly not
trying to impress anyone – how unusual!' The visit
turned out to be a church-changing event for us. A
whole book could be written of all that happened. One
startling healing miracle, among so many remarkable
blessings, happened to an elderly lady who received
sight back in a blind eye – something I had never
believed I would ever see in an Anglican church!

He left his ministry with us

Someone commented afterwards: 'We have had many
visiting preachers who have blessed us and when they
have gone they have taken their ministry with them,
but John Wimber came and left his ministry with us.'
John was himself surprised at the positive impact of his
visit to both these 'renewing' churches. We were
delighted to see (and experience) such powerful lay
ministry being modelled for us. This was very significant.

In the UK the charismatic movement which had
influenced many Christians profoundly since the 1960s
was turning into a preaching bandwagon. We had benefited greatly in our individual spirituality from their
teaching. Many had been filled with the Holy Spirit and
received 'gifts', but now there was a great longing to see
how it could be worked out in the life of the local
church. To be real it had to be local. There were no
model churches where people could go to see 'the
saints' actually ministering in the gifts and power of the
Holy Spirit. One felt these splendid teachers had opted
out of the local church because they could not convert
the theory into practice at that level.

John's visit changed all that for us. He was more
than an answer to my prayer. We had seen and experienced the potential for lay-ministry in the power of the
Holy Spirit that weekend. He was soon back in England

once more, in 1982, and went on to South Africa. Again there were powerful responses. He also flew over especially to pray for David Watson, by then diagnosed with cancer. As we all know, physical healing was not granted. John was heartbroken when David died. But he kept returning, simply teaching what the Lord had been showing them in their local Anaheim fellowship and always bringing a team with him to model the ministry he was leaving behind wherever he went.

Famous course at Fuller's

Peter Wagner invited John to pioneer a new course at Fuller in the January of 1982, believing that the School of World Mission was in danger of over-concentrating on the behavioural sciences and the technology of church growth. Peter became increasingly convinced that they were in danger of overlooking the sovereign work of the Holy Spirit in the ministry of world missions. The course was called MC510, and it was the first course of this nature to be offered in a major accredited seminary anywhere in the world. They never imagined that the course (taught on Monday nights over a three months' period), which was repeated each year for four years (1982–85), would attract as many theology students as mission students.

John lectured on such subjects as the Kingdom of God, the biblical records of the miraculous, different world-views, spiritual gifts, contemporary faith-healers and the relationship between modern evangelism today and evangelism in the power of the Holy Spirit with signs and wonders following. Then John would invoke the Holy Spirit on the class and minister as he sensed God leading him. There were some quite amazing signs and wonders following these 'clinics'. Robert Walker, of *Christian Life* magazine, had flown out from Wheaton, Illinois, to attend the first course and write a report on it. Walker was so impressed that he dedicated the entire

October (1982) issue of *Christian Life* to MC510. It was published with a dramatic cover: MC510 ORIGIN, HISTORY, IMPACT: COULD THIS NUMBER AFFECT YOUR FAITH? The issue sold out faster than any other religious magazine and orders for reprints were numerous. It quickly became known as 'the sold out issue'.

Open doors to wide world

This seminary experiment was still in its infancy but it now became a centre of public attention across the Christian world. Robert Meye, Dean of Fuller Seminary School of Theology, was reported as saying to a joint faculty meeting, 'I know of only two seminary courses that have become famous. One was the course on dogmatics taught at Basel by Karl Barth and the other is the MC510 taught by John Wimber at Fuller here.' John was a risk-taker (he would often tell us faith was spelt 'R I S K'). He took huge risks of faith, publicly (not least by making himself so vulnerable). This, of course, often made him a hostage to fortune, but the impact was felt worldwide as many churches began to enter into the blessings of those risks and rediscovered their faith in the midst of their vulnerability. Of course no Christian teacher is ever beyond criticism, but John was soon being sniped at and misquoted maliciously by a certain brand of Christians who feel they are doing God a service by that kind of thing. He was often urged to fight back but he dismissed the idea, saying 'I don't think the Lord would have responded that way – it's not our thing.' But apart from criticisms true or false, after MC510 some serious theologians began to take John seriously.

Wimber was soon being invited to teach on '*Signs and Wonders*' on most continents. He made a return visit to London in 1984 and a further visit in 1985 going to London, Sheffield and Brighton. After that he came to the UK probably every year for the rest of his life, not to mention his other visits to the rest of the world. He taught and modelled overseas just what he ministered back at home: a ministry which increased in momentum as year succeeded year. In 1993, John was diagnosed with cancer and underwent a difficult period of treatment, but he insisted on getting back into his travelling ministry as quickly as possible. His son Chris came over to England with him pushing him in his wheelchair. He seemed to be gradually regaining his strength and fitness, when he suffered a stroke

His hero was Jesus

John died of a massive haemorrhage on November 17th 1997 following a fall in his house, while still recovering from by-pass surgery of the heart. He was sixty-three years of age. He was certainly looking older than his years. He had often said that it was not the age of the car that counted but the mileage! John had faithfully run the race and finally finished his course. Some time before he died he talked publicly of the trauma of living with uncertainty during his bout with inoperable cancer two years previously. 'When all is said and done, dying is the last, worst thing that any of us will face. As Christians, however, we need to recognise that it's also the best thing. Going to heaven is what we signed up for. That's not so bad, is it?'

Looking back on his times of illness and difficulties he said: 'I don't know about you, but I haven't done so well with "prosperity" in life, in times when everything's good. But believe me, everything gets focussed when I'm in trouble. Do you know that prayer: "Oh God, oh God, oh God . . .?" ' His simple, honest, self-effacing ministry had been unique in our generation. He so often described himself (on the platform) as just a fat man trying to get to heaven, but he was, of course, a very talented musician, an apostle, a prophet, an evangelist, a pastor and a teacher who married

Pentecostal experience to evangelical teaching.

John was also the eventual founder of a new denomination who led us into new forms of worship; he was a deeply spiritual thinker, a joint author of many books, a model healer, a trainer of leaders and laity alike. He was a most generous friend to many. Who can ever remember being allowed to pay when John took them out for a meal? He was a wise counsellor of leaders, a relaxed inspirer of youth, a major church planter, a gifted administrator and businessman, a preacher of righteousness. He shared his insights willingly for the blessing of the whole church; his focus was ever 'the Blood and the Book' as he often used to remind himself – the cross and the Bible. His guide was the Holy Spirit. He listened to God. John would never be anyone's hero. He wanted all to know and worship his Hero – Jesus Christ.

When he died, he left behind his wife Carol, three sons and a daughter and many grandchildren. His eldest son Chris, a long-time cancer sufferer, has since followed his father to glory.

Such is the background for the chapters that follow. In them different scholars and leaders draw our attention to different aspects of the ministry that John has bequeathed to the Church of Jesus Christ for its permanent enrichment.

Watson's tribute sums up the person

In his book *Fear No Evil*, which David Watson wrote just before his death, he described John Wimber as

> a large, loveable, warm and gentle person, reminding me of a teddy-bear. He also had an able mind, wide Christian experience, and shrewd spiritual discernment. Every now and then in my travels I meet someone whom I feel I can really trust – someone who loves me and accepts me as I am, who is not try-

ing to use or manipulate me, and who is full of godly wisdom. There are not many like this but John Wimber is one.

Source books

Gunstone, John, *Signs & Wonders – the Wimber Phenomenon* (London: Daybreak, 1989).

Gunstone, John (ed), *Meeting John Wimber* (London: Monarch, 1996).

Springer, Kevin (ed), *Power Encounters* (London: Harper Row, 1988).

Wagner, Peter (ed), *Signs & Wonders Today* (Orlando, Fla.: Creation House, 1987).

Wagner, Peter, *The Third Wave of the Holy Spirit* (Ann Arbor, Mich.:Servant Publications, 1988).

Wimber, John and Springer, Kevin, *The Dynamics of Spiritual Growth* (London:Hodder & Stoughton, 1990).

Wimber, John – video-recorded testimony 'I'm a Fool for Christ's sake' – 1984.

Personal recollections from conversations over 16 years with John and Carol Wimber.

2

THE FAMILY MAN
BOB AND PENNY FULTON

*Bob Fulton is married to Penny, Carol Wimber's youngest
sister. Bob was once a youth pastor on the staff of the
Quaker Church to which John Wimber was also first called
as an associate pastor. He joined John Wimber in the founding of the original Vineyard Christian Fellowship and later
planted out another in Yorba Linda. For some years he has
been the international co-ordinator of the Association of
Vineyard Churches. Penny is a gifted speaker and for a time
headed up the women's work for the Anaheim Vineyard
Christian Fellowship. She also co-founded a Vineyard
Christian Fellowship with her husband in Yorba Linda*

Penny Fulton's perspective
What makes a man a 'family man'? What idea do we get
in our head when we use this phrase? Personally, I
think about someone who loves his wife deeply,
beyond expression, and gives her respect and honor as
they live their life out together. On top of that, I would
add that he loves his children enough to discipline
them, train them and play with them with the full
knowledge that he received his family as a treasure
given from God. This is my idea of John Wimber. But
before I explain my reasons for saying this I must
recount my experience from years ago.

The first time I met John Wimber was in the streets

of Catalina Island, California. He was walking with my big sister, and my other sister and I (the two youngest of six) were following closely. I was nine years old and very interested in my 'big' sister's boyfriends. I immediately decided that this one was the best of them all and he soon became the favorite of the family. After my mother met John at dinner one night, she remarked that Carol was going to marry a man who was an 'adult' – in her experience most men were little boys!

Poor John. The moment he married Carol we all made him the father. Our own father had died a year earlier and John was such a 'father' type person that it was an easy transition. I suppose being the youngest caused me to emotionally connect to Carol and John as my 'parent' types more easily than it was for the rest of the family. I began emotionally depending on both of them as role models in my life.

John was just as interested in our wellbeing as Carol was. When one of the siblings was going through a hard time, he was there with fatherly advice and support. My brother, Tim, moved into their home during his teenage years because he wanted more stability in his life. John welcomed him and let him live with their family as long as he needed to. It was John who tried to teach him boundaries and ways of making good decisions. He really did act like a father. It's easy to understand how people automatically looked to him as such. During a tough time in my teenage years, I didn't hesitate to call Carol and John. I'm not even sure if they invited me to live with them, I just knew I was welcome at any time. I asked to move in with their family when I was seventeen years old, and they immediately made room for me. At the time, there were four children and the house was filled to capacity. I slept on the living-room couch, and felt grateful for this loving home. I had just become a Christian and John constantly mentored and prayed for me.

During this time I was having conflict with my mother. One night we all prayed together about this, and while praying, John reached over to me, put his hand on my shoulder and assured me I would never have to move back home if I didn't want to. He was never bothered by me living in his home, making everything more crowded. He treated me as he did the whole family. When I think about how hard it is to have extra people in your home, it is amazing to me that he was so inclusive with me, especially when the kids were so young: Stephanie (the baby) was still in her first year, Sean just over two years old; the two boys were beginning primary school. On the other hand, this is how it was with John Wimber all the way to the end of his life. He welcomed people, always, to share in his family: his greatest treasure.

While I was living with the Wimbers, I think the most delightful time of the day was when John first came home from work. He couldn't wait to play with the kids! They would wrestle on the floor and giggle until they were speechless. Sean, John's third son, was especially close to his father. He would go to his arms the minute John came through that door and stay there until dinner was served. After dinner came bathtime (John always helping), and the kids would all get their pajamas on . . . except for Sean, who would only wear his father's T-shirts. The playtime would then continue until bedtime. All the kids were red-headed, like their father. Sometimes we would style Chris's hair (the first-born) into the latest teenage style, making sure he could look 'cool' in the future when the need arose. We all had such fun! This was the nightly routine, except for Fridays when it was a little earlier because that was the night they had Bible study in their home.

The Bible study had begun before I lived with them. It started with me coming over for weekends, before I moved in more permanently, and a man from their church would come over to answer my questions. John brought his mom and dad to listen to this man also. The Bible study was soon given over to John to run (not even a Christian of one year yet), and it grew so big he had to move it to the church, where there were bigger rooms and more chairs.

One evening, while at home with the Wimbers, a young man named Bob Fulton came to visit. He came over to talk to me about entering a Bible college, now that I had become a Christian. Carol and John thought very highly of this young man, and that first evening he visited, they quietly excused themselves while he was talking to me. They went to their bedroom, knelt down and prayed that this would be the man that I would marry. God answered that prayer, and not only did we turn out to be family but best friends too. After we were married, John and Carol insisted we stay with them when our first baby came in order to receive care and help. Looking back at that time, I can't figure out where they slept because they gave their bed to us!

And our church life began! The Bible study that John was leading grew to several a week. The church had already hired my husband as Youth Director, and now they saw the anointing on John. He was hired as Associate Pastor and continued teaching in any home that he could get into. He began teaching on 'Husband and Wife' relationships, so I opened our home, invited our neighborhood, found a home that would do child-care and John came the minute I asked him. He was soon the expert on family relationships. He probably felt a little 'out of his league', but the wonderful thing about John was that he always welcomed Carol's input, his kids were crazy about him (they never went through that typical 'teenage hate your parent years'), and he loved his family above anything else, so we trusted him as an expert. On Sundays we were often in his home for dinner after church. It was John who did the inviting, who went by the store to get the wonderful bakery rolls and meat, and John who loved to include everyone in his family. He was never exclusive. His family was always there with the friends he wanted over. His mom and dad were constantly invited too, and no one felt left out.

As his ministry grew, the new church (eventually to become the Vineyard movement) started, and he began traveling more and more. His kids were growing up and had children of their own. The day John looked forward to the most (and which eventually took place), was the day he would be able to take all his kids with him along with their families on one of his ministry trips. His four children had all married people who longed to serve the Lord, and the trips were their delight. Finally the day came when John took the four children and their spouses along with him as he ministered. Almost all of them were in England with the grandchildren at one time, and another time they all traveled to Sweden. I remember John wanting to discuss the topic of blessing coming to a member of the family. He used to say, 'Has God given me prosperity, or has God given "us" prosperity?' He was trying to make a point of the fact that if he is blessed, then it makes sense that his whole family is blessed, because nothing was more fun for him than sharing his blessing with them (whether they were still at home or married with their own home).

John's children were the apple of his eye, and once in a while his teachings in the UK included nearly as many stories of the grandchildren as there were illustrations of 'signs and wonders'. He was loving and generous, and if he thought any of us had any need at all he would be there with money or things the minute he had the opportunity. None of the kids (or me for that matter) could mention wanting anything without John trying to get it for them. He took such pleasure in giving

his kids what he could. At one point, John's daughter
Stephanie had to have surgery. His heart ached for the
her, and then he found out there was a beautiful dress-
er that she had previously admired. He bought that
piece of furniture and had it in her house before she
came home.

On Sunday afternoons John began the tradition of
taking his children to a restaurant after church. The four
children, their mates and the eleven grandchildren
were included. World leaders would come to visit the
church, and John would set aside time to spend with
them. If this time ever ran into Sunday, he always
included his whole family. He never separated visitors
from the family dinners. John's value for his family life
was the forefront of his choices. If a visitor was present
at these times, he met with John and the family – grandchildren included. The fun with the family was never
interrupted; it just included more people sometimes.

When I look back at these things in John that were so
important (and immovable) I realize what a rock he was
to his family and also to his community – the church
community as well as the worldwide church he served.
When he chose family life without apology, it freed
those watching him to do the same. He was not intimidated by expectations of 'important' people. He did
what he valued and believed in with no apology. He
was a family man first. Carol and the children were his
priority above every other responsibility, and also the
love of his life. If he had free time, his playtime included taking the kids out to breakfast. If he had a free
couple of weeks, he would get tickets for the kids and
grandchildren to go to a play together. He was a man
who loved God with everything in him, believed that
God gave him responsibility and relationship with his
family first, and worked out obedience from that foundation. Although he taught these things in those early
Bible study years, it was the way he worked it out that

was so impressive. He always said, 'At the end of the
day, all you will have are the relationships God gave
you. Care for what God gave you and you'll be all right
in your old age.'

John looked at the ministry that God gave him as
separate from character issues in his own life. He felt
God took pleasure in him when he chose to be kind to
his family, when he worked hard to have a 'soft
answer', when he repented of any hurt he caused. As
far as his healing ministry went, or anything else like
that, he knew beyond question that this was God and it
was up to God to do the ministry of 'signs and wonders' when and if God wanted to. It was his everyday
choices of kindness, considerate behavior and sensitivity to his wife and family that he measured himself by.
There were times he lived out these values and times
when he failed. If he felt he didn't live up to these values, he always listened to correction. I never saw a man
try harder to change than John that last year of his life.
He made a point of asking Carol where he was offensive and repenting when the need arose. I noticed that
he was doing everything in his strength to change any
behavior that might be hurtful. When he thought he did
offend someone, he told all his friends about his 'bad'
behavior until he somehow got it corrected. Maybe that
was why he held family values with such high regard.
He never thought of himself as approved by God
because someone was healed or because it was a great
night of ministry. He had that part settled. The ministry
was God's; it had nothing to do with him. The everyday
choices he made before God concerning his actions
were what made a man righteous or not. Recently I
asked Stephanie, what was it in her dad that contributed to her choosing to walk with the Lord. She answered
that it was his integrity. The way John paid his bills on
time, took care of his family even if he had to work in a
ditch (he was close to that once), and the high standard

he kept of providing for his family above any other pursuit caused Stephanie to have a high respect and honor
for the God John served.

Bob Fulton's perspective

Penny has described how she knew John as father and
family man. Now my distant past (I've known John and
Carol for thirty-five years) is not as sharp as Penny's so
I will refer to the qualities of John as husband and father
that most impressed me.

Most people who read this book knew John as a
speaker at renewal conferences, or they knew him as
the founder of the Vineyard movement. His picture was
often on the cover of Christian magazines and numerous articles were written about his ministry. Did this
notoriety change Carol or John's approach to family
life? From my vantage point I would say it changed
them very little from what Penny has described.

One day after a very fruitful ministry trip, John was
telling Carol about all that God had done and the great
Christian leaders he had met. He was relating how they
were saying very complimentary things about him and
the way he was being used by God. Carol looked at him
and said, 'Oh man of God, please take out the trash.' To his
family and those close to him, he was still just John
Wimber: husband, father and friend. I can only think of
a few times, over the last eighteen years, that we would
talk about 'the great way God was using him'. If anyone
started to talk of his notoriety, he, Carol or one of us
would change the subject. John knew this prominence
and visibility wouldn't last long but he would *always* be
a family man.

His children knew of the demands on his time and
energy, but they also knew they were his highest value.
If he was having a meeting with Christian world leaders and any of them called him, his secretary would
always connect them immediately because she knew

his desire toward them. If any of the grandchildren were visiting him and came in to say hi, John would introduce them to the group, and then at the appropriate time they would leave. Many times when John was ministering to someone, praying for God's blessing, healing, deliverance, etc. if one of the families came in, they could join the ministry time, just watch or leave. I learned much from the way John included his children and grandchildren in his whole life. It was not compartmentalized into family and ministry.

Often he told us – the Vineyard leaders who were doing renewal conferences – *to stay in the pulpit, don't buy a tent and take your show on the road. Hopefully many will do what we're training them to do and soon those leaders will teach it to others. After a time many will be doing smaller conferences in their country and we won't be in demand anymore. God will also raise up others with new emphases and the people will follow them. So don't neglect your families, either genetic or church for this renewal ministry.*

In the thirty years I have been leading in the church I have seen so many leaders sacrifice their families for the ministry. Often John would tell me that at the end of the day all you'll have is Jesus, your family and friends. For those who are following you now, your ministry will become a distant memory. Keep an intimate relationship with those close to you so you will have friendship with them in your late years.

It's been said that the glory, gals or gold are what stumble most leaders, especially if one is very famous. It is 'heady wine', so to speak, to become a visible leader. It seems the more useful one is to the church, the stronger the temptations become. This is especially true for those who have a prominent ministry in the wider church. John always exhorted leaders quite plainly, to 'keep their zippers up or their skirts down, hands out of the till, and heads out of the clouds'.

John had his share of temptations and as they came,

we would talk of them. But his relationship with Carol was especially important to his overcoming these temptations before they became sin. He could tell her or one of his good friends what was troubling him and then it would lose its grip on him. He believed he should share every thought with his wife. He didn't teach that everyone should do the same, but for him it was very important, to keep him from being overcome by glory, gals or gold. He knew that simply to battle it by himself and confess only to Jesus, would be to lose many of these battles. As it says in Ephesians 6:12, 'our battle is not against flesh and blood, but against principalities, against the authorities, against the powers of this dark world and against the spiritual forces of evil in the heavenly realms'. If some temptation was getting a hold in his mind, it was brought out into the light by confessing it to Jesus and the church, and it then lost its grip on him.

I believe it was his openness to confess a temptation and his honesty to admit something was getting a grip on him that helped him to overcome. God also used those close relationships to challenge him, if God revealed something to them. We were ruthless with him because we knew he didn't want to fall as he had seen other leaders do. Of course he relied on the power of the blood of Jesus, Scripture and the presence of the Holy Spirit to put to death the deeds of the body, which caused victory to come time after time. John desperately wanted to end the race a winner in these battles.

I often told John that the reason I could follow him over the last twenty years was because he repented easily and he relied on Scripture as the basis for his faith and practice. He was not perfect or sinless, but I was compelled by his heart for God, his family, the lost and the church.

3

FRIEND AND ENCOURAGER
DON WILLIAMS

Dr Don Williams was born January 29,.1937 in Long Beach, California. He was educated at Princeton University, Princeton Theological Seminary and Columbia University (PhD). He has written 11 books. The most recent is Jesus and Addiction *(Recovery Publications). Ordained* **Presbyterian,** *he is pastor of the Coast Vineyard in La Jolla, Ca and is married to Kathryn Anne Williams.*

It was the fall of 1987 and I was in the crisis of my life. While on vacation, I was fired by the elders from pastoring Mt Soledad Presbyterian Church in La Jolla, California. It was a 'palace revolution'. The congregation was stunned. I was devastated, sunk in depression. It was as if my insides had been tipped out. One minute I was leading a large church; the next minute I was unemployed. After the ax fell, I instinctively found myself racing to Anaheim and sitting with John and Carol Wimber. Why did I do this?

When I began preaching at Mt Soledad in 1980, the church was a shadow of itself. Under a hundred people gathered in an all-purpose building overlooking the Pacific. Unknown to me at the time, the Presbytery was preparing to close the church. Located in one of the wealthiest communities in the US, the dwindling congregation absorbed denominational funds to survive. After I began to preach, we grew to over a thousand members with three Sunday services and a network of home groups. This was originally fueled by a strong evangelical message, but in 1984 the Holy Spirit began to visit us in power. His coming was directly related to the influence of John Wimber.

The previous year (1983), my wife Kathryn and I were in crisis. We were reeling from a violent outside attack on our marriage. A caring friend encouraged me to visit John Wimber's class at Fuller Seminary, MC 510, where 'Signs and Wonders' were not merely taught, but caught through clinic experiences at the end of the lectures. He thought this might help bring healing to my pain. While I was unable to catch the class, I did find my way to the Anaheim Vineyard in the late spring. As I entered the parking lot of Canyon High School for the evening service, people were literally running toward the gym: not drifting in for church as usual.

Once inside, I was greeted by an auditorium filled with about 2,000 people, informally dressed. I slipped into the bleachers. A group of musicians mounted the platform at one end of the basketball court and began to play simple songs. There were no lyric sheets, no overheads, but virtually everybody began to worship. One song followed the other, often repeated. As I watched, I saw something new: a vast congregation singing to the Lord rather than to each other. Most were seated, some were standing with arms raised, some were kneeling. Many faces were wet with tears. Many were shining. Most were lifted heavenward. As a traditional Presbyterian, this staggered me. My worship context was three hymns punctuated with prayers, responsive reading, announcements and sermon. But here was non-stop singing for a half an hour. Because the songs were simple, I found myself tentatively joining in the repetition.

After worship, the large man at the keyboards, who I identified as John Wimber, got his Bible and began to speak. From my days in the Jesus Movement of the sixties, I expected a pop sermon from Revelation on the end of the world. I got a thoughtful sermon on the Kingdom of God, come and coming and our place in it 'between the times'. Skeptical me was impressed. Then came the 'ministry time' which included a barrage of 'words of knowledge' or prophetic words indicating people God wanted to heal that night. Scores responded and exited to a side room where a ministry team was ready to pray for them. I went into the Southern California night saying to myself, 'I don't know what worship is, but whatever it is, this is "state-of-the-art" '.

Next Sunday I was back with several musician friends from our Presbyterian church to experience worship again. After the service, a former student of mine at Fuller Seminary, Wynn Griffin, who was now doing research for John Wimber, spotted me and introduced me to John. After exchanging pleasantries, John asked me if I would like to visit him during the next week. I jumped at the chance and our friendship began.

The following Wednesday morning, I drove through the streets of Yorba Linda to the Waggoner House to keep my appointment. Ushered in by John's assistant, Blaine Cook, I found myself sinking into a couch in what looked more like a living room than an office. I felt at home as I poured out my pain. John listened intensely and told me that the Lord had urged him to see me. We spent a couple of hours together, which included an ordered-in lunch. John prayed for me and then said, 'Don, I want to give you everything that the Lord has given to me.' What could this mean? I would only fully know over the years, but after having said that, John took me to a storage shed and loaded me up with volumes of teaching cassettes, books and music tapes. I later realized I had over a hundred dollars worth of materials. Right there, John began to teach me and encourage me. I was to give away everything that God

was giving to me. What a lesson for an up-tight, controlling, competitive pastor!

What John did for me that day he did for untold others. Episcopal Rector Mike Flynn remembers 'the sheer
generosity of the man'. When Prue and Richard
Bedwell visited John from England, they stayed at a
sleazy hotel near the airport and hardly slept. John was
horrified. He personally put them up at the Raddison
and paid their bill on the next visit. Bishop David
Pytches recalls that of the hundreds of meals he had out
with John, he was only able to pay once. Quite a record.

As I left John that afternoon, he invited me to come
back the next week for the National Vineyard board
meeting in his office. 'Just hang out with us, if you like.'
Having worked with denominational Byzantine
intrigue for most of my ministry, I couldn't believe his
openness and generosity. So I popped in, met the board
and listened to their discussions. I found a group of
men, mostly veterans of the Calvary Chapel branch of
the Jesus Movement, talking earnestly, laughing hearti-
ly, exchanging reports of God's power in their midst,
and praying for each other and the churches they over-
saw. Where were the hidden agendas? Where were the
theological obscurities designed for 'inclusiveness'? I
couldn't find them. Everything seemed real, new, biblically referenced, experimental and experiential.
Everything was also exploding. Here was John, drawing this Presbyterian pastor into his inner-circle, with
no plans or agenda for me. He simply liked me and
wanted me around. He was ready to be my friend when
I really needed a friend. I was amazed that I got John as
my friend.

More invitations came. John was taping a series on
the 'Gifts of the Spirit' from 1 Corinthians each week at
a home nearby. Would I like to come? You bet I would!
Here I learned for the first time that the Spirit's gifts
were situational, given in the moment, rather than con-

stitutional, one per Christian (on the average), given for all time. I threw out my 'Gift Inventories' with this insight.

I will never forget one evening service that summer. John was in the middle of his sermon. He recalled going to a hotel in Chicago the previous week and turning on a pornographic movie. Then he stopped and said, 'The Lord told me not to finish the story.' He abruptly moved to a ministry time. Next Sunday night John recalled the incident. He explained, 'The Lord told me not to finish the story because I hadn't told my wife Carol. I told her. Now I can finish the story.' I was staggered. What national church leader would be so honest and so current with his congregation? All those I knew shared after the fact only 'victories'. Here was a man I could trust.

John sparked my interest in the healing ministry of Jesus and its place in the church today. I was intrigued, but not convinced. But my paradigm shift, the change in my perception of reality, was at hand. John was teaching a Healing Seminar at the First Baptist Church in Bakersfield. Would I like to drive up with him for the weekend? I would, indeed.

So, on a warm Friday morning, off we went up the 5 Freeway, north out of Los Angeles. As we drove, John began to question me on some Christological issues. He confessed to not being a theologian. He now had to rework his theology in light of what the Holy Spirit was doing. John wanted my help in thinking through things. Because of my training, I was able to suggest several approaches to ideas that were troubling him. I found John teachable, non-defensive, ready to stand corrected by biblical truth in an evangelical context. I thought, 'I have something to give to John. I was honored, excited, welcomed as a peer and as a teacher. Part of deep friendship is honest, intellectual challenge. David Pytches remembers John as easy to argue with;

he would listen, laugh and agree to disagree (over things like infant baptism). John and I were in the give and take of our relationship which was to become our style over the years. I felt valuable. John was grateful. It was quite a ride to Bakersfield.

Once we got to the church, we were joined by a ministry team from the Anaheim Vineyard. John taught several sessions on healing. He demonstrated that Jesus' ministry is for today by calling people out of the audience with specific illnesses. His teams prayed for them up front. Often he would get words of knowledge, even as bold as 'seven women with vaginal warts'. These were confirmed by John's associate, Blaine Cook, who was hearing the same things and leading the ministry team.

Again and again, the power of the Spirit was physically evident as people were prayed for. Some would tremble, some would sink to the floor. Many were healed. I moved from an observer to a believer that weekend, almost ready to become a practitioner.

As we were heading home, I asked John how he prepared to pray for the sick. I expected to hear, 'I fast, I intercede, I confess all of my sins.' He replied, 'I drink a diet Coke.' This was John. Unpretentious, matter-of-fact. He never worked the crowd. He never drew attention to himself as the anointed special agent of God. He always gave the ministry away. His passion was to equip the whole church to do the works of Jesus. In his phrase, John wanted the church to be 'naturally supernatural'.

At the same time, John personally prayed (often with Carol) for thousands. Anglican missioner, David Watson, leader of the renewal in England, became perhaps John's best friend outside of family. David Pytches remarks that in him, John found a true soulmate. When David was dying of cancer, John flew himself, along with John McClure and Blaine Cook, to England to pray for David and then had him come back to California for eight days of soaking prayer in the Wimbers' home. John practiced what he preached. 'I want to give you everything the Lord has given to me,' he promised.

I asked John how he learned to pray for the sick. Apart from the Bible, he said that all he knew he learned from Francis MacNutt's book, *Healing*. I not only read that book, I attended a Methodist renewal seminar in San Diego where Francis (an ex-Roman Catholic priest) and his wife Judith were teaching. They were wise and loving communicators, ministering in understated power. I was impressed.

The next week, Francis vacationed in La Jolla and offered to lead a service at our church. That Sunday night he taught on Jesus' healing ministry, demonstrated that it was for today by praying for a few people and then spent the next several hours praying for over a hundred who were there. I watched it all and thought, 'This is just like the New Testament.' But it was here in my church! John convinced me that this ministry is for today and Francis brought it personally to us. We were on our way.

What I was experiencing with John and Francis, I wanted fully for our church in La Jolla. I had come to John in personal crisis; he put me into ministry crisis. How could I translate this concrete ministry of Jesus into a traditional, evangelical Presbyterian church? John gave me a key answer. He said, 'Don't mess with Sunday morning. People want the service to be predictable. If you start to change it they will be upset. But you can do anything with Sunday night. No one cares about that service.' John was right. Our Sunday evening meeting averaged twenty-five people, all singles. Who cared? So I thought, here we can shift to Vineyard worship, pray for the Holy Spirit to come, minister to the sick, and let the rest of the church go on as usual. I was naive. After we started to do these things, the Spirit fell and attendance grew to over 300. Often we would pray for hours into the night with people strewn over the platform. Substantial numbers came to the Lord. Prophetic words were spoken; people received the gift of tongues; it was a mini-revival in La Jolla and John was pastoring us through it as he did scores of other churches experiencing renewal.

In early 1985 I asked John if he would bring a team and hold a week-long conference at our church. He agreed and we hosted 'What Is the Holy Spirit Saying to the Church Today?' Blaine Cook and others joined John in ministering to a standing-room-only crowd. The Spirit came in power. Many were healed and filled with the Spirit. On Thursday night during worship I was outside speaking with John. Suddenly Mark McCoy, our worship leader, appeared. Laughter was breaking out in a corner of the room as the worship ended. What was he to do? John stepped inside, took a look and said, 'Leave it alone, it's the Lord.' Soon wave after wave of laughter engulfed the over 500 seated there. An Oriental student from Occidental College, seized with spasms of joy, walked about touching others and the joy seized them. John said, 'This is the Spirit because it is healing. We have had an intense week; now God is giving us relief.' When 'holy laughter' broke out in the Toronto Airport Vineyard years later, John had given me a context to reference this work of God.

John not only became a friend and mentor, he also was there for people in my life who were beyond my ministry abilities. Here he was truly an encourager. A man in our church who had been active in the entertainment industry was gay. As he confessed his struggle, he also wanted to be free. I called John, 'Would you pray for this man?'

Up we went to Anaheim for an hour of intensive prayer. A dear friend became HIV positive through a dirty needle. I called John. We went to the Wimbers' home and Carol and John took this on. The Spirit came; a powerful ministry time resulted. We could see his infected glands shrink as we prayed. My friend never developed AIDs. Ten years later, he is in ministry with a wife and family. As I write this, I wonder, 'How many people came to John for personal prayer? How many thousands of hours were lavished upon them?' John, like Jesus, lived the poured-out life. 'I want to give you everything the Lord has given to me.'

As our Presbyterian church grew spectacularly, John asked me to share in a major international conference in Anaheim. This led to further invitations to speak there, especially on the theology of the Kingdom of God which John urged me to develop fully. After one conference, he suggested that I put the material into a book: *Signs, Wonders and the Kingdom of God* took shape by his direction. John always challenged me beyond my comfort zone. He took me with him and pushed me out. John spelled faith RISK and he taught me to risk for the Kingdom.

Now in 1987 here I was in Anaheim with John and Carol, broken-hearted, pouring out my loss and rejection after being asked to resign as the pastor of my church. The trigger for this was a confrontation with the key elder (the biggest giver in the church) over a moral issue in his life. As we talked heatedly, he said, 'Does it have to end like this?' I didn't catch his drift, but what he meant was he would campaign behind closed doors for my removal. He did and I was gone. The church was in shock as I said farewell the next Sunday. I could have moved down the block with hundreds of people and started my own church. I could have fought the elders' decision with Presbytery (the higher judicial body). But I felt the Lord saying, 'Don't split the church. Go home and be quiet.' I told John this. He and Carol listened and comforted me. As I left Anaheim that difficult night,

John said only one thing to me, 'If you need money, let me know.' ('I want to give you everything the Lord has given to me.') What a friend!

The months of quiet passed as I finished my book on the Kingdom of God and prayed for the next step for Kathryn and myself. Morning after morning I sat in the silence and cried out to the Lord. As my severance pay was ending, I vividly remember praying,

'Lord, what do you want me to do?' I had heard nothing. My prayer trailed off: 'Lord, what do you want . . . ' Then in the stillness God spoke, 'I want you.' This broke me. I wanted to hear – 'I want you to do this or that'. What I heard was the call to relationship, 'I want you'. What John had spoken into my life about intimacy with the Lord was coming to pass the hard way. I remembered John saying, 'Never trust a man who doesn't walk with a limp.'

One afternoon in this interim period, I went to the beach with our dog. When we returned, Kathryn greeted us at the door. 'I was in the kitchen and the Lord spoke to me. We are to plant a Vineyard Church.' I knew this was God for two reasons. First, Kathryn is not the typical pastor's wife. She has always struggled with the ministry. She wouldn't come up with this 'word' on her own. Second, I heard John say one day that when he wasn't hearing from the Lord he would pray for God to speak to Carol. With this thought in mind, without telling Kathryn, I had been asking for two weeks for God to speak to her. Now my prayer was answered.

Within twenty-four hours John and Carol were sitting in our living room. We had several hours of conversation about our coming into the Vineyard. As it ended, John told me that they had had prophecies in the Anaheim Vineyard for the last two years that I would be joining them. John said, 'The Lord told me not to tell you this when you were fired. He told me not to inter-

vene when you were vulnerable. Now I can tell you.'
This was the encouragement I needed now. John had
obeyed the Lord and allowed me to go through the
breaking process. This prepared me for the future. My
best friends care more about my relationship with God
then they care about comforting me. John was one of
those friends.

Over the years, John and I talked about many things.
He and Carol were there when Kathryn and I were in
crisis. He intervened on my behalf with his massive
authority when necessary. John confided in me: his
struggles with the church, his fears for his family, his
failing health, his mistakes and miscues in leadership,
the hurts he bore from the attacks of others and those
who departed the Vineyard, the triumphs as 'naturally
supernatural' reversed the grip of rationalism and ces-
sationism which held so much of the church in
bondage. John shared his regret that the Vineyard as a
movement had not been more successful in evangelism.
I take this as a mandate for its future.

While John and I did not see each other regularly,
we never had to catch up emotionally when we were
together. We had instant intimacy which came out of
deep love and trust. John welcomed me and my gifts
into the Vineyard. He valued my theological sense. He
knew how I struggled to fully embrace a biblical world-
view which was so easy for him. He watched me and
helped me turn good theology into practice. John
embraced me as a peer. He learned from me when
needed. At the same time, I was submitted to him as my
pastor, my mentor, my coach. We were bonded in a
deep, God-given friendship.

John's huge capacity for friendship, based on his
giving spirit, in the words of David Pytches, was also
his 'snag'. Others read John's giving heart as an implied
permanent commitment. He could not be committed to
so many thousands. As David said to me, and I share in

this, our advantage was that we were not looking for John to be our father.

John has left his mark on the church in the late twentieth century. But for me, John has left his mark on my heart. I wept through his memorial service as I saw the videos of his teaching, sang the love songs to Jesus which he had written, watched Carol give the finest tribute I had ever heard – to a Christian leader and a dear husband. Here was a man who wanted to be a fool for Christ and go to heaven. He did it, sailing through the battle with his flags flying.

I know this sounds like bad theology, but heaven is more desirable to me now that John is there. I want to see the twinkle in his eye again. I want to see him sing to the Lord in his jazz style from the keyboards. I want to revel in his humor as I ponder his wisdom. I just want to be in his presence. Now I know that all of this is very human, from our side, but this is how I feel as a stranger and an alien here, on my way home.

When I think of John Wimber, I recall what Theodore Weld, the abolitionist, wrote about his upset with the evangelist, Charles Finney. Weld said, 'I know that Finney is not a perfect man . . . but yet take him for all in all, when shall we look on his like again?' As with Finney, so with Wimber. When shall we look on his like again?

4

WORSHIPPER AND MUSICIAN
MATT REDMAN

*Matt Redman was present at the first John Wimber visit
to St Andrew's Chorleywood in 1981. As his musical
talents developed he was given responsibility for the
musical direction during the evening worship there for
several years. Since its inception Matt has also led the
worship regularly at the large annual 'Soul Survivor'
youth conferences and latterly at the annual New Wine
Christian family conference. Matt has produced many
popular CDs of his own composition all enshrining
the values imparted by John Wimber.*

One of the greatest and most notable distinctives of the
Vineyard movement has been its worship music. Walk
into any Vineyard setting – whether that be a conference or a local church, and you'll find, right at the heart
of everything else that goes on, time set aside to worship God and meet with him through song. As a group
of cultural anthropologists from the University of
Southern California once observed, 'Nearly every meeting of the Vineyard, from home fellowships to training
meetings for counsellors, begins with half an hour or
more of singing songs'. John Wimber, of course, had
been a talented and successful musician from early on
in life, but it was not his heart for *music* that prompted
him to lead the movement into such a whole-hearted
embrace of song. Instead, it was his heart for *worship*.

Initially there had been no connection between these two areas – music and worship – in Wimber's life. Quite the opposite in many ways. Before becoming a Christian, John had spent much of his time pursuing music and the music industry for his own means. In 1962 he was involved in the founding of the Righteous Brothers, a pop duo made up of Bill Medley and Bobby Hatfield. Wimber played the saxophone in the backing band for this popular group, who in 1964 were booked to support the Beatles at the start of their American tour in San Francisco. It was later that year that the Righteous Brothers released their well-known single, 'You've lost that loving feeling'. Many people have wondered if there was any spiritual significance behind the naming of the band, but as Wimber pointed out, the word 'righteous' in the title had nothing to do with being holy. It was in fact the in-vogue way of describing something which the audience felt to be 'cool' or 'hip'!

Shortly after his conversion, Wimber was prompted by the Lord to lay down all that he had built up for himself as a successful musician. As he explained in one interview:

> When I became a Christian I was a musician with two albums I had produced in the US Top Ten; it was the establishment of my career after thirteen years of hard work. But God spoke to me in the two-line parable of the pearl of great price: 'I want it. Give it to me.' He didn't say 'Give it to me and then I will give you a career as a pastor, or some music that will bless many nations of the world.' He said 'Give me everything. Liquidate all your assets and I'll give you the pearl' . . . The pearl is Jesus.'

Later on, as the first Vineyard congregation began to learn about the role of music in worship, these musical gifts would begin to operate again; this time towards the glory of God, and an expectancy to meet with him.

The history of this discovery of 'worship' in the Yorba Linda (now Anaheim) Vineyard, began in September 1976 with a small group of people simply meeting in a home, who were desperate to encounter God. Among those initially present were Carol Wimber, Bob Fulton and Carl Tuttle. They followed no formality or complex liturgy – the agenda was simply to 'pray and sing some songs'. As Carol Wimber recalls:

> What we began with in worship was nothing except the word 'worship' . . . We sang many songs, but mostly songs *about* worship, or testimonies from one Christian to another. But occasionally we sang a song personally and intimately addressed to Jesus, with lyrics like 'Jesus I love you'.

As Carol explains, it was during these kinds of songs that people really began to experience God deeply. They soon began to understand that these times went way beyond the singing of uplifting songs. Where once songs had been used just as a vehicle to get people 'in the mood' for the sermon, they now become the 'main event'. It was an opportunity to touch the heart of God – both to bring before him an offering, and to sense his glorious presence.

Although John Wimber himself didn't attend these meetings until around the fourth month of their existence, they soon evolved into the style and values of worship that he and the Vineyard have become renowned for.

Wimber placed worship firmly at the top of the Vineyard's agenda, declaring in their church statement that: 'Our first priority is to give God's love back to him in worship'. He saw worship as a twofold activity – firstly as communication *with* God through the basic means of singing and praying, and secondly as the communication *from* God through teaching the Word, and other kinds of vocal utterances such as prophecy and speaking in tongues. As Wimber himself said, 'Worship is incomplete without both of these dimensions.' But most strikingly of all, John Wimber and the Vineyard promoted a new expectancy to meet with God intimately through song. This had emerged right in the earliest stages of the Vineyard, as described already by Carol. John constantly encouraged the church to pursue this intimacy, which he described as 'the highest and most fulfilling calling that men and women may know'. This intimacy, however, was not a means of portraying God as some kind of 'celestial chum' – it was strongly accompanied by a desire for God to be appropriately revered. As Wimber humorously, yet pointedly, observed, 'Sometimes I think we treat God like he's our pet; we scratch his head and fondle his ears . . . and forget who it is we're serving and worshipping.'

Wimber soon developed a model for this worship, which he saw as a continuum with at least five phases. He explained, 'As we pass through these stages we are headed towards one goal: intimacy with God.' This continuum, which has come to be known as the 'Vineyard model' for worship, is summed up below:

Stage one: **'A call to worship'**; In other words, a message directed towards the people being led in worship, and/or towards God. This is a time of invitation.

Stage two: 'Engagement'; In Wimber's own words. 'The electrifying dynamic of connection to God and to each other.' John Wimber firmly believed that although an individual may have times like these alone in private, when the church comes together the manifest presence of God is both multiplied and magnified.

Stage three: 'Exaltation'; Many different expressions of praise then start to flow from the hearts of the congregation. As Wimber simply explained. 'If you draw near to *God*, you're just going to want to praise him!'

Stage four: 'Adoration'; The expressions of worship then become more tender in nature. It is a time to bring love songs before the throne of the God of love.

Stage five: 'Intimacy'; this is our destination – God's intimate presence amongst us. Wimber passionately explained, 'We need a visitation of God. We need his presence and his work among us . . . and I believe it will come out of worship. We don't worship *for* that though – but it's a by-product.' Wimber would often challenge and encourage congregations with the words, 'Come prepared for an audience with the King.'

Before long, God was using Wimber and his team to minister these values in worship to many places around the world. It was in 1981, for example, that Wimber brought this teaching, theology and practice of worship to England. The whole 'signs and wonders' topic was radical, challenging and eye-opening for so many who attended these initial meetings, and yet the approach to worship that was offered was equally enlightening. Many recall the uncompromising value of spending quality time in bringing adoration to the Lord. The style modelled was a flow of unhindered and uninterrupted worship songs, each taking the congregation one more step along the journey into the depths of God's presence. Wimber himself would model this, often playing the piano, and then getting up straight away afterwards to preach. When challenged on one occasion about the amount of time being spent in song, Wimber defended his decision by commenting that even if no one else needed to, he personally needed to worship God and spend that time meeting with him.

Nowhere is John Wimber's heart and passion for intimacy in worship reflected more strongly than in his outstanding love song, 'Isn't He beautiful', written nearly two decades ago. Apparently, the song was composed following a call one day for Wimber to go and collect a visitor from the airport, which was miles away. He had just arrived home, worn out, and he lost his 'cool' with his family. Driving to the airport he soon felt convicted, realising that his family had done nothing wrong. Grieved that he had taken out his frustration on them, he repented before the Lord. Turning to worship he began to sing out to Jesus of his beauty and wonder. A song was born:

> Isn't He beautiful, beautiful, isn't He?
> Prince of Peace, Son of God, isn't He? . . .
> Yes You are wonderful, wonderful, yes You are,
> Counsellor, Almighty God, yes You are, yes
>   You are . . .

There is a fantastic story of how, on one occasion, a Jewish man walked into a Vineyard meeting whilst this song was being sung. Having no previous inclination towards Christianity he was struck by the repetition of the line, 'Yes You are, yes You are'. He heard the congregation chanting 'Yeshua, Yeshua', the Hebrew name for Jesus. Shortly afterwards he turned to Christ.

Wimber penned many other congregational songs, notably 'To seek your face', but even more importantly he invested in worship leaders at the Vineyard who were producing many fresh worship songs. After a conference in Australia, Wimber was criticised for not including enough songs which referenced the cross in the conference songbook. He accepted that, to a degree, the criticism was a valid one, and on returning home he gathered many Vineyard music writers and encouraged them to meditate upon the cross and study some of the classic theological works on Christ's redeeming work. Not surprisingly, more songs focused on the centrality of the cross soon began circulating.

Input into these worship leaders went way beyond the songs – he was concerned with the heart of those who were being trusted with leading worship. As Wimber himself explained. 'From time to time you run into a problem when you get into specialised [leadership] areas such as music . . . because you can find people who have tremendous ability but don't have the character.' On one occasion, in an interview for an English worship magazine he emphasised:

> The difficulty will not be so much in the writing of new and great music; the test will be in the godliness of those who deliver it . . . We learnt a lot from our experiences of God's initial outpouring in the Vineyard in 1979 and the following years. We had people who were just not ready to be used of God in a highly public way, although you would have thought they were from their gifts; they were gifted, they just weren't very godly . . .

In the same article he went on to stress:

> Historically every move of God has produced new music. Sometimes the music actually precipitated revival, sometimes it occurred during revival, but it was always present in the aftermath . . . Think about it; if worship leads every move of God, where do you think the enemy will attack? And do you think that he will have mercy and not attack at the point of weakness? If you think that you don't know anything about him, and you don't know anything about the art of warfare.

Such forceful words illustrate once again that Wimber's approach to worship was far more about matters of the heart than matters of music.

The effects of what God trusted John Wimber with as worship pastor, worship leader, songwriter and musician are far reaching, having touched, and are still touching, many parts of the church worldwide. It is estimated that 80 per cent of all the churches in the USA today are including 'Vineyard' songs in their public worship. Speaking personally, I have been affected by his approach in various different ways. In May 1981, when I was aged seven, my father died. Two months later I was taken along to some of Wimber's first meetings in England, at St Andrew's, Chorleywood, my home church. Memories of that time can be summed up simply – there was 'life'. I grew up within that environment – a church impacted with a new and dynamic lease of life within its worship. My testimony will be the same as thousands of my generation; that as I regularly embraced intimacy in worship, God drew near to me, at the same time healing the wounds of the past as I sensed his presence.

I am privileged to be working with a youth organisation called Soul Survivor, which attracts many thousands of young people, and has adopted these Vineyard worship values. Time and again we see the Lord changing lives as his people become involved in such intimate worship; a model brought to us originally by Wimber and his team. I particularly recall a youth gathering in the early 1990s when three young guys independently came up to their leader during the time of worship. Without any encouragement to do so, one handed in a knife, the other a pair of knuckle-dusters, and the third a packet of condoms. They had been overwhelmed by the presence of the Lord, as we approached him with our intimate worship songs. They couldn't escape repentance.

Many around the world will be able to testify to similar experiences – powerful yet intimate encounters with a living God through worship in song. Wimber was used by God to usher in a fresh approach to worship. He offered the church a biblical and practical framework for approaching the Lord through song. Among many aspects of the Kingdom that Wimber was entrusted with for the church, this must surely be one of the most significant. These truths about worship that John Wimber faithfully preached and practised, have enlightened, refreshed and strengthened so many of God's people.

5

THE EVANGELIST
EDDIE GIBBS

*Eddie Gibbs is Professor of Church Growth in the
School of World Mission at Fuller Theological Seminary,
Pasadena, California. He has been in the US since 1984.
His most recently published book is* Winning Them
Back, *Monarch, 1993. He is currently writing on the
subject of church growth in postmodern cultural
contexts under the title* Transforming Transitions,
to be published in the autumn of 1999.

My first contact with John Wimber was at Fuller
Seminary in January 1978 when I was visiting the cam-
pus for a two-week intensive in the Doctor of Ministry
Program. John had been invited by C. Peter Wagner to
contribute to his course on church growth by leading
some afternoon sessions on church leadership and
management. John's expertise as a church consultant
was beyond doubt, but he made his greatest impression
on the class as an evangelist. He confessed to the classroom full of pastors that he loved to catch fish, but he
couldn't stand the thought of having to clean them!

Before leaving for the United States, David Pytches,
the vicar of my home parish of St Andrew's,
Chorleywood, had said to me, 'If you find anyone you
think can help our church move forward, feel free to
explore the possibility of a visit.' So I had a preliminary
chat with John. On a subsequent two-week visit I discovered that the advertised lecturer had retired and

that in his place David Watson would be teaching the
course on church renewal. That was in 1980.

During a lunch break David asked me where I
thought he should worship at the weekend. In reply I
said that rather than visit one of the well-known
megachurches, he should see what John Wimber was
doing at the gymnasium at the Yorba Linda Canyon
High School as an evangelist and church planter. I
called the church on his behalf. Blaine Cook drove over
to collect him for the Sunday worship service, and the
rest is history. David Watson joined in the invitation
which led to John leading the first team to Britain to
visit St Andrew's, Chorleywood and St Michael-le-
Belfry in York.

I believe that David Watson and John Wimber
struck up an immediate relationship, not only because
they bonded as friends, but because they shared the
same insights, namely that the renewal of the church is
a prerequisite for effective evangelism and that renewal would only be sustained through an unshakable
commitment to evangelism.

Neither had grown up in a church-going environment, and both had to come to terms with the institutional church as new Christians. John Wimber was converted out of the pop music culture. He described himself as a fourth generation unbeliever who was raised as
a pagan. He came to Christ at the age of twenty-nine
when his life was falling apart in Las Vegas. David
Watson came to Christ as a cynical unbeliever with a
family background in Christian Science.

John's gifting as an evangelist

John was attracted to Jesus and had bought a Bible
which he was reading avidly. His major obstacle was an
inability to relate to the church-going, hymn-singing,
jargon-ridden community which he encountered. The
pop-culture and conservative evangelical cultures rep-

resented two worlds with no contact and little mutual understanding. Soon after he committed his life to Christ, the Lord began using him to lead others to faith and during the next seven years he had the joy and privilege of leading hundreds of people to Christ.

While he believed that every believer is called to be a witness, he recognized that not everyone is gifted by God as an evangelist so he did not make the mistake of projecting his giftedness on to other people. I remember him saying that the evangelist is not only given a burden to share the gospel, but has a 'spiritual antenna' (his phrase) sensitizing him as to who is ready to hear. He referred to himself as a spiritual midwife who knew when the time for birth had come. He recognized that God has to prepare the heart of the individual, otherwise it is a waste of time, and even counter-productive, to intrude into their lives. He would caution the zealous evangelist when they were wasting their time trying to sow on concrete. This understanding of the evangelist's task helped him to be sensitively bold, responding to the leading of the Holy Spirit, without becoming offensively brash.

A second gift which he displayed as an evangelist was the ability to listen to the other person. He asked questions and sought their opinion. He gave individuals his full attention even when there were severe time constraints. He was genuinely interested in their views and respected each as a person of intrinsic worth. He was a vulnerable and deeply compassionate man, able to weep with those who came to Christ out of intense suffering or deep conviction of sin.

Having spent his early years in the pop-culture of the 1960s, John was tolerant of other people whose lifestyles he could no longer condone now that he was a Christian. He was both unshockable and compassionate. He realized that a legalistic approach was of no help to people caught in addictive behavior patterns.

Only the gospel, and not the law, had the power to change lives. This attitude is of vital importance for the evangelist to be effective in a neopagan, postmodern setting. The heart of the message is the Good News of God's grace, rather than the bad news of God's impending judgment on sinful humankind.

A presentation of the gospel was not a ten-minute pre-packaged, take-it-or-leave-it deal, but a genuine dialogue, exploring the relevance and ramifications of the gospel for each individual. Modeling his ministry on that of Jesus, John addressed people's felt needs with patience, honesty and integrity. That gracious and caring approach gave him permission to probe deeply. He was the kind of person you counted it a privilege to be with, because you felt you could trust him and you came away enriched. He was on close terms with the Lord, wanted to get to know you, and thereby positioned himself to make the introductions, which is the heart of the evangelist's task.

Although a person of passion and deep conviction, he was not up-tight or intense. He was relaxed and informal in style whether in personal conversation or addressing a large gathering of people. John enjoyed life, had a twinkle in his eye, and a sense of fun which regularly bubbled to the surface. In his presence faith was infectious. He was a gentle man whose quiet calm perhaps owes something to his early years in the Quaker movement.

Church planting as a means to evangelism

It is not surprising that he formed early links with the Calvary Chapel movement in Southern California, which had grown out of Chuck Smith's ministry to the Jesus People of the 1960s. John Wimber realized that traditional churches were unlikely to reach out to the Vietnam era generation. The decade of the 1960s was to prove a watershed period for the mainline churches in that, with the exception of the Southern Baptists, they all peaked in membership around the midpoint of the decade, and then went into a severe decline which has continued to the present day.

In retrospect we now see this as the beginning of a cultural shift of mega proportions as Western societies moved from modernity to postmodernity. I don't think that John would have analyzed it in these terms, but his instincts were perceptive, some would say prophetic.

After working with Chuck Smith he eventually separated amicably, rather than face increasing tension over the place of healing and deliverance as essential aspects of evangelism in the contemporary context. In his search for a theology to explain his experience and convictions, John became greatly influenced by George Eldon Ladd's emphasis on the gospel of the Kingdom. He realized that the Kingdom not only represented a future hope but a present reality. He came to a further conclusion that Jesus operated out of his humanity and not his divinity, otherwise he could not have reassured his disciples that their ministry was to be a continuation of his own. Therefore, to use John's phrase which has become part of the vocabulary of the Vineyard, we are 'to do the stuff'.

John recognized that evangelism was not a lone-ranger confrontational activity, but rather something which was at the heart of the local church. In other words, it had to be undertaken in much the same way as the early church practiced its evangelism in the first century – in a relational context by a community readily accessible to unbelievers because it lived out its faith in their midst.

Power evangelism, in those early days of the Vineyard movement, wasn't something confined to the sanctuary; it belonged on the street. So when believers met in restaurants they prayed for people. On planes as they journeyed to conduct seminars around the US and overseas, they split up and ministered to the people around them. Many have heard John's stories of how he and others in their team were given gifts of knowledge which enabled them to gain the attention of fellow-passengers by speaking to them so directly about their life situations that they became aware that God loved them enough to bring someone alongside with a life-changing message.

John had a vision for planting churches in their thousands, churches which would demonstrate the risk-taking vitality of the churches of the New Testament. He saw that it took a witnessing group of believers to minister to unchurched, counter-culture North Americans. It was out of this evangelistic concern that the Vineyard movement was founded. Their sanctuaries were located in school gymnasia and converted warehouses – spartan places where people did not have to dress up to attend, where they could come and go as they pleased.

The worship style consisted of soft-rock worship songs, followed by folksy exposition and application of the Scriptures, over which John, with his laid back style and casual dress, presided with such skill and charm that unchurched visitors were quickly set at ease. As a good evangelist he knew his audience, was fully aware of the kind of things going on in their lives and of their expectations. This was not a struggle for him, because he simply had to delve into his own pre-Christian experience to identify with their struggles and aspirations.

The church spent no money on fancy buildings and did not rely on publicity to draw the crowds. The church relied on the witness of individuals and friendship networks to bring along those who were seeking Christ for whatever reason. And they did not have to wait for a church service to be ministered to. The Vineyard congregation had been trained and empowered for ministry, and members were constrained by the Holy Spirit and followed the guidance of the Spirit in seeking out the lost. They took bold initiatives in confronting people in the name, grace and power of Christ wherever they were: in restaurants, parking lots or in one of the many kinship groups.

The challenge that John faced was whether he could maintain that radical stance in the context of the Orange County Christian subculture. Orange County has the reputation of being the Bible belt of Southern California. His growing prominence in charismatic circles, reinforced by his regular appearances on the Trinity Broadcasting Network, resulted in the 'floating Pentecostals' drifting towards the Anaheim Vineyard in significant numbers.

The average age of the congregation began to increase. The 'floaters' brought with them their stereotypical expectations and self-focused spirituality. Their commitment level was not so high. A further complication was the fact that the evening congregation had large numbers of occasional visitors and regulars from other congregations who came to the Vineyard for a spiritual uplift. While such spectatorism is inevitable and to be welcomed to the extent that visitors are able to learn and to take insights back to their own churches, it is still a considerable drain on ministry resources.

The growth of the Vineyard movement came about not only through the planting of new churches, but with existing independent churches wanting to affiliate. The challenge the movement faces is to retain its original evangelistic vision and to adjust from the challenge presented by the baby boomers for the very different, and even greater challenges which will be encountered in reaching the baby busters, or generation-X, and the Millennials which are the youngest group to be labeled.

I remember John himself saying in the early 1980s that he did not know whether the Vineyard movement would outlast him. My prayer is that it will, because the need for church-based evangelism by groups who are prepared to move into the turf of the counter-culture groups is even greater now. Furthermore, within a few more years, those counter-cultures may become the mainline cultures of the post-modern era.

Power evangelism

On this point John was criticized by some for moving too far in his emphasis on signs and wonders and for failing to recognize that we still have to live with the tension of the 'now' and the 'not yet' of the Kingdom, played out with his own chronic health problems and the course of events which lead to his death. However, John was credible as an advocate of the importance of signs and wonders because of a total absence of sensationalism and a determination to be both honest and clinical in his approach to the healing ministry. He never told people to ignore their symptoms and he counseled those who asked whether or not they were healed to consult their doctor. Furthermore, sometimes an overemphasis is necessary in order for the wider church to take notice and to face its own avoidance or rationalizations.

John was never enamored with signs and wonders simply as spiritual phenomena or as an end in themselves. In Vineyard churches and in the seminars held around the world, ministry did not take place on an elevated platform as a public spectacle, but among the congregation with circles of people involved. In his book *Power Evangelism*, he wrote, 'While signs and wonders are what many visitors first notice about our church life, my understanding and experience of them come from an investigation of the kingdom of God – not out of a thirst for the supernatural.' They represented a pushing back of Satan's control of people's lives, and therefore had the closest tie with evangelism as the announcement of the Good News of the Kingdom.

To underline the point that John was not enamored of signs and wonders for their own sake, I cannot resist telling the story of a visit we both made to a hillbilly, snake-handling church in rural Georgia in 1983. We were together in Atlanta teaching a church growth class at the invitation of Peter Wagner. Peter had written to me in England suggesting that it would broaden my ecclesiastical horizons to pay this church a visit. I replied to inquire whether as I had had no prior experience with snakes I could practise on worms first! Unfortunately, there was no known worm-handling church for me to check out.

John and I sat on the back row – perhaps for similar reasons that newcomers choose the back row in churches even where snakes are not welcomed. The country preacher conducted the service and preached with snakes around his neck and arms – rattle snakes, copperheads and water moccasins. One of the snakes, it was announced, had been caught only that afternoon, and didn't know how to behave in church. I noticed that the country preacher appeared to be more nervous reading the Scriptures than he was handling the snakes!

At the end of the service, when the snakes had been returned to the safety of their boxes, a sick woman came forward for prayer. The preacher invited John to come to the front to pray for her. No sooner had he begun to pray when the preacher let the snakes out of the box again, with one bobbing and hissing perilously close to John's outstretched arms. He survived the ministry time without being bitten, but on the way back to the hotel confessed that he hadn't felt much spiritual power present that night!

As we have already noted, John was concerned to place healing and deliverance ministries within an evangelistic context. It was he who popularized the term 'power evangelism'. It was not a ministry to be exercised by celebrity preachers operating in full view of TV cameras. Rather it was a ministry in which all were to observe at close hand, and to be trained to exercise with discernment. It was to be a powerful demonstration of the presence of God in our midst, of the power of the gospel to mend broken lives, and of the Holy Spirit's convicting and converting power.

To this end John often took a back seat during ministry times, leaving it to members of the congregation. He managed and mentored by wandering around. He believed that the manifold ministries had to be restored to the people of God for 'power evangelism' to be released. For too long, in his view, the debate among evangelicals had swirled around 'presence', 'proclamation' and 'persuasion' evangelism. His model cut right through the debate because the signs and wonders declared the presence of the living Lord in their midst, which provided a heightened expectation to hear the Good News of God's love proclaimed in the power of the Holy Spirit. Each reinforces the other to heighten the persuasion.

Renewal of the church for authentic evangelism

John Wimber and David Watson both pastored churches which emphasized renewal and evangelism. This indissoluble link prevented their charismatic emphasis from becoming either trivialized or domesticated. In seeking to lead other churches into renewal they faced the same challenge. Each had come to empowerment through an experience of brokenness, tears and anguish of soul.

While teaching with John Wimber in Atlanta we talked about this. I asked John whether he thought he could bring people to where he now was within the time limits of a two- or three-day seminar. People are challenged, have their vision enlarged and become excited, but can they enter into the power without the pain? John replied that there is no short-cut. Jesus' disciples, after three years of personal mentoring, were told not to depart from Jerusalem until they had received the promise of the Father. The deepening of the relationship must precede the bestowal of the power, otherwise the consequences can prove disastrous. I write this not in criticism, because I have faced a similar perplexity in relation to church growth seminars which share insights without developing the necessary skills to apply them effectively. It takes spiritual maturity, faith and discernment to relate mountain top experiences to the urgent demands of ministry in the valley and the dull routines of everyday life. Yet, despite the brevity of the courses which John and his team conducted, many church leaders who attended did go through the important paradigm shift, which was subsequently translated into the life of their congregations. Some describe the history of their church in terms of 'pre' and 'post' Wimber!

One of the challenges facing any renewal movement is to ensure that renewal is not sought after as an end in itself. Those wonderful worship songs addressed to Jesus have a powerful impact both in terms of renewal and evangelism. This is something David Watson shared with John, when he spoke to him of the 'Celebration Evangelism' which had become associated with his ministry, conducted in many of the great cathedrals of England. But those songs of adoration can, over time, degenerate into sugar-coated sentimentality. This occurs when people become so self-focused that they are no longer using the occasion to seek God's face and join the seeking Savior in his continuing mission to a lost world. I agree with those who believe that John Wimber's place in history may be alongside that of John Wesley. But for that to happen the Vineyard movement in the US and worldwide must renew its commitment to his evangelistic vision and burden.

In this regard, it is fitting to end this chapter with another memory from the early 1980s. After visiting Chorleywood, David Pytches and I accompanied John to Holy Trinity, Brompton for an unforgettable mid-week meeting. The hall was crowded with between 200–250 people present. John began by inviting the presence of the Holy Spirit.

Within a few minutes we became aware of a man shaking. John paused, to explain that God was doing a deep work in that person's life, and that if it became disturbing the team members would take him outside for ministry. After a short while, it seemed that half of the audience was overcome by the presence of God with many shaking uncontrollably. At that point John said, 'Oh dear! This is getting messy! So I invite you to gather around any on whom the Spirit has come and to minister to them as the Spirit leads. Meanwhile we will walk around to provide any assistance you might need.'

As John walked around exercising the gift of knowledge, he said of one young man, 'Take that one out' and as he was being carried through the french windows, John added, 'God is giving to that man the ability to tell people about Jesus'. At the time there was nothing to indicate what that young man's future ministry would be. He was a barrister in the city of London and, as he later reported, had been very cynical and skeptical about the team from California. But that night in 1982 he received a powerful anointing of the Holy Spirit. Today Nicky Gumbel is known throughout Britain and around the world as the Director of the Alpha course. This evangelistic program has been adopted by denominations across the theological and ecclesiastical spectrum, and has been the means of countless thousands coming to know Christ through the fellowship of the church and in the power of the Holy Spirit.

John had a rare gift as a Christian leader, which was

to be ambitious for the people around him. He was trusting to a fault. Whatever holes we may pick in his theology, his ministry has had a profound influence on churches across denominations. Today there is a new generation of leadership in place, many of whom have been influenced by his insights and his personality. For above all, John had his Savior's concern for the lost, and in his service John was prepared to risk his reputation. His life and ministry provide an abiding legacy to all of us whose first instinct is to play it safe.

6

FATHER FIGURE AND PASTOR
ELEANOR MUMFORD

*Eleanor Mumford studied history and art history at
St Andrew's and Edinburgh Universities before training
at Cambridge as a teacher. After 5 years of teaching, she
married John in 1978. She helped to start the SW London
Vineyard where she serves on the staff. She enjoys
teaching and training within the local church and
the wider Vineyard movement, but loves best
being a mother to James and Marcus.*

It is a most extraordinary thing that a man whose own
father left home on the very day he was born, and
whom he never saw again, was later to become a 'father
in the gospel' to so many younger men and women
both within his own family and across the wider
church.

Paul wrote to the Corinthians, 'Even though you
have ten thousand guardians in Christ, you do not have
many fathers, for in Christ Jesus I became your father
through the gospel' (1 Cor 4:15). There are many of us
in the Vineyard movement today who would consider
John Wimber to be the father-figure that Paul clearly,
and quite unapologetically, was to many in the church
at Corinth. As indeed he was to Timothy, the young
church planter and pastor at Ephesus to whom he
wrote, 'To Timothy my true son in the faith' (1 Tim 1:2).
John would have hated hagiography and would have
taken exception to our accolades. He would have been

the first to point to his own faults and failings in being a parent, as he was quick to do in any other area of his personal life, but the truth is that with John's death, I, with others, have lost a father quite as precious to me as I suspect Paul was to Timothy.

Any account of John's life as a father figure and a pastor will inevitably be highly personal, based as it is on relationship. My own father was a good man, a God-fearing, church-going Presbyterian, who loved his daughters dearly although he was rarely able to say so. My mother would frequently tell me how much he loved me, but was his only emotional representative in my life. He was, I now think, a highly emotional and passionate Scotsman, but he considered his own faith very private, and anyone else talking about theirs as highly embarrassing. When I became a Christian in my mid-twenties, having been to church every Sunday since birth but never having been told the gospel nor understood the cross of Christ, I became far less a cause for parental pride and rather a source of family embarrassment. As I embarked upon my Christian life with the same passion and vehemence with which I had previously mocked my Bible-believing and Spirit-filled friends, life at home became increasingly difficult. Losing both their interest and approval in so many ways, I was dismissed by my father as having become fanatical, which hurt me deeply. It was at this point that I first met John and Carol, and looking back now, I am deeply grateful to God for all the influence John had upon me as a father-figure and pastor. I loved him very dearly and can only say, as Laban did to Jacob in the Old Testament, 'The LORD has blessed me because of you' (Gen 30: 27).

My husband, John, first visited Wimber in Anaheim, Southern California, in the spring of 1982. The airless gymnasium that they used as a church building was a marked contrast to the architecturally impressive,

mock-Gothic Anglican church in central London where
John was about to start a new job. However, the ten-day
visit proved life-changing. He loved the intimacy of
new and startlingly simple worship songs; was profoundly affected by seeing ordinary people, not least
Wimber himself, ministering to one another with
extraordinary effectiveness, be it in small mid-week
groups or in large gatherings on Sundays. He found the
informality refreshing and the sense of excitement
infectious. He had previously written to Wimber, on the
recommendation of David Watson, to invite himself to
visit the church, but had received no reply – not unchar-
acteristically, as we later discovered. Defying every rule
of etiquette or requirement of convention, he flew west
anyway with a single telephone number in the pocket
of his well-tailored blazer! Two or three days into his
visit, feeling a little embarrassed and out of place, he
went for lunch with Wimber who immediately welcomed him with characteristic friendliness, paid the
restaurant bill as he always insisted upon doing,
assured John that he fully believed that the Lord had
planned and orchestrated the visit, and thereby put him
completely at his ease.

John spent his whole visit quizzing Wimber, filling
notebooks which he still treasures and asking probing
and awkward questions of people, so typical of the
sceptical Englishman abroad. But I suppose Wimber
recognised in John a genuine longing to learn, and he
returned to the United Kingdom with his suitcase
bulging with books, cassette tapes and inspiration. If
Wimber looked a little like Santa Claus, he shared other
characteristics of his, too. From that day forward they
became the firmest of friends, their relationship developing into one in which Wimber felt as free to confront
as to compliment.

For myself, I met Wimber a year later during one of
his early visits to London. John and I were by then

working on the staff of a church in central London, and
we were loving it. We took a group of our friends to an
open meeting at Holy Trinity Brompton where we sat
in relative safety, so we thought, near the back. I had
never been to a meeting like it and had never seen nor
experienced the Holy Spirit working in such evident
power. It was both disconcerting and rivetting. Wimber
taught from the Gospels of the reality of the Kingdom
of God, that God was able to do today at the hands of
his own church deeds no less remarkable than those
done two thousand years ago at the hands of his own
Son Jesus.

Towards the end of the meeting, in a way that was
refreshingly unpretentious, he described to the whole
congregation a number of ailments from which he
thought various people in that room were suffering.
One of these, a relatively minor complaint common
among women, applied to me. I was appalled, coming
as I did from a family where such parts of the body
were never mentioned or admitted to in private, far less
named in public! However, the dye was cast and I felt
compelled to go to the side-room where I would be
prayed for. (It should be said that John led this part of
the evening with great sensitivity and a high regard for
people's dignity; I always loved the masterly way in
which he could be both honest yet protective, true to
what God was telling him yet sensitive to the vulnerability of people.) My worst fears, however, were about
to be realised.

I was met by a bearded Californian covered with
extraneous hair, dressed in a sleeveless teeshirt and
considerably shorter even than me. As he chewed on
his gum and puffed spearmint in my direction, he
prayed for me. No sooner had he finished than he
encouraged me to go and start praying for the sick
myself: I had received blessing from the Lord, so what
better than to give some of it away immediately? I

returned to the main meeting but was unable to stay in
my seat at the back, because my earlier scepticism had
now given way to fascination. John took me to Wimber,
who was praying for people at the front of the room
and asked him to teach me everything he knew by taking me alongside.

The next couple of hours were a turning point in my
life. Wimber literally took me by the hand and taught
me how to pray for the sick. Up till that point it had
never occurred to us that this was something teachable
and transferable. (Only later did we re-visit the New
Testament and discover the way in which Jesus trained
the disciples to preach the gospel, lay their hands on the
sick, and cast out demons, just as Wimber did.) He
prayed for a couple of people while I watched, and then
casually invited me to pray for the third, stopping occasionally to explain what he saw happening. It was all
done in a way that was both sensitive as well as incredibly practical in a down-to-earth way, completely
devoid of any hype that so often causes us Anglo-
Saxons to cringe. You might say that what began as a
hand-holding exercise evolved into intelligent tutoring,
and was followed by the encouragement to me to take
risks for myself.

I remember thinking at the end of those two hours,
'If all this is true and the power of God is available to
heal the sick, to care for the broken, to comfort the sad,
to encourage the defeated and so forth, then what else
would one want to do between now and the Return of
Christ?. . .' In that sense, he was an inspiration to us, yet
he never lost sight of the practical and the obtainable.
He modelled, in a fatherly way, something that was
both compelling and possible. He was always a trainer
and never a superstar, always wanting to equip others
in the church, never to shine himself as a solo artist. He
helped me realise, as indeed he did for hundreds like
me, that – incredibly – it is possible to be used by God,

even though so often we perceive ourselves to be normal and ordinary.

John Wimber had a highly developed sense of family, extraordinary in one so deprived as a child. He only discovered the existence of his own two half-brothers, George and Bill, shortly before he died. Finding and getting to know them over that short period gave him profound pleasure. At his funeral in November 1997, his whole family gathered on the platform to pay their own tributes. John and Carol have four children, all married to men and women following and serving the Lord together, and eleven grandchildren, every one loving Jesus and well able to say so. The sight of them all surrounding John's coffin was a most moving tribute to a fatherless man whom God had raised up to be so much loved in his own home.

He was immensely proud of his sons Christopher, Timothy and Sean and of his daughter Stephanie. He loved to regale us all of tales of their lives and exploits, enjoying what a one-time Anglican Bishop of Salisbury used to call, 'FSOC' (Favourite Subject Own Children). Possibly the greatest agony John ever had to suffer – of which there were not a few – was to watch his eldest son Chris battling with incredible bravery against melanoma cancer. He, John, had survived cancer not five years before, only to learn soon afterwards of Chris's illness. It was a terrible blow about which he spoke freely and always poignantly.

Shortly before he died John telephoned Chris, who was himself dying, to tell him just how much he loved him. He went on to tell him what a remarkable work he had done leading the Vineyard Music Group, turning it into a flourishing company and documenting the worship of the Vineyard that was so precious to John. He told Chris at great length how proud he was, as a father, of his son's business achievements and of the tenacity he was showing in the face of great suffering. John

spoke eloquently for many minutes into the answer-
phone. As Debbie, Chris's wife, later reported, she and
Chris hoped so much that whoever got the heart-warm-
ing message felt blessed and wonderfully well-
fathered, since the message never ever reached Chris
himself. John had dialled the wrong number!

John adored his many grandchildren and they
would hover around him like bees around honey.
Whenever he arrived home after travelling, he would
gather the family together for lunch after church, one of
the things he loved best; and the children were always
central to the party. As each grandchild approached his
tenth birthday John would prepare to take him on one
of his trips abroad. Visits to London were a highlight.
He aged unnaturally quickly towards the end of his life
and the eight- and nine-year-old grandchildren would
watch the process with increasing apprehension. One of
them even approached Carol to check whether she
thought that John would live to take him on his next
trip to London, or might it be wise to lower the age
limit?! Many of the children wrote poems or presenta-
tions which they read at John's funeral with the most
evident affection. John really was the all-time and
archetypal grandfather to a generation of small children.

He also had a remarkable capacity for absorbing into
an already strong family unit the spouses his own children married. He had a particular gift for making his
new daughters-in-law feel accepted, embraced and
admired. Each one of them, Debbie, Sharon and Kristy
flourished as new brides, young mothers and godly
women. John believed in and loved each one dearly, yet
differently, and was able to draw out the potential in
them that they might otherwise never have known.
They and Danny, the son-in-law whom John greatly
respected, assumed an important place at the heart of
the family and he always felt the richer because of each

one of them.

It always struck me that John well understood how to treat women, both within and beyond the immediate family. For him, Carol was the brightest star in his own firmament and he would often tell us so. He obviously loved her devotedly, but he also held her in very high regard. He knew that she could think clearly and would express herself incisively. We all knew that much of his own thinking was sharpened on the anvil of hers. Far from threatening him, it was to him an appropriate source of pride and often amusement. Carol would sometimes challenge him in a meeting, or argue with him in public, and would never let him get away with much. We all, and not least John (most of the time) loved her for it.

He became nothing less than a father to Carol's younger sister Penny, when she went to live with them in her late teenage years, met her husband Bob through them and went on to marry from their home. John was a key figure in Penny's life, her own father having died when she was only a small child. Their relationship was incredibly close and John once spoke publicly of the way in which he had learnt about love through the lives of both Carol and Penny.

What John did within his own family he reproduced in the wider church. Paul reminded Timothy in Ephesus, 'If anyone does not know how to manage his own family, how can he take care of God's church?' (1 Tim 3:5). John saw himself as a father, first to the church at Anaheim, and later to many churches as the Vineyard movement grew both within the United States and beyond. He understood well the principle of sowing and reaping. What he sowed into his own family, often with tears in earlier years, he latterly reaped with the greatest of joy. He also grew to understand what fatherhood, in the purest sense, meant. He realised that no son or daughter, whether within the

smaller family or the larger church, can have a sure
sense of their own uniqueness until they hear it spoken
from their father's lips.

Over the years John became nothing less than a
father to me. Just before he died, I went on my own to
spend a week with him and the family, for he had just
been through major heart by-pass surgery and was not
recovering well. It was a memorably happy week for
me, albeit sad to see him so weak and incapacitated, but
we spent time together every day which is all the more
precious in retrospect. Little did I know that within two
weeks of my return to England he would be dead. I
know that John loved me and felt free to tell me so, constantly affirming and encouraging me. He also knew
that it was appropriate to confront and to correct me on
occasions, which I didn't much enjoy at the time, but
came to value greatly later. He was interested in the
smallest details of our lives. He loved our two sons,
who were never happier than they were with him. I
know he used to pray for them and that he genuinely
enjoyed their company. He would laugh at their jokes
and listen to their stories, with all the indulgence of an
honorary grandfather.

It so happened a few years ago that he was the first
guest to stay in our newly-refurbished home in southwest London. He seemed to take real delight in all that
we had done in the house, and I remember being
incredibly touched that he telephoned Carol, at home in
Yorba Linda, during the night when jet-lag kept him
awake, to describe to her every last detail and to catalogue even the colours of the cushions. He had a creative streak in him that enjoyed designing a garden for
their new home in California, and he was not backward
to come forward with suggestions for ours! My own
parents, being both frail and faraway, were never able
to visit my home after I was married as I had always
longed that they should, so once again the Lord used

John to make good the gaps for me.

Many people have tales to tell of his incredible kindness and outrageous generosity. Jackie Pullinger has said that John was nothing less than a 'father in the gospel' to her and to her people in Hong Kong. Another friend tells of an occasion when John visited his home in England at a time when his teenage daughter was taking what might be described as a 'sabbatical from God'. She avoided the morning service, but badly wanted her lunch. There she met John for the first time, who once again exhibited the intuitional fatherliness we loved him for, particularly when he and Carol invited her to visit California and to share their home for the summer.

Five years ago one of our own colleagues went to the airport to collect John, something which he loved to do, but equally something John would have no particular reason to remember, one might think. Four years later that same man drove him to our house after a meeting and they renewed their acquaintance. 'Of course I remember who you are. You're the David I've been praying for.' No young leader in the church at Corinth could have been more thrilled. Several years ago John went to visit a New Frontiers church in Brighton one Sunday morning, and on his way into the building with his hosts, he stopped on the steps outside to chat casually with small children. To the surprise and delight of some of the congregation, when later he stood up to speak, they recognised in him the affectionate father-figure as he metamorphosed into that morning's visiting speaker.

Over the years, I have talked to countless people in numerous places who have all said, quite spontaneously yet independently of one another, that they felt as if John was a spiritual father to them. All of them had in common the extraordinary fact that, although they had never actually met him personally, nevertheless they respected and genuinely loved him – something, surely, which is only explicable because it is God-given. The Lord raised John up to become a 'father in the gospel' to hundreds, even thousands, of people whom he never personally knew, but to whom he felt a profound sense of commitment.

John Wimber had about him all the warmth and generosity of a father. Almost without realising it, it seems, he gave to many, many people the security to be themselves and the safety to develop in the Lord. He did all he could to give away all that God had invested in him, and freely blessed the generations that were to follow in his own family but also across the church. The part he played in our lives was both endearing and empowering. As a father-figure and a pastor John loved every expression of the body of Christ and as Terry Virgo, a close friend, said at a memorial service in London, 'With John's death we have lost a father and a great friend in God'.

7

BIBLE TEACHER
RICH NATHAN

*Rich Nathan is senior pastor of Vineyard Christian
Fellowship of Columbus, Ohio, a church of more than 3,500.
He has been an Association of Vineyard Churches Regional
Overseer for several years and serves on AVC's National
Board. Rich co-authored the book,* Empowered
Evangelicals *(Servant Press) with Ken Wilson and
is currently working on a new book on the church.*

The source of John's message: the Gospels
What made John Wimber's Bible teaching different
from typical conservative evangelicals or charismatic
teachers? One of the main differences was that Wimber
drew his messages, in the main, from a different source.
Conservative evangelicals have historically focused
most of their attention on the Epistles. This focus, of
course, has a very long history in the church. The book
of the Bible that served as a catalyst for the evangelical
revival was Paul's Letter to the Romans.

For example, a worldly-wise young North African
man named Augustine was led to the book of Romans
when he heard a boy randomly crying out, 'Take and
read!' Augustine's Bible happened to be open at the
book of Romans – chapter 13:12–14 – which spoke
directly to his dissolute lifestyle. The experience trig-
gered his conversion. Centuries later, Martin Luther, a
monk in the order named after Augustine, experienced
a similar conversion as he encountered Paul's teaching

on 'a righteousness that is by faith from first to last' (Rom 1:17) from the same book. Two hundred years later, the Great Awakening was sparked when an Anglican cleric named John Wesley listened to a reading from Luther's commentary on the book of Romans. Wesley felt that his 'heart strangely warmed' as the power of God's grace invaded his soul. Little wonder then, that the letters of Paul, especially Romans, would have such a prominent place in the teaching of the churches, which identify with the Protestant Reformers.

The Pentecostal emphasis on baptism in the Spirit with speaking in tongues brought a renewed emphasis on the book of Acts, and various gifts passages such as 1 Corinthians 12–14.

Much of the teaching in the Pentecostal and charismatic streams of the church are drawn from these portions of Scripture. The neglect of the Gospels in the teaching of the church was substantially altered as Wimber dusted off the Gospels and allowed them to challenge our preconceptions about the supernatural world and the power of the Spirit.

For conservative evangelicals, this meant recapturing a view of Jesus' humanity and his miracles as a model for the church today. In the past, conservative evangelicals tended to view the supernatural elements of Jesus' ministry as an expression of his divinity. He could do these things, in short, because he was God. Certainly the miracles of Jesus are important evidences for his divinity. Yet Wimber made out a powerful case that Jesus performed these works of power as a human being, led by the Holy Spirit (see e.g., Luke 4:1, 14; 5:17). (This statement is not meant in any way to take away from Jesus' full divinity or to teach some kenotic theory of the Incarnation.) While Jesus was fully human and fully God, Wimber showed from the Gospels that Jesus relied on the promptings of the Spirit for his ministry. Wimber never tired of pointing out Jesus' utter dependence on the Spirit. Jesus made a point to underline his dependence: 'I tell you the truth, the Son can do nothing by himself; he can do only what he sees his Father doing, because whatever the Father does the Son also does' (John 5:19).

For charismatics, Wimber's use of the Gospels took spiritual gifts outside the prayer meeting and into the marketplace. As Wimber frequently said, 'The meat is in the streets.' What did this mean in practical terms? Within the charismatic movement of the 1970s and 1980s, one of the primary expressions of renewal was the 'prayer meeting'. A typical prayer meeting would have the participants meeting 'in the round' to maximize the sense of participation. Elements of the meeting would include singing, interspersed with vocal praise and punctuated perhaps by a message in tongues, followed by an interpretation, a prophecy (in which the speaker would address the group in the first person, 'The Lord says . . .') and 'singing in the Spirit' (the assembly singing together in the same key, some in their native language, some in tongues).

The Gospels, however, show Jesus not using spiritual gifts in a charismatic 'prayer meeting'. Rather, Jesus modeled exercising gifts in the public square. From this perspective, when Jesus told the accusers of the woman caught in adultery, 'If any one of you is without sin, let him be the first to throw a stone at her' (John 8:7), he may have been speaking what Paul later called a prophecy in his description of various gifts of revelation (see 1 Cor 12:8). Or when he told the Samaritan woman that she had five husbands, he spoke, again, by a word of prophecy. His insights concerning the Kingdom were what Paul later called 'the message of knowledge' (1 Cor 12:8). Wimber's perspective on Jesus' use of spiritual gifts prompted many Christians to seek to exercise gifts of the Spirit not only in the church meetings, but also in the opportunities for ministry at work, in their neighbourhoods, at school and in the wider community.

The heart of John's message: the Kingdom of God

Wimber taught the profound idea that in Jesus Christ the Kingdom of God has truly invaded this world and has not simply 'drawn near'. In other words, Wimber taught that there has been a true change of affairs affecting this present evil age, even though this present age was not entirely destroyed or removed. It is absolutely the case that the most profound change took place on the wooden cross at Calvary where Jesus bled and died for the forgiveness of our sins. All evangelicals, whether charismatic or noncharismatic, agree that Jesus' mission at his first coming was chiefly 'to give his life as a ransom for many' (Matt 20:28).

But it is no denigration to the chief mission of Christ, that is, the salvation of sinners, to state that Jesus' first coming was not exhausted by this central fact of the forgiveness of sins. Jesus also came to bring about the invasion of the Kingdom of God, namely God's rule and reign in eternity, into our present time and space. Thus, Wimber regularly said, 'Don't be surprised that in Jesus' first coming, the things awaiting eternity – namely, the healing of the sick, the recovery of sight for the blind, the end of poverty and hunger, the reconciliation of broken relationships, the deliverance of demonized, the raising of the dead – were all brought by Jesus into human history.' In Christ, *eternity broke into time*.

Wimber described Jesus as a glorious relay runner who took the torch of the Kingdom of God from the Father's hand and carried it into this world, into our age, lighting the torch of eternity in our time. The torch was passed to the apostles, who were commissioned to do and proclaim the very same things that Jesus was doing and proclaiming. As Matthew reports: 'Jesus gave [the twelve disciples the] authority to drive out evil spirits and to heal every disease and sickness, commissioning them to preach this message: ' "The kingdom of heaven is near." Heal the sick, raise the dead, cleanse those who have leprosy, drive out demons. Freely you have received, freely give' (see Matt 10:1, 7–8).

Jesus also gave the same commission and authority to the seventy-two, a group of followers obviously broader than Jesus' core of twelve disciples (see Luke 10:1, 8–16). And the apostles not only proclaimed the gospel by preaching and healing, but they also taught the disciples they made to proclaim the gospel by preaching and healing. Wimber pointed out that non-apostles such as Stephen, Philip, Ananias, and congregations such as the ones in Galatia, Corinth, Philippi and Jewish Christian congregations (in the Book of Hebrews) all experienced and practiced the ministry of the Kingdom, which included not just the proclamation of the forgiveness of sins, but also the healing of sickness and the driving out of demons.

But Wimber's message and transparent life (his cancer and heart problems, his stroke and his family problems) contained no shallow triumphalism. Though we experience the thrill of eternity, which includes having our sins carried away and having 'tasted the goodness of the Word of God and the powers of the coming age' (Heb 6:5), in this time before the second coming Wimber was, like Paul: 'Hard pressed on every side, but not crushed; perplexed, but not in despair; persecuted, but not abandoned; struck down, but not destroyed. [He] always carr[ied] around in [his] body the death of Jesus' (2 Cor 4:8–10).

Wimber's experience of the thrill was, therefore, always tempered by his communication of the agony, and his belief in the power of God always ran side-by-side with his experience of pain and suffering. Wimber made sense of power and pain, therefore, through the grid of the *already* and *not yet* of the Kingdom of God. It was his belief that we will not see *total* healing of our racial and ethnic divisions until the Holy City Jerusalem comes down from heaven (see Rev 21:10), but we can experience *substantial healing* of our divisions now (see Eph 2:14–17). Likewise, Wimber taught that we will not experience the eradication of disease until the second coming of Christ (see Rev 21:4). Nevertheless, we can expect many mental and physical healings (see Jas 5:13–16). And Wimber suggested that even the resurrection of the dead, which will be fully accomplished at Christ's second coming, should occasionally be seen in this age (see Matt 10:8; Acts 9:40; 20:7–12).

The model of John's message: words and works

It took me quite a while to get over the initial shock of experiencing John Wimber's method of teaching. Unlike any Bible teacher that I had ever heard before, Wimber didn't believe the teaching time was over when he closed the Bible. For him, Bible teaching was inextricably linked to the ministry of the Spirit. Anyone who came to a Wimber conference probably remembers their shock at observing this bearded, laid-back Californian, 'do ministry' after his Bible message was done. At least for me, the model that I had grown up with was the pastor leaving the pulpit after the Bible message was completed to greet parishioners at the back of the church. But Wimber's methodology was modeled on the example of Christ himself and the apostles.

What Wimber saw in the Gospels and, indeed, throughout the whole New Testament, was the continual link-up of the preached word and the exercise of spiritual gifts, such as healing, deliverance and prophecy. Wimber used to call Jesus' methods 'show and tell'.

Jesus spoke the words, Wimber would say, and then he did the works. Thus, some of Wimber's favorite teaching passages were texts such as these,

> Jesus went throughout all of Galilee teaching in their synagogues, preaching the good news of the kingdom, and healing every disease and sickness among the people. News about him spread all over Syria, and people brought to him all who were ill with various diseases, those suffering severe pain, the demon-possessed, those having seizures, and the paralyzed, and he healed them.
>
> (Matt 4:23ff)

Wimber taught that Jesus not only taught and preached the message of the Kingdom, but that he also demonstrated it with works of power. Jesus not only modeled 'teaching the word and doing the works', as Wimber pointed out, but he also commissioned his disciples to follow his example. Thus, Jesus said, 'As you go, preach this message: ' "The kingdom of heaven is near." Heal the sick, raise the dead, cleanse those who have leprosy, drive out demons' (Matt 10:7–8).

Words and works were not only the method of Jesus and the Twelve, but also the method that Paul used in spreading the Kingdom of God. As the apostle Paul wrote in the book of Romans,

> Therefore I glory in Christ Jesus in my service to God. I will not venture to speak of anything except what Christ has accomplished through me in leading the Gentiles to obey God *by what I have said and done* – by the power of signs and miracles, through the power of the Spirit. So from Jerusalem all the way around to Illyricum, I have fully proclaimed the gospel of Christ.
>
> (Rom 15:17–19 emphasis added)

One of the highlights for people who attended any meeting led by John Wimber was the 'ministry time'. Ministry time always followed a lengthy, well-exegeted message taken from a selected biblical text (as noted before, Wimber's favorite passages were from the Gospels).

I personally had the opportunity to listen to Wimber on over one hundred occasions. I never saw John do ministry without first opening up God's Word to his people. He fundamentally believed in the power of the Word of God to change lives. But unlike some conservative evangelicals, Wimber believed that God's intention for a congregation was not exhausted by the teaching of the Scriptures. Thus, John added what he called 'ministry time', which was a time for a person to receive physical healing, deliverance, guidance, or whatever else the Holy Spirit purposed for that individual immediately following the message.

John never 'hyped' the ministry time by promising great things. Rather than attempt to elevate people's emotions, Wimber on many occasions actually exhorted folks to 'dial down' their emotions and simply allow God to do what God purposed to do. John was well aware of the effects of mass hysteria and manipulation. Thus, he did everything within his power to be non-manipulative and non-assertive during ministry times.

Still, one of John's lasting contributions to the body of Christ will be his model of Bible teaching: always coupling the preaching of the Word with the doing of the works of Christ.

The fruit of John's message: staying power

A revival or renewal, even if it began as a genuine work of God, loses its staying power without the systematic study of the Scriptures and an appreciation for theological reflection. Like the days of the Judges of Israel, an earlier move of God can quickly become forgotten by the children and the grandchildren.

> After that whole generation had been gathered to their fathers, another generation grew up, who knew neither the LORD nor what he had done for Israel. Then the Israelites did evil in the eyes of the LORD and served the Baals. They forsook the LORD, the God of their fathers, who had brought them out of Egypt. They followed and worshiped various gods of the peoples around them. They provoked the LORD to anger.
>
> (Judges 2:10–12)

The charismatic movement has suffered the problem of 'no grandchildren' often in its brief history. Early in Pentecostal history (about a year before the meetings at Azusa Street that spread Pentecostalism throughout North America), a significant revival took place in Wales. Between September 1904 and June 1905, it is estimated that over a hundred thousand Welsh were converted under the preaching of Evan Roberts and others. Chapels, barns and every other conceivable meeting place were filled night after night as people worshiped, praised God ecstatically, and listened to testimonies by recent converts. Often the meetings were not scheduled in advance. It has been reported that people were simply drawn to the meeting places by the leading of God's Spirit.

Newspaper accounts of the Welsh revival reported enormous short-term results from the revival meetings. The crime rate dropped dramatically throughout Wales, as did gambling and alcohol consumption. Anecdotal stories are told of pit ponies at coal mines who had to be retrained to respond to new vocabulary, because previously they had been trained to respond to their owner's cursing and swearing. Yet despite the many wonderful events of 1904 and 1905, Evan Roberts and other leaders of the revival neglected expository teaching of the Bible. They failed to encourage the study of the Scriptures in their meetings and treated theology as a 'fleshly discipline'. As a result, when World War I broke out just a decade after this extraordinary revival, there were just a few pockets of believers remaining in the Welsh chapels. By the 1920s, visitors to Wales said that one could find virtually no evidence that a revival had ever taken place. How extraordinarily tragic! But experiencing the Spirit unsupported by teaching the full written Word of God is like water spilled on the ground. After a brief time, the ground dries up and no sign remains that water was ever poured there.

Better and more lasting things can be expected to result from Wimber's ministry, because it was always undergirded by teaching the eternal Word of God. Through John Wimber, people received not only an experience, nor even a charismatic personality, but a true message from the Scriptures. And it is Wimber's biblical teaching that will give his ministry staying power. For as the prophet Isaiah said, 'All men are like grass and all their glory is like the flowers of the field. The grass withers and the flowers fall, but the word of our God stands forever.'

8

THE PROPHET
JACK DEERE

*Jack Deere was professor of Old Testament Exegesis and
Semitic Studies at Dallas Theological Seminary from 1976-
1988. He then served as an associate pastor at the Vineyard
Christian Fellowship of Anaheim until 1992, before pastor-
ing the First Presbyterian Church in Whitefish, Montana
until 1996 where he lives with his wife and three children.
Jack is now working on a number of writing projects and
conducts a conference ministry with Paul Cain and Mike
Bickle. He is the author of* Surprised by the Power of
God *and* Surprised by the Voice of God.

John Wimber would probably laugh at the title of this
chapter, for he never really considered himself a
prophet. Others referred to him as a prophet or even an
apostle, but he seemed more amused by this than anything else. When Leesa and I were first getting to know
John, I asked him if he thought he was an apostle. He
smiled as if he knew something I didn't and said, 'No'.

'Others call you an apostle. Why don't you?' I asked.

'Jack, one day I'm going to heaven and will stand
before the Lord for his personal evaluation of my life. I
don't want to hear him say, "So you're my apostle?"
You see God has never said to me that I'm an apostle,
so it doesn't really make any difference what my admir-
ers say.'

If fear of that future divine encounter kept John from

calling himself an apostle, it was an underestimation of
his gifts that kept him from thinking of himself as a
prophet. He had no trouble calling his friend Paul Cain
a prophet and even publicly extolling Paul's gifting.
Often I heard him refer to members of his church as
prophets even though they were much less prophetical-
ly gifted than himself. In spite of his own personal reti-
cence to say so, John Wimber was a prophet. He was
not a scripture writing prophet nor an inerrant one, but
nonetheless a real prophet for our times.

The prophet in action

Prophets know the secrets of people's hearts. At
Samuel's first encounter with Saul he told him where
his father's lost donkeys were and then asked him to
spend the night promising to tell Saul the secrets of his
heart on the next day (1 Sam 9:19–21). The first time I
went to a conference with John was in Ashland, Ohio,
in 1986. After he finished teaching, a young couple
approached him asking for prayer for the wife's
abscessed tooth. While he prayed, both of them were
smiling, feeling privileged to have John Wimber personally praying for them. Then without any warning
John said, 'Lord, would you heal that infected ovary?'
Through their tears they asked, 'How did you know?
How did you know?'

'The Lord told me,' he answered.

When we walked away, I asked, 'John, how did you
know?'

'The Lord told me.'

'Yeah, I know, but how did you know?' I asked
again. I was stunned. I had never seen anyone do anything like this. He was so unreligious, almost casual
about it. And his confidence in the voice of the Lord
was unnerving to me. He didn't ask if she had an
infected ovary – he blurted out a prayer for it. How did
he know?

Before he could answer me again, someone ran up to him asking him to come quickly. We were led to a man about sixty years old, slumped in his seat, with contorted face and hands, and a frantic wife sitting beside him. I thought he was having a stroke or heart attack. John looked at him for a second – I was about to offer to call an ambulance – and then he leaned down and whispered something in the man's ear. The man nodded his head 'yes'. Then John prayed, 'I break the power of this darkness over my brother.' Break the power of what? I don't remember the rest of the prayer. I got lost on the first phrase. Can Christians do that? Is it legal to go around breaking darkness? Can you make the darkness mad doing this sort of thing. I wasn't exactly sure what the darkness was, but I didn't think it was a good idea to irritate it. When I came out of my musings, I heard John say to the wife, 'He'll probably be like this the rest of the night, but don't worry. The Lord is dealing with him. You'll have a new husband tomorrow.'

'What was that all about?' I asked as we walked away.

'The man was under the bondage of a sexual sin,' said John.

'How did you know?'

'The Lord told me.'

'Would you please stop saying that and tell me how you knew? I mean was it like an audible voice or what?'

'No, it was just an impression.'

'A strong, overpowering, clear impression no doubt?'

'Actually, no. It was so faint I almost didn't pay attention to it. Except in these situations I've trained myself to notice even the faintest impressions. They could lead you to the key that will unlock someone's bondage.'

I was overwhelmed. I felt like I was beginning my Christian education all over again, but this time with a prophet not a professor. I watched John do these kinds of things in conferences all over the world as well as in his own church. Sometimes he could look at people he had just met and tell them their gifting and even something about their future.

Like the Old Testament prophets he was also skilled at discerning the Lord's present priorities for the church. He was one of the first to recognize God was changing a model of ministry widely embraced in the church. The 'man of faith and power for this very hour' model was about to enter a divinely planned obsolescence. In the place of a single anointed servant, the Lord wanted a congregation of ministers trained in their gifts, knowing their calling and on active duty (Eph 4:11–13). So John built a church like this. He was definitely ahead of his time.

Persecuted and misunderstood

And like others who were ahead of their time he was persecuted and misunderstood. John was a prophet not a theologian. This made him an easy target. Sometimes those who regarded themselves as divinely appointed definers of doctrine were better at defining God's love than they were at showing it to John Wimber. This is one of the chief occupational hazards of being a professional definer – defining takes precedence over experiencing. It was natural for them to look at prophets of the Bible as subjects to define rather than models to imitate.

John was concerned to imitate what he saw in the Bible, to let the supernatural flow through his humanity. But others who were more concerned with defining the supernatural didn't pay much attention to how it was filtered through the humanity of the biblical prophets and apostles. In their theories, rigid lines separated the humanity of the biblical servants from their supernatural acts. In John's experience, he often felt divine revelation coming to him in such a faint way that it was almost disguised as a merely human thought. And when he acted on the faint impression, it turned out to be true. But he would have never known for sure if he had not acted, not had the courage to risk looking like a foolish failure.

Sometimes when John tried to explain the process, he got into trouble. And being a trainer made him also an explainer frequently in trouble with the definers. Once when someone asked John how these incredibly specific words of knowledge came to him, he replied that it was like a 'hunch'. His reply was taped. After hearing the tape, certain members of the merciful, who by their own confession had never experienced any communication from God other than what they had read in the Bible, ridiculed him without mercy. They said he had reduced the Word of God to a hunch. Privately John felt terrible about these accusations, but he never showed that publicly or retaliated against his detractors. Everybody who knew John, knew that he held the highest view of the Bible. For him it was the inerrant, infallible, absolutely authoritative Word of God. He thought every private revelation had to be submitted to the authority of the Bible, and nothing contradicting its statements or principles could be admitted as true. But John wasn't a Bible scholar. He was a churchman and an equipper of believers. He wasn't an educator; he was a trainer. And this frequently left him at the mercy of educators who had more knowledge to spare than mercy. For whatever reason, they seemed more intent on discrediting than understanding; thus forcing John to bear another of the true marks of a prophet – persecution by the religious (Lk 6:22–23). I heard him preach several good sermons on enduring persecution. Perhaps they were good because he never had to go very far to find his material.

Another thing that is characteristic of prophets is

that they recognize other prophets. John did more than this. He reacquainted the church with a form of prophetic ministry that it had been resolutely ignoring, or worse, despising for a long time. Even in the charismatic church which had a theoretical belief in prophecy, there was often a tendency to disdain the gift. It was frequently practiced on Sunday mornings at the most elemental and general levels in King James' language, e.g., 'Yea My people I love thee and will bless thee'. Or if the prophet were in an angry mood it might sound like this, 'Yea My people have I not said unto thee that I am about to spew thee out of My mouth'. Or in some cases, prophecy was used to control people even to the point of arranging marriages. And, predictably, these marriages often failed. I have met a number of those prophetic casualties. So it's not difficult to see why many in the church were less than enthusiastic about the gift of prophecy. They hadn't seen much that resembled the biblical examples of prophecy. John Wimber's specific words were the most remarkable examples of supernatural revelation that many of us had seen, but John didn't consider himself a prophet. Then John met the prophets.

Meeting a Kansas City prophet

When John first met one of the 'Kansas City prophets' in 1984 he was eminently unimpressed. By 1988, when I came to work for John at the Anaheim Vineyard, both he and the Vineyard were at a low point. Some key leaders were going through very difficult times. Some left the ministry. John was having severe problems with his heart. He was even making frequent jokes about his death. His youngest son Sean had been losing a battle with drug addiction for years. This was the context when John met Paul Cain in December 1988.

John had heard about Paul and wanted to meet him, but it took months to coordinate their schedules. Paul wanted to meet John because he felt the Lord had shown him something he wanted to do for John and the Vineyard. In the privacy of the Wimbers' living room, Paul's opening words were, 'The Lord says to you," 'Grace, grace, grace" ' John was shocked. He had expected a rebuke or judgment. Next, Paul said that if John would call the Vineyard to repentance and a higher level of holiness, the Lord would change the Vineyard by the next time that John addressed the whole Vineyard. That date had already been fixed, August 1989. The Lord had another, more personal promise for the Wimbers. If John would issue the call for holiness, the Lord would deliver Sean from years of rebellion and drug addiction. And he would do it within the next nine months, i.e. before John addressed the national Vineyard conference. Years of rebellion would be ended in a matter of months.

John told me later that Paul had not acted very much like an awesome prophet. He didn't prophesy in King James' English. He was soft-spoken and unassuming, even a little disorganized. But John didn't judge Paul by what his eyes saw or what he heard with his ears. If he had, Paul would have come up short from the perspective of style and manner. Nor did he judge Paul's words by their content alone. This would have guaranteed an immediate, uncritical acceptance of the message. Who wouldn't want to believe that God would bless their movement and deliver their son? But John was a prophet. So he evaluated Paul and his prophecy with the discernment of the Holy Spirit. Through the witness of the Spirit John believed what he had been told and did what was required of him by the prophetic word.

I was there the following June when Sean was set free. It was wonderful. And I watched a renewal come to the Vineyard as they responded to John's call for repentance. It was also wonderful.

John had been so blessed by prophetic ministry that

he wanted to introduce it to everyone. He began to have prophets speak and minister in his conferences. Not everyone agreed with this move. Some of John's friends had serious misgivings about the prophetic ministry in general. They thought it was too subjective and that it would inevitably diminish the authority of the Bible. Others had been hurt by the prophetic, or they knew someone who had had a bad experience with prophets. One prominent leader warned John to drop it immediately. He told him that he knew leaders who had been household names throughout the church until they got involved with prophets. They lost their ministries overnight because of their infatuation with revelatory gifting. It was too risky. John had worked too hard and had too much to lose.

Too Pentecostal

Others accepted the prophetic ministry in principle, but rejected the particular prophets with which John had become involved. A common criticism from this camp was that the prophets' theology or preaching style was 'too Pentecostal'. In these discussions 'Pentecostal' was never defined, and so it was impossible to know how one could avoid the error of becoming 'too Pentecostal'. It seemed that too Pentecostal simply meant more Pentecostal than the objector considered himself to be. A number of my friends from another life thought I had become too Pentecostal also. This worried me for awhile until John told me not to worry about it. He said he was singularly convinced that in my case I had a significant amount of ground to cover before I would become too Pentecostal.

Actually the charge of being 'too Pentecostal' is just one of a whole class of vague ill-defined objections that allows someone to dismiss a ministry without really examining it closely. I know a Presbyterian official who rejected the ministry of laying hands on sick people in a church service and praying for their healing. His sole reason for doing this was, 'That's not Presbyterian'. Never mind that people, like an eight-year-old boy suffering from severe asthma, were healed. It just wasn't Presbyterian. Let the little boy keep his asthma so we can all be good Presbyterians. Not to pick on the Presbyterians, the examples could be multiplied *ad nauseam* from other denominations. Haven't we all heard, or even made similar objections using our own particular traditions as the reason for rejecting something. These kinds of objections have no real substance. They usually amount to nothing more than, 'I don't like it. It's not what I'm used to.'

Unhappily most of us are too insecure, too afraid of change, to be completely above this kind of thoughtless rejection. On more than one occasion I even heard John Wimber say, 'That's not Vineyard'. But in his best moments he always used better criteria for making judgments. In reality, it was John who taught me to avoid the facile objections of the status quo mentality and to ask the only really important question, 'Is it God?' Never mind that it's not Vineyard – does Vineyard have all the truth? – is it God? What if God wanted to do something that wasn't Anglican? Would the Anglicans give their consent?

Since John had often been the victim of this type of criticism, and since he had personally experienced the fruit of being too Pentecostal, he didn't pay much attention to the complaints about the prophets' Pentecostal style, whatever that was. But the warning that he was risking his whole ministry by promoting the prophets was more serious. John knew this from the moment he first brought prophetic ministry onto his stage. The first time he took the prophets with him outside the United States, some of the religious leaders there told John that the prophets were too Pentecostal and that they didn't want them back in their country. John thanked the lead-

ers for coming to him privately, said he understood
their fears, and he would comply with their wishes – he
wouldn't come back to their country. 'No!' they said,
'You misunderstand us, dear brother. We want *you* to
come back, we just don't want *them*.'

'No, I understood you perfectly. You've misunderstood me. If you don't want the prophets, you don't
want me,' he said.

Just like that, John was willing to risk his whole ministry in that particular country for what he believed to
be God. That was how John handled the warning from
his friends that he was risking his whole ministry by
bringing the prophets on board. John lived by risking
for God. More than once he had thought God was asking him to give up everything for the pearl of great
price. Each time the risk had paid off. In the prophets he
saw another invitation from God to risk everything for
a pearl that the body of Christ urgently needed. John
took the risk and paid the price. He bore the brunt of
the merciless criticism from the guardians of religious
tradition who are seldom right in these matters but
never in doubt. He took the wearying lead in resolving
the controversies in his own circles created by his
change of course. The pay-off came in the numbers of
people who were strengthened, encouraged and
renewed through prophetic ministry. The Vineyard
movement itself was revived and its influence extended. After John had incorporated the prophets into his
conference ministry, Vineyard Ministries International
enjoyed the largest conferences in its history.

During this stage of his life, the humility that John
expressed was nothing short of inspirational. He had
always said that the ministry was not about us; it was
all about Jesus. So when he thought that it would bring
more glory to Jesus, he let his own ministry fade into
the background in order to give some of the other
prophets a greater platform. In doing this he was imi-

tating John the Baptist who lived by the dictum, 'He must increase; I must decrease' (Jn 3:30). The spirit of prophecy drives prophets to testify about Jesus (Rev 19:10). I believe this is what drove John Wimber, what made him a prophet, and such a wonderful father of the prophets.

His enduring significance

Who ever would have thought that a fatherless son from Missouri would father hundreds of spiritual sons all over the world? But it happened. I was privileged to be one of those sons. The Lord used John Wimber to give back a fatherhood that was stolen from me in my youth. So many young men in my generation found in John a father who delighted in us, believed in us, and brought out the best in us. Some of us weren't always the most grateful sons. Some of his sons even turned against him. But he never turned against them. And they were always welcome to come home.

If we live long enough to see the history of the twentieth-century church written, we may well find John Wimber being credited with changing the church more than any of his peers. He gave back ministry to the people. I never heard him use the word 'laity'. In his eyes, every Christian was meant to be a minister. He restored worship to a place of primacy in the church. Now churches all over the world have worship leaders instead of song leaders and music directors. More than anyone I know, John has helped to restore the ministry of healing to the conservative evangelical church. Church leaders and seminary professors alike found him to be a creditable witness to the contemporary supernatural healing ministry of the Holy Spirit. Similarly, the resurgence of prophetic ministry can largely be traced to his influence.

But above all, John was a spiritual father who wasn't afraid to be real. I saw so many people, sick of being religious and ready to give up, discover a new intimacy with God through John's unreligious transparency.

He had all the fundamentals, but they didn't come in a religious package. This irritated some leaders and even made others declare John an enemy. But the rest of us loved him for it. Not so much by listening to John, but rather by watching him, I learned how to be kind to my enemies, care for the poor, be willing to risk and suffer humiliation in trying to follow the Lord. Most of all, I learned what it feels like to be a son loved by a proud father. I never had that before I met John. Now I'll never lose it. But still, I would give anything to have him back.

9

CHURCH PLANTER[1]

STEVE NICHOLSON

*Steve Nicholson has been pastoring the Evanston
Vineyard Christian Fellowship in the Chicago area for
the past 22 years, which affiliated with the Vineyard in
1985. Steve has been personally involved in the planting
of 3 churches and the Evanston Vineyard has planted
10 daughter churches. Currently Steve is leading the
Church Planting Task Force for the AVC which is
overseeing the planting of about 100 churches annually.
He is currently working on a manual on how to coach
church plants. Steve is 45, married with 3 children.*

John Wimber loved church planting because he loved
seeing people give their lives to Christ and become fully
participating members of local churches. He knew that
church planting was one of the most effective ways of
seeing that happen. He knew that, according to the
studies, new churches were far more effective at reaching and incorporating people who had no previous
church affiliation. And he knew that new churches with
new styles and methods were needed to reach groups
not being reached by existing churches.

When John Wimber worked for the Fuller Institute
of Church Growth (1974–78) he attended a funeral that
had a great impact on his life.[2] He related that this
funeral was unique in a number of ways. First, it was
quite large and lasted all day. About 20,000 people.
mostly Puerto Rican representing fifty-six churches,

attended in groups of 1,000 throughout the day. As they paid their last respects they wept and laughed in honoring the deceased. Second, what had died was a church. Those who attended the funeral were the spiritual descendants of those who had been sent out from the mother church to plant other churches. One pastor stood up and shared that in the last year alone, the mother church had planted eleven churches and was like an old 'bitch' dog that had given birth one too many times. Third, those who had come back for the funeral had nothing but good to say about the church that had given them birth. There had been no splits, no fights and no festering disagreements. The members had been saved, discipled and sent out to do it all over again, and again and again.

Wimber remembered that the pastor of the church that had died was weeping throughout the day as he saw that his dream to plant churches had become a reality. This man had understood the evangelistic impact of new churches and had literally spent himself to win the lost. The pastor felt he could now go home a fulfilled man, having done what God had put him on the earth to do.

Wimber was profoundly touched and reflected later. 'That day God burned a passion into my soul for renewal and growth. I knew that whatever God called me to do, it had to be marked by a willingness to give everything away. I prayed, "Lord, if you ever call me to minister in another church, I promise it will be a sending church." '

In 1977 Wimber got his opportunity. That was the year that God led him to take a Bible study group and form what was first called the Calvary Chapel of Yorba Linda (later the Anaheim Vineyard). The church grew quickly, attracting a large number of young people. One of the young couples, Todd and Debbie Hunter, became the first church planters to be sent out from that church.[3]

Todd and Debbie were newly married and had just graduated from college. They were born and raised in Southern California and had gotten saved in the Jesus Movement of the late 1960s and early 1970s. They were deeply impacted by their experience in Calvary Chapel and especially in John Wimber's Calvary in Yorba Linda. They wanted to share that experience with other baby boomers (post-war modernists) so they approached John about wanting to plant a church.

What started out as nothing more than an impression that they were to go 'East' eventually wound-up becoming a specific call to Wheeling, West Virginia. Wimber tried very hard to persuade them not to go to Wheeling, arguing in favour of a large growing city like Houston or Kansas City. But Todd was so convinced they were to go there that in the fall of 1979 the Hunters and another couple naively journeyed to a very different culture from Southern California, found a place to live, got jobs in the community and proceeded to plant the Calvary Chapel of Wheeling (later the Wheeling Vineyard).

In the next ten years God used the Hunters not only to plant the church in Wheeling, but also to be catalysts for the planting of dozens of other churches throughout the American Midwest, a region that now has nearly one hundred Vineyard churches.

In May 1982, John Wimber, his church and several other related churches left the Calvary movement and joined the fledgling Vineyard movement, initially started by Kenn Gulliksen. Recognizing John's call and greater leadership abilities, Kenn turned over leadership of the new movement to him. Not only did this put John in charge of the newly formed movement, but it put him into a leadership role with catalytic church planters like Kenn Gulliksen and Jack Little, who along with many others went on to plant a number of

Vineyard churches in various parts of the country.

Shortly after this John had an incredible experience with God in answer to the prayer he had prayed at the church funeral. He described the vision he saw in the first issue of *First Fruits* magazine.[4]

> Several years ago God spoke to me in a vision concerning the planting of 10,000 fellowships. In this vision I saw a map of the United States with thousands of little lights all across the country. Some in the Mid-West, Denver, Chicago, Kansas City, etc: a large number across the Sun-Belt from Los Angeles to Phoenix to Houston and on into Florida. The New England states from Maine to New York City were covered as well as the Pacific Northwest clear down to Southern California. Thousands of little flashing lights! I asked God what this meant. He told me that each light represented a new fellowship that He wanted to start. I thought I had gone berserk. It must be me. I'm only making this up. As usual, God was persistent and patient and I was slow and resistant. I am now convinced that God has called me to encourage the planting of these 10,000 fellowships.
>
> Where will they come from? Some we will adopt (i.e. existing churches who wish to become Vineyards). To some we will be foster parents (i.e. they will stay who they are, and we will provide assistance as requested). Others we will give birth to. It is in this later grouping that most fellowships will be planted. God has initiated: now it is up to us to follow.

A vision for planting churches was now plain and being clearly articulated. John had been commissioned to start a church planting movement.

It wasn't long after I first came in contact with John Wimber that I heard about this vision. When I heard it, something powerful was sparked inside me. I thought that this was a vision worth spending one's life and energy for, a vision that had the potential to really have an impact in the nation, not to mention thousands of peoples' lives. I had previously been interested in church planting and had myself already planted churches, but hearing this vision turned me into a 'church planting maniac'. It became my favorite subject I became far more intentional about wanting to plant churches. I found myself looking for potential church planters in every possible situation. And I've talked to dozens of others who were similarly inspired and impacted by the same vision. For many of us the desire to play a part in achieving this vision was a prime reason for becoming more committed to the Vineyard.

In 1984, John Wimber and Bob Fulton put on a seminar for all the would-be church planters who had suddenly presented themselves to the Vineyard. A practical, step by step model for planting new churches was presented and taped.[5] These tapes were circulated and referred to by hundreds all around the world and used to help in the planting of more new churches than John could even know about.

In 1986, John asked Todd Hunter to do a survey of church plants, both successful and unsuccessful, in order to identify common factors and develop a profile for identifying successful church planters and also some direction for more effective training of church planters. The results were published in the Spring 1988 issue of *Equipping the Saints* called 'Successful Pastors: Are They Really Different?' This survey has had a major role in the development of church plants not only in the Vineyard, but also in many other movements.

But the vision for church planting was not limited to the United States. In the vision of the blinking lights, John had also seen the light jump over the ocean and land in the United Kingdom and from there it went all over the world. John already had begun an important connection with the UK. In 1981 he had met Canon David Watson, which resulted in an important ministry trip to England. During this trip God began using Wimber to powerfully renew and revitalize established churches, beginning with the Church of England parish known as St Andrew's, Chorleywood. Before the first team made this trip to England they had been having prayer meetings at Bob and Penny Fulton's house. During that time Bob had a dream about ministering in the streets of England and saw a whole series of churches popping up. He believed that the dream meant that the Vineyard would be planting churches in countries outside of the US.

When they arrived in the UK they told David Watson about the dream, but his response was 'No, that's not what this is about at all.' He pleaded with John not to plant churches but to work to equip the existing churches there to move in power. He knew that it would be difficult to pursue both renewal and church planting. The result was that John agreed to a moratorium on church planting, not only in the UK, but also in other countries where John was invited through the connection of David Watson's Anglican friends. John was holding large meetings with thousands of pastors and church members in attendance. In preparation for these meetings he made agreements with the leaders not to allow Vineyard church planting in their countries. If he were planting churches, the renewal could easily be perceived as a backdoor attempt to recruit members for the church plants. In fact, the renewal part of John's ministry in the United States was adversely affected by the great increase in church planting which took place in the years 1984–1987. Because of the moratorium, John was able to maintain a positive relationship with a wider range of pre-existing churches in countries such as the UK and Australia. The renewal work was able to go on for a much longer time.

But John soon found that it was more difficult to
'keep the lid on' church planting than he had anticipat-
ed. In 1985 he was approached by a young Anglican
curate and his wife, John and Eleanor Mumford. The
Mumfords had been powerfully touched by God in
Wimber's meetings and for various reasons were convinced that God was calling them to leave the Anglican
Church and to be a part of the Vineyard. They asked
Wimber for permission to plant a Vineyard church in
England, and he told them 'No'! Instead, Wimber invited them over to Anaheim for three to six months with
the idea that they would have an opportunity for training in preparation for a return to plant or pastor a
renewed Anglican church. The Mumfords arrived in
Anaheim in November 1985 and for various reasons
their stay was extended until June of 1987. The stay in
Anaheim only served to increase their sense of connection and belonging to the Vineyard and not to the
Church of England. But they felt called to the UK, not
the US. This left them in a confusing quandary, as John
was adamant about no church planting in the UK and
keeping Vineyard church planting confined primarily
to the US.

During this time the Mumfords were forming
stronger relationships with other Vineyard leaders who
began to feel that the Mumfords were really being
called by God to the Vineyard in spite of the church
planting moratorium. Finally, at a Vineyard board
meeting in the spring of 1987 general agreement was
reached that God was overruling Wimber and calling
the Mumfords to return to the UK to plant a Vineyard.
John Mumford recalls that later that day as Wimber
prayed over them to commission and release them for
the church plant, he began the prayer with something
like 'Lord, we've done everything we can to stop these
people from planting a Vineyard church and put obsta-

cles in their path and yet You seem to have continued to
call them in this direction, so we're going to release
them . . .'

Wimber found this situation to be profoundly
embarrassing. But feeling that he had no choice he con-
tacted a number of church leaders in the UK (David
Watson had died previous to this) to 'renegotiate' the
moratorium. Most of them were understanding and
supportive, and so the church planting moratorium in
the UK was ended. In June 1987, the Mumfords
returned to London and began their work to start what
is now the Southwest London Vineyard. Soon others
were joining them in various church planting efforts in
the UK. But the church planting moratoriums in
Australia and Germany were not ended for another ten
years or so.

Even though the Vineyard has been through many
ups and downs in its short history since 1983, church
planting has remained an ongoing legacy of Wimber's
vision. The number of churches has grown in every
year since its inception in spite of the loss of churches
which died or left the movement during various controversies. Most of this growth has been through church
planting rather than the adoption of existing churches.
At the end of 1983 there were thirty-two Vineyard
churches, all in the US. By the end of 1997 there were
148 in the US and 238 in other countries – a total of 686
churches. John's prayer at that funeral had been
answered! He had not only been allowed to start a
church-planting church, but also a church planting
movement.

Wimber's influence in church planting was, however, not limited to the planting of Vineyard churches. His
vision and ministry also played a part in encouraging
church planting efforts all over the world and in many
denominations. Anglican churches impacted by
Wimber have found a number of ways to 'church plant'

either by taking over defunct parishes or starting new 'fellowships' of various sorts. Church planting among other groups was revitalized or helped through Wimber's influence. His teaching on building churches for church planters has been used by many to strengthen and multiply churches. And John Wimber was happy about it all, because he always felt called to 'love the whole church'.

John's vision was fulfilled in kind, in that he saw his ministry, his church and his movement become characterized by the Kingdom-oriented sending and church-planting that God put in his heart. But the vision isn't yet completed. There are many lights, especially if one counts all the churches and leaders impacted by his ministry. But there are not yet 10,000 lights. There is still more to be done. There are still thousands of ordinary men and women, all over the world who are in desperate need of Christ and for a church that will lead them into a dynamic relationship with him. There are still thousands of communities who desperately need a biblically-oriented church that will be open to ministry in the power of the Holy Spirit. So what comes next? Where to from here? I think John would want us to follow the example and command of Jesus found in Matthew 9:35–38:

> Jesus went through all the towns and villages, teaching in their synagogues, preaching the good news of the kingdom and healing every disease and sickness. When he saw the crowds, he had compassion on them, because they were harassed and helpless, like sheep without a shepherd. Then he said to his disciples, 'The harvest is plentiful but the workers are few. Ask the Lord of the harvest, therefore, to send out workers into his harvest field.'

Notes

1. I am indebted for much of the historical sections to an as yet unpublished manuscript on the history of the Vineyard by Bill Jackson. a Vineyard pastor in California.
2. John Wimber. 'Sent into the Harvest Field', *Equipping the Saints*, September/October, 1987.
3. Todd Hunter, 'Culture Shock', *First Fruits*, May 1984: 'Church Planting: Listen and Obey', *First Fruits*, June 1984.
4. John Wimber, 'Do You Know?', *First Fruits*, May 1984.
5. This tape set was originally put out by AVC under the title *Advancing the Kingdom Now*, but was later changed to *Church Planting: God's Heart for Expansion*.

10

SIGNS AND WONDERS
DAVID PYTCHES

British Roman Catholic journalist and broadcaster Peter
Jennings has told the story of his remarkable healing
from sarcoidosis, 'a rare and potential killer disease
with no known cure', though at the time of his writing
there was still some residual damaged tissue.

He had been diagnosed with sarcoidosis at the
Queen Elisabeth Hospital in Birmingham where he
returned for a check-up less than forty-eight hours after
John Wimber had prayed for him. Fresh blood tests and
a Kveim test showed no trace of the disease. A further
X-ray showed the lymph gland to have made 'a tremendous improvement'.

At the eye hospital the following day, Dr Baig was
surprised to find no trace of any nodules in Jennings'
eye. In a taped interview he told Jennings: 'When I
examined your eye (at first) under the microscope I
found inflammation and the iris was filled with minute
nodules. I was very surprised that all the nodules had
completely disappeared. I wrote, "NO NODULES!" in
large letters in your notes and thought it was very
unusual to have seen such a big improvement in the
condition of your right eye in such a short period of
time. Medically I couldn't give a reason why the nodules in your eye had disappeared so quickly.'[1] Dr David
Lewis, a social anthropologist, has commented that this
healing was inexplicable within the frame of reference

of ordinary medicine.

I remember John telling me, after he had prayed for him, how he was feeling exhausted as he left the meeting that afternoon when Peter Jennings approached him for prayer and John promised that he would try to see him later. John had actually got into the lift to go to his room when he sensed the Lord nudging him to go back and pray for Peter there and then, so he turned back in simple obedience to God to find him. This was John trying to practise what he preached.

Relaxed model

Those who attended John Wimber's first conferences when he taught on 'Signs and Wonders' were totally bowled over by the ease with which he moved into ministry after his teaching. He fully believed he was following Christ's example for training disciples by healing the sick and casting out demons – teaching and then doing it, words and works. It seemed too simple and yet what he was doing resonated with what we had all been reading about in the Scriptures for years.

This was radical stuff indeed for many evangelicals who, though they claimed to believe in the authority of Scripture, no longer expected power to be manifested in miracles and healings after they had preached the Kingdom of God. Not surprisingly, therefore, most of John's fiercest critics came from the evangelical quarter of the church and more that one of them perceived such ministry as taught by Wimber as 'the devil's plan for the demise of evangelicalism'![2] It was all very reminiscent of the opposition Jesus himself had experienced when they accused him of blasphemy, casting out demons by Beelzebub and being mad. Possibly one of the most prevailing objections to healing the sick has been the accusation that it was presumptuous. Clearly some could become consumed with the love of power and allow such a perversion of God's will to override

the power of love. Justification for this criticism of presumption was supposed to be based on Jesus' own
refusal to 'perform' at the dictation of those who asked
him.

Jesus clearly refused to provide signs for those who
simply came asking for them. He said that no sign
would be given them 'except the sign of the prophet
Jonah' (Matt 39), referring to his own death and resurrection. Many like Herod wanted to meet Jesus hoping
'to see him perform some miracle', but Jesus would not
even answer him (Luke 23:8,9). Jesus would never provide a sign at the whim of man but only at the will of
his Father – which explains why, after two occasions
(Matt 12:38 and Matt 16:1) when he rebuked those who
came demanding signs, he continued providing them
(if we follow Matthew's chronology). He fed the five
thousand, walked on water, healed the sick (Matt
14:13–36) and healed a boy with a demon (Matt 17:14).
Jesus always did what his Father wanted him to do
(John 5:19) – indeed he did nothing else.

A shared ministry

John Wimber never wanted to exercise this ministry
alone; he soon had many others involved. He taught
that we could never do this in our own power – but
only in the power of the Holy Spirit. John was teaching
just what Paul had written about to the Corinthians:
'The kingdom of God is not a matter of talk but of
power' (1 Cor 4:20). This power was available to the
church to advance the purposes of the Kingdom of God.
Clearly one dimension of this power was manifested in
healings and deliverance from evil spirits. These healings etc. were signs of the powerful nature of the
Kingdom of God and were significant for church
growth – a matter of major concern to most of John's
audiences. John believed that healing the sick had to be
understood as part of the Great Commission (Matt

28:18–20). This was quite novel to those like ourselves
from many traditional churches who had overlooked it.
I remember back in 1961 discussing church planting
with an Assemblies of God missionary in Chile and asking him how he thought I might go about it, since with
my background I was feeling ill-equipped to start. My
friend seemed very confident in his reply. 'No problem!' he said and explained that all I needed to do was
to rent a shop on a main road going into town and
advertise a healing meeting and everything would soon
start moving. I smiled, but to my shame I inwardly dismissed his counsel as vulgar presumption – in any case
where would I get the money to rent a shop? Of course
I realised later that he understood a lot more than I did
on the subject. In those days we prayed for the sick to
get them ready to die in peace, but we really did not
expect anyone to get healed by the power of God. It's
interesting to follow how John came to this New
Testament position.

The significant factors in church growth

Whilst John was researching the subject of church
growth a number of senior overseas missionaries
attending his lectures at Fuller reported that signs and
wonders were major factors for church growth in their
area overseas. Seeing the power of God operating in
deliverance and healing had caused many to turn to
Christ. What was more, these missionaries explained
they had found it very difficult to talk about the signs
and wonders they had seen with their church friends
back in the USA. Their friends simply could not believe
them. This exactly tallied with my own experience sharing in England about people having their teeth miracu-
lously filled in Chile.

We are still hearing reports today showing the significance of signs and wonders for church growth.
Paddy Mallon, from St Thomas' Crookes, Sheffield,

recently returned from a visit to a certain area in Nepal where he found that 45 per cent of the new converts there had come into the Kingdom through a healing and 45 per cent through deliverance from demons. A significantly high percentage!

World-view

As Wimber was pondering this feed-back Charles Kraft, also on the staff at Fuller, told him how, in the course of seeking to serve the Lord in Nigeria, he had prepared studies on the Epistle to the Romans which he delivered to a local Christian congregation there. After a while the leaders became frustrated with Kraft's teaching and complained that his studies were irrelevant. What they really wanted to know, they said, was how the gospel might help them to deal with the evil spirits which were troubling them in their villages night after night.

We in the West were evidently missing out on something significant with our Western world-view – the way our culture normally sees and understands the world around us.

The excluded middle

John was also impressed by Paul Hiebert, a professor of anthropology at Fuller and a former missionary in India. Hiebert was known for his theory of the 'excluded middle'. He taught that the world-view of most non-Westerners was three-tiered. The top tier was full of cosmic forces and personalities. The bottom tier was all the things that make up human existence – birth, eating, drinking, working, marriage, sex, sickness and death. But there was another tier – a reality being reckoned with by a vast number of the world's inhabitants – that reality was comprised of the supernatural forces which impact everyday life (spirits, demons and ancestors etc). This middle tier also included the people who have particular insight into, or authority over spirits (witch doctors, mediums, exorcists etc). Since the Western world, with its rational mindset, has no place for this middle view, Hiebert termed this 'the excluded middle'.

Those who have been brought up with a 'two-tier' view of life and believe themselves truly enlightened regard 'three-tier' people as superstitious, slightly inferior or mad. The West has made gigantic leaps in science, based on its rational world view, but has very little perception of the spirit world which affects us cosmically and personally. Hiebert soon realised that this Western world-view, with its 'excluded middle', has greatly limited our theologians, our leaders, our churches and our missionaries.

John Wimber was also reading Eldon Ladd on the Kingdom of God. Was it here already or was it yet to come? Ladd clarified to John that the Kingdom of God was here already though it was not yet here in its fullness and glory. There was also another kingdom. Lucifer was a fallen archangel and did not compare with God in power and authority, but it was obvious that there was a clash of kingdoms involved, with Satan in rebellion against God. This kind of confrontation was evident in Scripture and the effect of Jesus' ministry in this conflict could be summarised in one verse: 'how God anointed Jesus of Nazareth with the Holy Spirit and power, and how he went around doing good and healing all who were under the power of the devil, because God was with him' (Acts 10:38). It was Jesus who actually referred to Satan as having a kingdom when he asked 'How then can his *kingdom* stand?' (Matt 12:26) and Paul is evidently describing the devil as '*the ruler of the kingdom* of the air, the spirit who is now at work in those who are disobedient' (Eph 2.2).

'Kingdom Advancers'

All these converging insights drove John back to the New Testament where he saw how Jesus preached the good news of the Kingdom repeatedly, and followed his preaching invariably by healing the sick or casting out evil spirits. Then John looked again at the Acts of the Apostles and discovered that the apostles (and evangelists) either healed the sick first and then preached (cf. the healing of the lame man at the temple gate gave Peter the opportunity to preach to the gathering crowd with great effect) Acts 3 and 4:1–4, or they preached first and then healed etc. Acts 8:5–8. The New Testament church was growing rapidly (though not exclusively – e.g. Acts 17:16–34) as a result of this kind of ministry.

Paul had gloried in God because he had been able to lead the Roman Gentiles to Christ 'by the power of signs and miracles, through the power of the Spirit' (Rom 15:19). He referred to a similar ministry in his first Corinthian letter when he wrote about his ministry 'with its manifestations of the power of the Spirit so that your faith might not rest in man's wisdom but in God's power' (1 Cor 2:4,5). Clearly the Galatians also were familiar with this kind of ministry. Paul made a point in his argument with them by referring to the miracles done amongst them: 'Does God give you his Spirit and work miracles among you because you observe the law, or because you believe what you heard?' (Gal 3:5). Again, the writer to the Hebrews refers to the salvation to which 'God testified . . . by signs, wonders and various miracles, and gifts of the Spirit distributed according to his will' (Heb 2:4). Paul also spelt out how the gifts of healing (along with other gifts) were evidently available to the church (1 Cor 12).

This ministry in the power of the Holy Spirit was a continuation of the ministry of Jesus (Acts 10:38). Jesus

had trained and commissioned the Twelve to go out
and preach the Kingdom, heal the sick and cast out
demons (Luke 9:1); he did the same with the seventy-
two (Luke 10:1); casting out demons was evidently
implicit judging by their report back (v 17). Then he
commissioned the disciples to make new disciples and
teach them to obey everything he had commanded
them to do (Matt 28:18–20).

Wimber saw that healings and deliverances were
clearly 'Kingdom Advancers' in the New Testament.
He saw that the apostles obeyed and went out and did
as Jesus had bidden them (Acts 3:7 and 14:10); the evangelists healed also (Acts 8:6) and he understood that,
according to the witness of so many missionaries, this
was happening in the less-developed countries of the
world. John began to look at models nearer home. In
the process of puzzling it out practically, he was used to
heal his wife Carol in 1977, but he knew it had not been
him who healed her. 'My part was passive – secondary,'
he explained, 'the Lord was active – he is the Lord who
heals (Ex 15:26)'. It was done in the name of Jesus
through the Holy Spirit.

Teaching the new Vineyard to heal

Once John was back into church leadership again having taken over the little flock ejected from the Quaker
church, he began teaching on healing with conviction
but initially with little effect. He had learned much
from Francis McNutt's *Healing*. John persisted for
months in praying for sick people, but with no positive
encouragement to pass on to the church. Finally, when
he had almost given up hope, he experienced a 'break-
through' – someone was healed (see Chapter 1). People
soon began coming to him for healing (and John soon
began to witness some remarkable healings in his ministry), but he did not want to model healing as a superstar. This was never how he had envisaged it and was

certainly not what he had taught. He wanted to involve
as many others as possible in this ministry.

His commitment was to 'equip the saints'. He eventually anointed a number in the Vineyard (see Carol
Wimber's tribute to John, p 303) and then prayed for
them to get on with it, which they did. And God blessed
them.

He brought this healing ministry with him over to
England on his first visit in 1981. Dr David Lewis later
observed how many others had exercised a healing
ministry and written on the subject, but 'what seems to
be more distinctive about John Wimber's ministry is his
practical training of large numbers of Christians in healing ministries of their own.'[3]

Blind eye made to see

One of the delightful and amazing things for me at the
time of John's 1981 visit to St Andrew's, Chorleywood,
was to have a lady there, almost blind in the right eye,
who recovered her sight after John's brother-in-law,
Bob Fulton, had prayed for her. It was just one of many
signs and wonders resulting from that first visit.
Wimber went on with his team to St Michael-le-Belfry
in York where David Watson was just handing over to
Graham Cray. Someone asked David how he would
explain the church-shaking visitation to the Archbishop
of York. He thought for a moment and said, 'I don't
think that should be too difficult. I'll report that the
blind receive sight, the lame walk, and the good news is
preached to the poor.'

John was simply trying to be obedient to God. He
never believed he had all the answers and he listened to
his genuine critics patiently and openly. With no idea
what a professional researcher might make of it all, he
allowed David Lewis, a trained social anthropologist, to
put out a questionnaire at one of his early conferences.
Lewis did a pilot study at Sheffield in 1985 and a more

extensive one at Harrogate the following year. His find-
ings, published by Hodder and Stoughton in *Healing:
Fiction, Fantasy or Fact?* (1989), proved to be more than
encouraging for John. John's model for healing was
very gentle. He was insistent that no one should ever
attempt to push anyone to make them fall when blessing what the Holy Spirit was doing in the person seeking healing prayer. He disliked 'catchers' waiting
behind people in case they should fall since their presence implied that people might be expected to do so
when being prayed for. But if God wanted to lay people
out on the floor without human assistance that was OK
by John. To John, pushing lacked integrity. On the other
hand, church leaders do have some responsibility when
a lot of people are falling over and some may even get
hurt in the process. The problem is easily resolved by
having at least two people together to pray for the sick
person.

John taught us to ask for the Holy Spirit (Luke 11:13)
whom the Father delights to give 'without limit' (John
3:34); to pray with our eyes open and 'track' the Holy
Spirit discerning what the Father was doing just as
Jesus sought to discern what the Father was doing (John
5:19), and then to try to do it also in the way the Father
wanted it done (John 12:49).

Misunderstanding or mistake

When David Watson became ill with cancer John flew
over from California with a couple of friends (all at
their own expense) to pray for him. David was astonished by such an expression of love from his friends.
They arrived at Heathrow and came straight to the hospital where David had been prepared in a private ward
to meet them. As they prayed for David, the power of
God came upon him in a wonderful way.

They prayed for him several times, and John con-
cluded their three- day visit with the words ,'Well

David, I believe the root of the cancer has been cut and
soon it will begin to die. I think we have done all that
we were meant to do'. Often people who had been
healed in other circumstances had experienced sensa-
tions of heat surges and vibrations of the body under
the power of God and David said he felt similar phenomena: this certainly seemed encouraging. Anyone
who has prayed for the sick, or even visited the sick, is
very much aware one eventually has to bring the time
to a conclusion and it is natural to be as positive as possible. There is not much else John could have said in
such circumstances, and he meant exactly what he said.
It was what he truly believed, though he was in fact
mistaken in his expectation. But he would never have
said specifically to David that he was healed as some
have reported.

'Fear No Evil'

When Wimber's visit to David was discussed in a
review of his book *Fear No Evil* (which he had dictated
from his deathbed) it was assumed from the reported
conversation that John had actually told him that he
was healed. This seemed so out of character for John to
have said such a thing, though we have all sometimes
said more than we meant to say. I had heard John teach
on the subject of healing many times and he urged people never to tell anyone they were healed. If the person
was healed he or she would know it. One of the reasons
for John's popularity amongst Anglicans in Britain was
the apparent integrity of both his character and his ministry. It was too late to check it out with David Watson
so I wrote at the time to David's wife, Anne, to see if she
had ever understood John actually to say that David
was healed. She confirmed that John had not.

John Wimber also taught 'healers' never to tell people to stop taking their medication. He was quite clear
that if people were healed they should go back to their

doctor who would soon take them off their medication if they were healed.

Five-step healing model
John had developed a very simple five-step approach for those starting out in faith in this healing ministry.

1. The interview.
When the 'healers' meet the sufferer, introduce themselves in as relaxed a way and listen to the sick person's story. The healers will probably understand little medical terminology, but all they are trying to discover basically, and as far as possible, is *what's the matter* in terms they can all understand.

2. The diagnostic decision.
At this stage the 'healers' are trying to discern if possible *why* the person is sick. Is it just a physical problem or are there other reasons *why* the person might not be getting healed up? There could be some emotional problem or even some sin – something as commonplace as resentment or unforgiveness. This needs very sensitive handling.

3. The prayer selection.
The next question is *'How do we pray?'* in the light of all we have picked up so far. At an early stage we need to ask the Holy Spirit to come to the sick person and to show us how to pray for the sufferer.

4. The prayer engagement.
We then ask God, ourselves, and the sufferer 'How are we doing?' We can talk to the people we are praying for, even when they may be under the power of the Holy Spirit. This part may also involve quite a long time of waiting and should not be hurried. We are trying to 'track' the Holy Spirit. There may be an immediate

healing in which case we give all the glory to God. Sometimes there is a partial healing and we may pray on for a while or encourage the sufferer to come back again for more prayer etc

5. The post prayer direction. When we think we have done all we should or could we have to bring the time to a conclusion. We will want to avoid statements which may undermine the sufferer's faith. Such phrases as 'Well, you obviously aren't healed or going to be healed', or 'God evidently does not want to heal you!' which might be what we think, but this could give the impression that the Lord is rejecting them in some way. The fact is we have experienced many cases of delayed healing and people have got better during the days following prayer etc. I developed a relaxed rounding off formula in such cases where I have no idea what has happened: 'Well, that seems to be as far as we can go for now. See how you go and if this has helped do come back for more prayer.'

Dignity of the sufferer

John strongly discouraged people telling the sick to have more faith (though he knew faith was essential, either in the people bringing their friend or relative for healing, or in the sick person him/herself, or in the person ministering the healing). He felt that that approach could tend to put the person down in some way. But he might with good precedent say 'According to your faith be it unto you'. Neither did John want to seem to be condemning people in any way who were coming for healing by suggesting they must be holding back on some unconfessed sin when healing did not happen. These things went against John's deep sense of compassion, mercy and the dignity of the individual concerned.

Again he was aware that in some cases sickness could be the direct result of sin (Mark 2:5 and John

5:14). His healing model was pleasingly gentle and surprisingly low-key. John had a theology for healing but he also had a theology for suffering which he had also taught about extensively even before he became sick with cancer himself. He knew his book of Job and he knew that even Jesus had things to learn through his suffering (Heb 5:8). John warned us that we would experience many failures as he had done; not everyone would be healed, but each healing, each deliverance, would be a sign of the Kingdom of God – a foretaste of the powers of the coming age (Heb 6:5). This was the message the world urgently needed to hear and which Christ entrusted to his church. The focus was never meant to be on the healing but on the powers of the Kingdom.

The best healing model

Wimber always maintained a totally orthodox Christology. He said he could work with any who named the name of Christ, however much their other ideas might diverge from his own, so long as they were one with him in their belief that the incarnate Christ was fully divine and fully human. John also believed that Jesus should be our example in the healing ministry. The healings recorded in the Gospels give many insights into Jesus' ministry. He did not heal out of his divine inherent power but in the power of the Holy Spirit (Matt 12:28) as he expected his disciples so to do. He did not start his healing and deliverance ministry until after his baptism in the Holy Spirit (Matt 3:16). In the synagogue at Nazareth one Sabbath, soon after his wilderness temptation, Jesus had read from Isaiah 61: 'The Spirit of the Lord is on me, because he has anointed me to preach good news to the poor. He has sent me to proclaim freedom for the prisoners and recovery of sight to the blind, to release the oppressed, to proclaim the year of the Lord's favour.' To their absolute amazement he followed this by saying : 'Today this Scripture is fulfilled in your hearing' (Luke 4:18–19, 21).

From this time on Jesus began ministering in the power of the Holy Spirit (Matt 12:28), in the context of proclaiming the Kingdom of God. When, after his resurrection, he was still talking to his disciples about the Kingdom, they asked him whether he was now going to restore this Kingdom. He answered that it was not for them to know the time when this would happen but that they would receive power after the Holy Spirit had come upon them and that they would be his witnesses 'in Jerusalem, and in all Judea and Samaria, and to the ends of the earth' (Acts 1:8). They would be empowered to drive back the powers of darkness and usher in the Kingdom of God.

Jesus commissioned the church to carry on his work. 'Anyone who has faith in me will do what I have been doing' (John 14:12). He empowered them to do the same in his name through the Holy Spirit just as he had done it in his Father's name (John 10:25) through the power of the Holy Spirit (Luke 4:18).

Healing in the highways and byways

Wimber firmly believed that the great commission had never been rescinded. It was still God's intention for today since Jesus had assured the disciples when he gave the commission that he would be with them always even to the end of the age (Matt 28:20). Though it is clear that the healing ministry is operative for God's people in the church today (the context of 1 Corinthians 12 implies that the gifts are given when the church is gathered) it is also operative for God's people when they minister at the temple gate, in the market place, along the highways and the byways. John Wimber happily prayed in a most natural way for the sick in aeroplanes, restaurants and the streets, if he sensed God telling him to do so.

Risky business

Of course, equipping the saints for this kind of ministry today seemed 'risky', but that was all part of the life of faith. Wimber's readiness to take risks for the Kingdom of God was both refreshing and inspiring to so many of us who were beginning to grow cynical about the very gospel we were preaching. Many churches have followed Wimber's example and taken up the challenge afresh, following the model of the Vineyard Christian Fellowship at Anaheim. This had been picked from the teaching at John's conferences around the world and his famous MC 510 courses at Fuller on 'Signs, wonders and church growth' which John conducted from 1982 to 1985 at Professor Peter Wagner's suggestion, and which attracted leaders from all over the world. Since then a number of other Bible seminaries have followed suit and included similar courses in their curriculum. Many wonderful healings and deliverances as a result have been witnessed, though it seems to be a common feature for all that they have experienced discouraging failures also; but the call is to be faithful which does not necessarily mean to be successful. We press on in this ministry because we believe it is the will of God according to the Word of God. Our own experience is that it has built up numbers in the church to such an extent that we have had to plant out churches several times. This is now a commonplace feature in the life of a number of churches of all denominations in the UK. Hundreds of healings have occurred across the country on a level that had never been seen in these churches before.

Still not doing it properly!

Some churches have seen remarkable healings etc. way beyond their church boundaries as they have gone out faithfully in God's name. But had more of us had the vision, time and courage to go further out into the secular world with this ministry, as John Wimber believed was what we were intended to do, I am sure we would have seen many more. Some, reading this book, may be prompted anew to take up the challenge which John spelt out for us in his first two books (co-written with Kevin Springer) entitled *Power Evangelism* and *Power Healing*,[4] which have been translated into many foreign languages. When the Lord told John that night in the Detroit airport Metropolitan hotel (see p 25): 'I have seen your ministry and now I want to show you mine', John believed the ministry of 'signs and wonders' to be part of that package.

Notes

1. Peter Jennings, *Equipping the Saints*, January/February,1987, p 10.
2. P. Masters, *Sword and Trowel* 1, London, 1987.
3. David C. Lewis, *Healing: Fiction, Fantasy or Fact?* (London: Hodder and Stoughton, 1989) p 10.
4. London: Hodder & Stoughton, 1985 and 1986.

11

THE COMMUNICATOR

GRAHAM CRAY

*Graham Cray is currently Principal of Ridley Hall,
Cambridge and has a commitment to seeing charismatics
doing theology. Formerly Vicar of St Michael-le-Belfrey in
York, Graham worked in partnership with, and then in succession to, David Watson. He is a member of the Advisory
Group of Anglican Renewal Ministries and of the Church of
England Evangelical Council. He is also on the governing
body of SPCK and Families and Under-Fives, is an Advisor
for CPAS and a trustee of Soul Survivor. He is
married to Jackie and has two daughters.*

In 1981, John Wimber and a team of young people from
his Vineyard Christian Fellowship made their first ministry trip to the UK. Over the Pentecost weekend at St
Andrew's, Chorleywood, their visit launched a ministry. St Andrew's and its New Wine events have since
became a significant resource for the renewal of the
church in the UK and further afield. Then John and his
team got on a train and came to York, to St Michael-le-
Belfrey, where I had become vicar to release David
Watson for his full-time travelling ministry. In York
God used the visitors to heal (and disturb) a church. St
Michael's had born much of the weight of the ministry
of local church renewal in the Church of England in the
decade before. We had found few peers and were tired
and in some ways wounded from the task. The ministry
of the Spirit through John and his team in those few

days was the most overt, powerful and gentle that I had ever seen or experienced. We were touched by God in deep ways and re-equipped to continue our ministry.

Something was communicated in that visit which raised the level of my expectancy of the Spirit and been part of my ministry ever since. I thank God for John Wimber and consider it a privilege to be asked to share in this tribute.

John was an excellent communicator, combining good content and a story-teller's gift, with a relaxed, humorous and self-deprecating style. However, this chapter will not focus so much on John's personal gifts as a communicator as on his understanding of the local church as a vehicle of communication, and of God's chosen means of communication through the church.

Culture as a bridge

John had an instinctive understanding of the relationship between gospel and culture. Ahead of the previous decade's more concentrated study on Western culture as a context for mission, he developed a set of church planting practices and a philosophy of ministry which was both theologically sound and in which the culture of the church acted as a bridge, rather than a barrier to the enquirer or new convert.

John never forgot what it was like to be an unbeliever. Converted as a 29-year-old rock musician he was a fourth generation unbeliever and therefore non church attender. He had no prior knowledge of the culture of the church or of the real content of the gospel. His experience of joining the church ('I gave up drugs for this?') taught him lessons he would never forget.

Later, his involvement with Fuller Theological Seminary and his work as a Church Growth Consultant provided him with a set of theological and conceptual tools and a great deal of data about the world church. In particular, having been converted into an anti-charis-

matic church, he was amazed to learn of the vitality and
growth of Pentecostal style churches in the Two-Thirds
World.

Finally, his involvement with Chuck Smith's
Calvary Chapel showed him an example of a form of
church for the children of the counter culture (the 'Jesus
People'). By this time rock culture had become mainstream for most young people and young adults.
Calvary Chapel saw large numbers of these young people come to faith in Christ. Its services were characterised by warmth and informality, and some of the
worship music was contemporary soft rock.

The shape and style of Vineyard churches grew out
of this mixture of experience and reflection, with the
Yorba Linda (now Anaheim) Vineyard as the trial
model.

John was both a prayerful and a reflective man. He
knew both his Lord and the Scriptures; he knew his cultural context and was able to bring the two together. He
never had to be a 'cross cultural missionary' in the sense
of breaking out of a stiff or antiquated church culture to
reach ordinary people. However, as he developed his
convictions about the centrality of experience of the
Spirit in the life of the church, he was quick to identify
the unnatural and hyped up nature of some Pentecostal
habits and mannerisms and the church culture to which
they contributed. The model and the values which he
established instead and then taught to others, enabled
many to review the culture of their own churches and
to remove unnecessary barriers to the gospel. In the UK
the growth and development of Holy Trinity, Brompton is a prime example.

Because the culture in which John worked in
California is also a main contributor to an increasingly
globalised culture, the Vineyard model has proved
adaptable to most parts of the westernised world.

The report of the 1997 Lausanne Consultation on

'Contextualisation Revisited' pointed out that 'there are many who still fuse the meaning and the forms of the gospel'. Any effective evangelistic strategy must ask questions about the culture of the church – what hurdles do people have to cross in order to get in? Is there a stumbling block caused by church culture in addition to the 'stumbling block' of the cross. Further to that, once people have joined the church what is the effect of the church culture which they absorb from week to week? Does it enable them to live as witnesses for Christ in the everyday world, or disable them by unintentionally socialising them into an alien world?

Under John Wimber's direction, the Vineyard Fellowships developed a laid-back and highly relational church culture which did not require believers to take a weekly trip through a timewarp. This church culture did, however, help people to refocus their lives around Christ, as Sunday by Sunday God was worshipped, the Scriptures were taught and the Holy Spirit was invited to minister. Despite John's increasing prominence internationally these churches were not structured according to the superstar pastor model. What mattered was Christ's ministry by the Spirit.

At one key point, John heard the Lord say 'I've seen your ministry, now let me show you mine'. Equipping for his ministry became and remains a primary value. Throughout the week training courses were run to equip members for practical discipleship and to identify new leaders. The Vineyard philosophy of church growth focused on the multiplication of a church's infrastructure to cope with numerical growth, assuming that new people would be attracted through the lives of the members if the culture of the church did not get in the way.

These two aspects: a church culture that was not hyped up or unnatural and a focus on Christ's ministry came together in the practice of worship. Worship lay at the heart of John Wimber's vision of the church. It was here that gospel challenged culture, by placing the worship of God in Christ above all other claims, loyalties or priorities. Yet it was also here that culture provided a bridge for the gospel through the expert but relaxed use of contemporary musical styles.

John's background as a rock musician equipped him to develop what Peter Wagner called 'plugged-in worship'; worship music in a soft rock style that was culturally accessible and appropriate for intimate worship. The style of music made by mid-seventies bands like the Eagles was put to the service and adoration of God. Baby boomers who grew up with rock music discovered it as a vehicle of Christian spirituality. Yet this was never at the cost of biblical faithfulness. A contemporary music style was put to the highest purpose to which the Creator's gift of music could ever be put. As John never tired of saying, 'We worship God because he is worthy of worship, and we were created for worship'. The music director for the Righteous Brothers used his gifts for the worship of God and inspired a whole string of gifted worship leaders and songwriters to do the same.

During the early 'Signs and Wonders and Church Growth' conferences in the UK, the initial response to the gentle intimacy of many of the songs may have been, 'Don't they know any fast ones?' but we were soon to value the songs and their underlying theology and to experience them as a gift for our context also.

Culture as a barrier

If John Wimber knew instinctively that some features of culture could provide a bridge for the gospel and should therefore have a vital role in the culture of the church, he knew just as well that other features were an offence, an active obstacle to the gospel and could have no part in the church's life. After all he had given up the drugs and other aspects of the addictive and self-indulgent lifestyle of his pop musician years. The music style could have a place in the Kingdom, but not the sin.

John's most significant contribution in this area was not so much about holiness, but about world view. As his convictions about signs and wonders and 'power evangelism' grew, they raised questions about the inability of Western Christians to engage in this ministry of the Spirit. With his strong connections to Fuller Seminary's School of World Mission, John knew that the expectation and experience of the supernatural was far more frequent in non-Western churches.

On the basis of Scripture, he came to understand that God communicated through his actions, not just through words. Above all he had communicated through the sending of his Son to live, die and rise for us. This of course is the heart of orthodox Christian belief. John's distinctive contribution was a rediscovery of the significance of Christ's incarnate ministry in the power of the Holy Spirit. Jesus had not done miracles so much 'to prove that he was God' as to model the ministry which redeemed humans were to exercise in the power of the same Spirit. God pointed people to his Son and to their need of redemption through his Son, by healings and acts of power, which revealed his love and compassion for fallen humans.

But if much of Christian communication was through God's actions by the Spirit, why was the church in the West so impoverished when it came to the supernatural?

Thus it was that John began to ask questions about the effect of the Western world view upon biblical faith, at much the same time as Bishop Lesslie Newbigin, himself just returned from thirty years' experience as a missionary in a non-Western context, began to question the Western church's cultural captivity to Enlightenment rationalism.

To the best of my knowledge, Wimber's work was initially quite independent from Newbigin's thinking. Newbigin's *The Other Side of 84* was published in 1983. *Power Evangelism*, published in 1985, makes no mention of his work, although it does critique Enlightenment rationalism. By 1987, in his introduction to *Riding the Third Wave,* John was referring to Newbigin's 1985 book *Foolishness to the Greeks* and clearly found Newbigin to be an ally. As if repaying the compliment, Bishop Lesslie was later to become a key theological advisor and teacher to Holy Trinity Brompton.

John held as a fundamental conviction that Christianity is a supernatural religion, but Western post-Enlightenment thought allowed no place for the supernatural.

In the early 'Signs and Wonders and Church Growth' conferences he consistently critiqued the world view underlying Western culture in order to point out how it distorted the reading of Scripture and disabled faith in the supernatural ministry of God's Spirit. Paul Hiebert, a Fuller Seminary anthropologist, had identified a blind spot in the Western world view which he called the 'excluded middle'; that is, a belief in the empirical world of our senses, and a belief (at least in theory) of a transcendent world beyond ours – most Westerners believe in God – but a blind spot towards supernatural forces on this earth. Through Hiebert's work, John pointed out the split in Western thinking between what Newbigin called the public world of 'facts' and the private world of 'values'. The notes for the first 'Signs and Wonders' conference I attended pointed out that 'Science worked in areas of experimentation out of proofs. Religion was left to faith, visions, dreams and inner feelings.'

John was not calling Christians to be irrational and to 'just believe' despite their education. He was challenging the conceptual basis of their thinking and believing.

He defined power evangelism as 'a presentation of the gospel that is rational, but also transcends the rational. The explanation of the gospel comes with a demonstration of God's power through signs and wonders.' What is challenged here is not God-given reason, but secular rationalism. John was not running from empirical data. He was pleased to allow Dr David Lewis of the Alister Hardy Research Centre to undertake research at his Harrogate conference in 1986. It is no coincidence that ministry times at these conferences were called clinics. They gave Christians an opportunity to experience what John was talking about and reorder their thinking as a result. Here John stood in the tradition of John Wesley and Jonathan Edwards who, at the dawn of the Enlightenment era challenged its scepticism, but made good use of its greater confidence in sense experience. They taught people to trust the inner witness of the Spirit as part of their teaching on assurance. As the sun set on the Enlightenment, John Wimber taught us to believe the evidence of our own eyes and the experience in our own bodies of God's healing power.

John was not calling us to add the supernatural to our list of possibilities, but to reorder our underlying world view according to Scripture. For his understanding of a world view he drew on 'Christianity in Culture', a 1979 work by another Fuller anthropologist, Chuck Kraft (who himself learned to minister in the power of the Spirit through attending the course John taught at Fuller in 1982). Other key intellectual sources were the Intervarsity apologetics specialist, James Sire, and a former student of C.S. Lewis, Harry Blamires. John was the first author I have read who described a world view as a lens through which we filter and interpret what we experience. 'Our world view is like a lens – it colours, clarifies, classifies, warps or excludes.'

The power of a world view lies in its being taken for granted. We are socialised into it as children and assume it is objectively true rather than one of many possible bases for interpreting life. 'Very few persons operating within a world view are conscious that they hold one.' 'We do not learn it so much as we absorb it.'

What was needed then was a change of world-view, a paradigm shift. This expression comes from the work of the Philosopher of Science, Thomas Khun. References to Khun's work are now commonplace in gospel and culture writing, being powerfully developed in the work of David Bosch, but again, John's work is the earliest in which I have seen the expression used. Similarly world-view theory has been helpfully developed by Middleton and Walsh in Canada and Tom Wright in the UK.

What has fascinated me in preparing this chapter has been to see how John was engaging with the same issues, from a different set of Christian academic thinkers. He had the great gift of taking the truths of the academy and putting them actively to the service of Christ in the local church.

To restore faith in God's supernatural power, John Wimber needed to be both a teacher of Scripture – particularly on the Kingdom of God and the significance of Jesus' ministry in the Spirit – and an interpreter and critic of culture and its underlying presuppositions. In his engagement with culture and his use of world-view theory, John was ahead of his time. As he exercised his most formative ministry he was doing far more than restore faith in the supernatural, he was also helping to prepare an appropriate missiology for an emerging post-modern culture.

We are entering a culture which is not so much secular, sceptical and rationalistic, as religiously plural and relativist. Spiritual experience is back in the public square, but any and every religious experience, for there are no longer any universally accepted maps of the territory. Churches which are rationalistic and sceptical of the supernatural will drive seekers after God into the arms of any number of cults and New Age groups. What we need are culturally accessible churches with a Christ-centred supernaturalism. John has left the church with an inheritance for ministry in the postmodern age.

Culture never stands still

God gave John Wimber to the church as part of his plan to alert us and equip us for ministry during a major transition in Western culture. That culture is not going to stand still. If we are to respect the inheritance he left us it will not be by slavishly copying or sticking to particular patterns of church or ministry. We must once again avoid the mistake of fusing the meaning of the gospel with particular recent cultural forms of it. West coast soft rock is already antiquated music to young Britons raised on ten years of electronic dance music. A hunger for ancient and esoteric spirituality in New Age groups again raises the question of the place of liturgy, without implying formality. The contemporary is increasingly a mix of the ancient and the very modern. 'Plugged-in worship' may now imply digital samplers, twin turntables and video sequences. We honour John best by following his principles of a culturally accessible church life rooted in a biblical world view, rather than by aping his culturally specific forms.

I do wish to honour him. He has been an inspiration in my intellectual engagement with culture, as well as in my commitment to minister in the power of the Holy Spirit. John communicated best by show and tell. He has shown me a way to integrate charismatic ministry and cultural analysis in one calling and I thank God for him.

12

THE ECUMENIST
GERALD COATES

*Gerald Coates was born in Surrey in 1944. After
a decade working in display and advertising, he started
a church in north-east Surrey, currently named Pioneer
People. His national Pioneer team currently care for
about 100 churches and lead various training and
evangelistic courses. He is best known as a speaker,
broadcaster and writer. His latest book is* Non
Religious Christianity *(Destiny Image/Revival Press).*

Walls came tumbling down

The wall that separates charismatic/Pentecostal evangelicals and conservative evangelicals, is plastered with mutual suspicion and papered (on one side at least!) with theological superiority.

Into such a divided house, stepped John Wimber, big time, in the summer of 1984. He had been to Britain several times before of course, but the Central Hall, Westminster meetings rocketed him into controversy and profile.

Yet here we are, barely fifteen years later, and an icon of conservative evangelicalism (Jim Packer) is writing a serious and constructive chapter in this publication on Wimber's theology. Why? How?

Signs and blunders?

John Wimber has not always been taken seriously. Some think he has been a serial blunderer (Signs and Wonders, Kansas City Prophets, Toronto Blessing) too convinced of his own theological certainties. Others think he lost the plot, allowing for bizarre behaviour of laughing, shaking, crying and falling to the floor in his own meetings and then exorcising Toronto from his network for doing the same.

Yet for all that, people including Kansas and Toronto people, loved him. His decisions often had the appearance of being cutting edge and sharp and insensitive. But generally they resulted in well-established mutual affection and appreciation. Even in what turned out to be his closing years, those he had fallen out with or those who had fallen out with him, held him in high esteem and fond affection.

Platform and personal graciousness

The reasons for this are several. When certain Christian leaders address their audiences, you could be forgiven for feeling that they appear to be addressing a mental health tribunal. Wimber by contrast spoke as though all of his listeners were personal fans and friends – while he must have known many were not. That is why so many found it hard to disrespect or dislike him. He knew that if you treat people like the enemy, they become the enemy. Can there be another man who has so many friends who disagreed with him, either theologically or over certain decisions that he had made? John and I first met at the famous Westminster conference of 1984. A mutual friend had encouraged a meeting between the two of us. As it happened, John and myself both arrived at Westminster Central Hall at the same time, but coming from different directions (prophetic?). As we walked up the stone steps, I reached across, offered my right hand and introduced myself. He responded with such delight, warmth and wide-eyed surprise, he made it look as though he had been waiting all week to meet me – which could not possibly have been the case.

Later that week, my friend the song-writer Noel Richards and I took him to my favourite London restaurant. 'When I asked John what he would like to drink, he named a wine which I ordered. Again and again I reminded the wine waiter that we were waiting, but, the wine never appeared – it was getting embarrassing. John quickly and quietly retrieved the situation: 'I'll be just as happy with a glass of tap water!' he said. He would rather have had a cloud-free evening of fellowship, friendship and fun than insist on his glass of wine in the environment of embarrassment.

Those two little incidents, one on the steps of the Central Hall at Westminster and one in the Menage à Trois in Knightsbridge, told me a lot about the apostle who did not believe in apostles and the hero who said that he did not want to become one.

Generosity of spirit

God has extended cosmic generosity to all who seek him, as well as to those who don't. John seemed to know that and exuded the same to those he met. That generosity of spirit sometimes led to problems. Some around him thought it was a license to do whatever one wanted. A large team came from Anaheim led by John Wimber. They divided up after the conference to minister in various churches including ours, during which time one of the team flirted improperly with several women who told me 'something was wrong'. I talked about it to the man in question and later I mentioned my concern to John Wimber.

During the following years of our friendship, John would often refer back to the sensitive, gracious and wise way that I handled the situation. Now, either my own memory cells are failing me or John Wimber has confused me with someone else, or there is that generous attitude being extended yet again. I had simply raised the concerns, out of loyalty to the Vineyard team and only later found out that the team member had been duly confronted and disciplined appropriately in his own Vineyard church. This is something, of course, that could happen to any network of churches and indeed it has. Again, despite my friendship with Mike Bickle (Kansas) and John Arnott (Toronto), and my taking a different view over the latter, John Wimber still came and spoke when we put up a large marquee in our town to accommodate the 'Toronto Blessing'. We had further enjoyable meals together between then and the time that he went to be with the Lord.

But John's generosity to others, and his willingness to make a platform for such people, caused him yet further problems. It resulted in his own ministry, and the Vineyard network of churches, living as though they were all in a fish bowl, with everybody scrutinising closely everything that was going on. What happened in Kansas was a classic.

Senior Pastor of Kansas Fellowship, Mike Bickle, had some heavyweight prophetic ministries in his church. Some of the words of knowledge that I have heard them give to friends of mine have been nothing short of amazing. But it was heady stuff resulting in large crowds and conferences, mounting accolades and the emergence of an unhealthy personality status. Wisely, Mike Bickle called in John Wimber to help, advise and stabilise things. During this time the Kansas City prophets, John Wimber and the whole issue of the prophetic rocketed into the public domain. Some criticisms of Gnosticism, theological naïveté and the prophetic taking precedence over teaching, may have been correct, but if so, Wimber did a good job judging by Bickle's later classics on Christology and prophecy.

However, the emphasis of profile in Vineyard magazines and conferences was the extraordinary gifting of
these prophetic people and the nature of Mike Bickle's
church. It seems that little time was allowed for theological discussion, or emphasis. Notwithstanding the
extrordinary level of blessing that came through these
ministries and the partnership they had in the gospel,
the bridge between KCF and Vineyard was just not
strong enough for the tonnage that needed to be driven
across it.

Numerous things come out in the light; not all bad
things. Light does not change anything, it just helps us
see things the way they are. The white light of
Vineyards' own promotion of certain people caused
relationships to strain.

Of course profile does not equal true significance,
but inappropriate profile can either enhance or endan-
ger a ministry and what it represents.

But there was one other thing about John Wimber
that needed to be asked. It is difficult to say how much
of this was his genetic make-up, or the West Coast laid-
back sunshine approach, or the work of the Holy Spirit.
Perhaps it was a mixture of all three.

Respect for individuals, love for all denominations

John seemed totally unimpressed with whether you
were Anglican or New Church, Pentecostal or Baptist.
Each person was treated as an individual, as a human
being. Each crowd was addressed because it was longing after God, his Word and his ways.

Today young people could not care less what church
other Christians go to or what denomination or networks they are a part of. Anyway the name of the group
does not tell you anything anymore. You could be
Anglican and be the most evangelistic and worshipful
body in town or a traditional, liberal irrelevance.

Equally you could be New Church and be the most dynamic fastest growing group in the area, or you could be disappearing up your own counselling courses and endless worship acetates.

Ahead of his time

Here John Wimber was way ahead of his time. Whilst valuing certain things in most Christian traditions, God never sees us or values us by denominational or non-denominational labels.

Perhaps that is why John was able to network and unite so many believers through his leadership conferences, public events, books and teaching tapes. While ecumenism was not a word familiar to the lips of the Vineyard constituency, John's broad appeal was just that and did much to create understanding and fellowship amongst various groups. Fellowship softens judgments of one another and its absence sharpens criticism. And John sought no status for himself. He simply set out to serve and empower the whole body of Christ and not just a few important, or self-important, titled platform speakers.

Embracing the legacy of a new beginning

So what are we to make of the Vineyard and its signs and wonders and colossal music/worship output? Or of the Wimber family and their remarkable influence but tragic losses? And what of the man himself, the charismatic theologian, interdenominational gatherer, effective communicator and father figure? He was at times annoying (as most leaders are!), but taught by example, that it is possible to disagree without being disagreeable. How different church would be if that legacy were embraced. He taught in circumstances, often beyond his control, but faith is not a way around pain but through it. For us to embrace both could mean that John Wimber's death is not an end, but for those that knew him intimately and for most of us who observed from a distance – it could be a new beginning.

13

THE BUSINESSMAN
IAN PRITCHARD

*Ian Pritchard worked with John Wimber in Anaheim, as
Conference Director for Vineyard Ministries International
for 7 years. In September 1991 he, and his wife Susan,
moved to Evanston, Illinois where he served on the pastoral
staff of the Evanston Vineyard. In June 1994 they were sent
to plant a Vineyard church in Croydon, England. At the
same time he become General Manager of VMI (UK) for
two years. He lives in Croydon with his wife and three sons.*

First encounters
As I drove through the streets of Yorba Linda, I recalled
the conversation I'd had with Bob Fulton at a hotel in
central London two months earlier. 'Be prepared,' he
had said. 'Make sure you have all the information with
you.' I remembered that I had been a little confused
talking to him. What did he really mean, 'Have all the
information with you'?

I was in California as the representative of a group
of church leaders from the United Kingdom: my mission was to discuss the details of the first major conference John was to lead outside the USA. Its theme was to
be 'Signs and Wonders and Church Growth' which we
had entitled, The Third Wave, and it was due to take
place at Westminster Central Hall in the autumn of
1984. The invitation to John had come from several
well-known vicars, pastors and leaders from a variety

of denominational backgrounds. What was more, John's close friend David Watson had suggested the conference in the first place. Surely that was all the 'information' I would need!

In any event, I was looking forward to meeting John Wimber. As I drove along the unfamiliar streets, on the 'wrong' side of the road, in search of 902 East Yorba Linda Boulevard – the address of the Wagner House – I wondered what I might expect on my arrival. From my previous experience of American corporations, I was sure it would be a splendid building. John would certainly have a secretary outside his well-appointed office. He'd be there dressed in a suit, ready and waiting for our important engagement.

I came to a stop light. There it was, the Wagner House – a house. Large, but nevertheless – a house! After parking the Chevrolet, I walked in through the backdoor and was met by the receptionist, sitting in the hallway. Something told me that my expectations were somewhat awry. Several others, casually dressed, were milling around. I was the only person wearing a tie!

Eventually, I was shown to the top of the stairs and into a room containing one sparsely-filled bookcase and a rather ordinary desk that had a phone on it and little else; a glass coffee table and a drab, yet functional, three piece suite where two people sat. One was Bob Fulton and the other was dressed in shorts and a colourful Hawaiian T-shirt. It couldn't be! Bob introduced me to his brother-in-law, John Wimber, who smiled broadly and invited me to sit – on a sofa next to the coffee table. If my mind was a pinball machine, it went on 'tilt'. Here was a man with no pretence, no false piety, no camouflage, no 'superstar' image. Openness and transparency were his hallmarks. He had no 'superiority complex'. He was refreshingly real, and what I experienced right then cut straight through all my personal religiosity and the legacy of my church background. With John, what you saw was who he was, a quality I shall always attempt to emulate.

I tried to look comfortable even though by this time I clearly was not. The usual pleasantries over, John asked me about the conference. After the first two questions, I quickly realised that I was out of my depth. He asked me all sorts of things that I had not even considered. To John, it was not enough that this conference was going to be a church event with a nice venue at the invitation of so many high profile church leaders. John had a habit of asking questions others either would not think of or were afraid to ask.

As I walked out of the building, I realised that John had given me my first lesson. The questions he asked . . . the way he dressed . . . his humble manner . . . surroundings that lacked any sense of ostentation . . . and an evident passion for Jesus and his Kingdom that was electrifying.

Many contemporary commentators have suggested that we can all recall where we were when Diana, Princess of Wales died. Like so many others, I also vividly recall my first encounter with John Wimber. I knew I had met an extraordinary and significant Christian leader, a man who was to have an enormous impact on my life – one that will last forever. Little did I know then that I would be working closely with him for the next eight years. Little did I guess that I would eventually plant a Vineyard church. Even less did I realise what the next thirteen years of close relationship would hold in store for me.

Vineyard Ministries International conducted over 120 major conferences (and over 500 smaller seminars) from 1984 to 1997, impacting hundreds of thousands of people. Many knew John Wimber for his phrase: 'I'm just a fat man trying to get to heaven', but what was he like behind the scenes? What was he like in the office environment? What sort of businessman was he?

Background

Seldom do you find a church leader who is gifted in as many areas as John was. Not only was he a pastor of a large church but he was also an excellent musician and songwriter and, a fact less widely recognised, an astute businessman as well. Perhaps it was because John did not come from a church background that he did not approach business in the way that the mainstream church expected.

His *modus operandi* came from three formative streams: his background as the manager of the Righteous Brothers; his experiences as an entrepreneur who had successfully started several business ventures; and his time as a Church Growth consultant for the Fuller Evangelistic Association in the 1970s. As a result, he was familiar with business processes such as the exploration of new concepts; goal-setting; formalising written plans and aiding personal development. However, throughout all of his dealings, John Wimber sought to play to an audience of one – Jesus Christ. He was a man with a passion to do what was right, with boundless energy to keep the offices and staff of several organisations on their toes and who, in all his dealings, acted with the greatest integrity.

The Father's directives

John always sought to emulate Jesus when he said 'I tell you the truth, the Son does nothing on his own; he does only what he sees his Father doing. What the Father does, the Son also does' (John 5:19). He first and foremost sought the Lord's leading. As he was fond of saying, 'I often pray, "Oh God, Oh God . . ." knowing that apart from him I can do nothing.' When he was in any doubt, he waited. John had many invitations to speak from all over the world. Sometimes people would try to attract John with secure financial commitments to pay his travel and grant a significant honorarium, or with guarantees of a large audience. Yet he remained true to his calling and would not be swayed from it. Sometimes he would wait for months before responding to invitations. Why? Because he was waiting for God's direction. He could not be manipulated and this at times gained him a reputation of being difficult to work with. Certainly it was frustrating for me, and others, at times!

'I am in favour of planning,' he used to say, '... after God speaks.' He never placed his primary reliance on professional management tools to the detriment of a reliance on the Lord's personal presence, initiative and guidance through the Holy Spirit. John always sought and expected the Lord's action and direction.

As such, he had a balance between the spiritual and the practical that was immensely attractive. He was passionate about God and the advancement of the Kingdom, in an unreligious, practical, planned and unpretentious way.

Strategic planner and thinker
'We should make plans – counting on God to direct us' (Prov 16:9 LB).

To John, planning was always important. He drew wisdom from the Proverbs. 'A wise man thinks ahead; a fool doesn't and even brags about it!' (Prov 13:16 LB). 'A sensible man watches for problems ahead and prepares to meet them. The simpleton never looks, and suffers the consequences' (Prov 27:12 LB).

In terms of theology, John Wimber was an evangelical traditionalist. In terms of praxis he was an original thinker. As such he 'broke the rules'. John was always kind, but he was equally frank and straightforward in his business dealings. He constantly asked questions, 'Is it working?' 'Where are the finances coming from?' 'Are the lost being saved?' Moreover, he dared to voice such thoughts as, 'If the church is not advancing – maybe Jesus is not building it!

As a result, at Vineyard Ministries International (VMI), we developed the following questions which we put to people who invited us to conduct conferences with them.

i) Why do you want the conference? Why do you believe it is God's timing to invite John Wimber and a ministry team?

ii) Who is involved in the inviting committee? Are they pastors and church leaders? Do they come from a variety of denominational backgrounds? (With passion John often declared 'God loves the whole church – that includes the Baptists, Catholics, Anglicans, Pentecostals, evangelicals – all of it. The Vineyard is secondary. We are just one vegetable in God's stew.' John was most interested in going to those places where we were invited by a whole host of pastors and leaders from different church backgrounds who were prepared to work together.)

iii) How does the conference fit in with the strategic plan for your churches and area? What sort of follow-up do you have planned? How is the teaching and ministry practice going to be integrated into the church?

iv) How many people do you expect to attend? On what do you base your projection?

v) Do you have a well-thought-out budget? How much will you charge the attendees? What will your costs be? Have you considered our costs?

This type of questioning was not limited to Vineyard Ministries International's conference activities. When we began to distribute Vineyard worship music through Mercy Music and then the Vineyard Music

Group, John asked similarly challenging questions. 'How do you plan to achieve your sales projections?'; 'How much of the income you receive from sales will you spend on marketing the product?' and he often asked for regular reports and updates.

This practice frequently met with resistance. Why? Because questions like these were way too practical for 'religious' activities. But they got people to think and, in turn, increased their effectiveness.

John believed that to refuse to address these pertinent and sometimes awkward questions would be like trying to play a game without knowing how to judge whether we are winning or not. It is an illusion to believe that we are successfully serving God without having measurements to discover whether we are or not. It is like playing football (soccer to our US friends) without the goalposts. You can pass well, tackle well, dribble well – but what are you shooting at? Are you scoring goals? John had a way of asking straightforward questions that challenged you on all fronts. What was more, his questioning practices provoked visionary thinking. He instilled a value of exploring all options, especially trying those things that had not been done before. His mission was to see the church of Jesus Christ advance, and he valued anything in the business arena that aided that purpose, and he expected compliance with agreed undertakings.

John also often spoke of the need to evaluate. Every programme, however good, needs to be measured and inspected from time to time. He continually recommended reviews and revisions, aware that what had worked two years ago might not work any more.

Yet he did not only demand this standard of business acumen from others. As he explored any new church programme or business opportunity he maintained his enquiring approach. What is more, as the Anaheim Vineyard Church expanded, the number of churches being added to the Association of Vineyard Churches (AVC) increased and Vineyard influence spread, the number of propositions he received soared. As such he had to be increasingly focused in his attempts to sift out God's plans from the myriad opportunities presented to him. His business decisions were made around four key factors: Purpose, Priority, Programme and Personnel.

Purpose

The key question was always: Does the event or activity facilitate the current objectives God has given us at this time? John knew he had been called to a very specific purpose. Its outworking changed over the years, and this in turn demanded continual reassessment of the organisations he was leading or the conferences he was conducting. Nevertheless he would not waver from his primary purpose. For example, in the early years, John felt that his main calling was to facilitate the renewal of the church in the Western world. As a result, he turned down many attractive invitations to other regions.

Priorities

Here the issue was: Is this activity the one to which we should be devoting our time, energy and money? There were always so many things that could be done, and it will always be true that needs outweigh resources. John continually made decisions on the basis of whether an invitation or opportunity made the best use of the resources available to him at that time, not on the basis of whether one particular invitation was more appealing than another. For those working with John, this particular quality often caused great frustration, as he would not be manipulated into action by the needs, real or supposed, of others. In fact, when things got fraught, he'd often call in to cancel a meeting that we had thought was critical, in order to eat out at a nice restaurant or go off and play a round a golf. He knew when he needed to juggle his priorities to make space for himself.

Programme

Again reflecting John's belief that his calling was to facilitate the renewal of the Western church, he developed a teaching programme for the conferences that would most aid this purpose. He taught on renewal fundamentals like 'Worship', 'Signs and Wonders and Church Growth'; 'Prayer'; 'Equipping the Saints'; 'Spiritual Gifts' and 'Evangelism in the Power of the Holy Spirit'. He insisted that conference materials and give-away books were all of the highest quality so they could benefit attendees long after the event as well.

In addition, time, energy and resources were devoted to building the Vineyard Music Group (originally called Mercy Music). The quality and style of product were intentional. In the early to mid 1980s, the Vineyard Worship tapes set a new standard that has since been emulated and even superseded by others. John wanted to impact the wider church with the Vineyard's intimate worship style. He wanted the church to sing songs that addressed God directly and personally as he believed this was fundamental for individual and corporate spiritual renewal.

Personnel

John was also strategic in his selection of personnel. He chose to work with those who were willing to unite behind the values he espoused. He had no problem in recognising that others were more gifted than he was in many areas. He was not afraid to enhance the organisations by surrounding himself with people whose abilities exceeded his own or complemented his gifts and abilities. He knew who he was and what God had called him to and as such was never challenged in his leadership by affirmation that others received. In time, well over 120 people were on the staff of the three main organisations – the Anaheim Vineyard Church; VMI and AVC.

John had no problem in seeing the church (and related organisations) as a business when the application of business techniques to church infrastructures was helpful. Our primary aims and strategic objectives were clear and defined. Our organisational structures and management strategy were intentional. Personnel were recognised and used in the arena of natural gifting whether it was 'visionary', 'managing' or 'maintaining'. It was evident that John's business background aided his thought process and decision making. Nevertheless, everything was always subject to the scrutiny of the Holy Spirit. And he realised that ultimately only God could build the church. We were to do what we could in all the ways we could to remove any roadblocks and therefore to help in the building.

Excellence

John Wimber sought to do his best in everything he put his hand to. All his staff were encouraged to do likewise. We were invited to continually learn and grow. We were exhorted to better ourselves and develop in the ministry God had called us to. Education was an important part of our development.

Likewise the product reflected this ethos. John saw no reason why church organisations believed they could settle for second best. Why did some believe the church could get away with serving up things half baked? We should be presenting ourselves as well as, or better than, our 'secular' counterparts. As such the materials presented at conferences were of a high standard. The music tapes cost a lot to produce and the final product reflected the investment. The books were carefully written. The audio and video cassettes were well presented.

In addition, facilities *were* important. In 1990 the three organisations moved into a thirteen-acre piece of land with just over 280,000 sq ft of space. It cost a lot of money, but then so too did the temple that God directed Solomon to build! None of the buildings were ostentatious. They were comfortable to work in and functional.

Both the buildings and materials were intentionally well presented. In themselves they bore testimony to the God we serve. But more importantly, out of these resources the ministry could flourish. As John demonstrated, 'if the investment is not made then the impact is limited'.

Leadership and management

Leaders have the willingness to work hard, to go beyond what can reasonably be expected. By stretching the definition of what is possible the leader proves by example that those who follow can do more than they think they can. Whenever a long-standing Olympic record is broken, experience suggests it will soon be broken again by athletes inspired by the record breaker's example.

C.J. Silas, Phillips Petroleum Co.

John Wimber was one such leader. He had an enormous capacity for work. He successfully led and managed three growing organisations. Just as Jesus took and taught the disciples by example, so John's philosophy was to train, deploy, monitor and nurture all he worked with. He sought to pass on to others everything he knew and the lifestyle he lived.

John frequently displayed an uncanny ability to

remember details – whether they related to something he'd requested, a report needed, or a financial issue. Often when his colleagues challenged him they found he was right and they were wrong. However it was not always the case! And we took delight in telling him! Fortunately, most of the time, John had a good sense of humour. He would be the first to admit he was not a perfect boss. But he did his best. When he made mistakes, he sought to openly admit to them, correct them and move on.

He had the ability to successfully juggle many things at once. It did not appear to matter if some things remained undone; it never seemed to adversely affect him. Perhaps it was because he refused to allow others' expectations of him to emotionally affect him. He knew that there was only one Saviour and it wasn't him!

John Wimber had a mission to bring to maturity and impart knowledge to all those under his care. He was genuinely interested in people's well being. He had no time for any 'superstar' image. He talked to all the staff. He helped when help was needed – whether it was stacking chairs or serving drinks.

Once, in Harrogate, I was unloading a large truck containing over 200 boxes (each weighing around 40lbs). It was late at night and a conference was due to start the next day. John Wimber, together with another Vineyard pastor and two other church leaders from the UK came out of the conference centre. Without a second thought, when John saw what I was doing, he said, 'Come on, let's give Ian a hand unloading boxes'. The Vineyard pastor followed suit. The look on the faces of the well-dressed UK church leaders was of utter astonishment, and their expressions betrayed their feelings. But to their credit they helped unload the truck. To John, whether unloading boxes for a conference or giving the keynote address, it was all part of the same Kingdom activity.

John was an equipper. He revelled in a learning environment. Just as certain failures characterised the early ministry of the disciples, so he did not expect his staff to be perfect. John displayed an admirable tolerance for people who made mistakes – just so long as they learnt from them. John always had an objective. He wanted to lift people to a higher level – to help them grow to their potential. In encounter after encounter, he would impart information or values. He gave space and permission for others to succeed. Often he could have done the job better but did not, preferring instead to turn over responsibility and stretch those in his employ. By his actions he taught that great leaders do not do the work of ten people but get ten people to do the work.

However, things were not always 'peaches and cream'! He once remarked that few were able to work alongside him for more than two or three years. Like the rest of us he had his character flaws. He was no 'people pleaser'. He used to say 'If you prune leaders when they are young, their roots will go deep and they'll produce more fruit over their lifetime.' At times we felt the outworking of his pruning!

He constantly stretched our horizons. Just when you thought you'd done a good job there was the push to move on. There was no time for self-gratification. If anything, one might say John was not too good on the 'encouragement' front. It was not because he did not appreciate you, but because he saw even more room for growth. A favourite encouragement of his was, 'You may be surprised at what you have managed to accomplish but you have potential for much more'. His life and ministry endorsed John Ruskin's statement: 'The highest reward for a man's toil is not what he gets for it, but what he becomes by it'.

Disagreements/conflict

There was conflict. It was expected. As John Wimber said,

> Whenever a church is obeying the words and doing the works of Jesus it is working in hostile territory and there attack must be expected. Paul exhorted Timothy, 'Endure hardship . . . like a good soldier of Jesus Christ' (2 Tim 2:3). A soldier's life includes hardship. A good soldier endures without giving up. He keeps going until Jesus returns.

Conflicts and criticisms from outside the organisations increased as the prominence of John Wimber and the Vineyard movement increased. John faced conflict in TV interviews; radio interviews; books and articles. Conflict and criticisms were, at times, painful to him. He did not know why some people disliked him so much, but he never felt pressured into responding in kind or to any specific criticism. Sometimes this caused misunderstanding, but John had a different agenda. He loved the church – even those people who disagreed with him – and would not get side-tracked from his mission by engaging in acrimonious debates.

Within the organisations conflict and disagreements also occurred. If they were over the vision and direction of the organisation they were swiftly addressed. In the same way, John acted quickly if he felt that an individual was seeking to build a personal power base. However, conflict arising from differing opinions about the best way of doing business was often encouraged. We had several meetings where a healthy discussion ensued. Different ideas were always acceptable as long as loyalty was assured. John rarely interfered with our decisions about the best way to accomplish our goals, and this in turn fostered personal vision and growth.

John placed a high value on unity and team playing

in the structure of the organisations. We moved forward together. There was no room for a 'territorial spirit'. Team building was encouraged. In VMI employees were taken on conferences to get the flavour of what they were contributing to. Even though John was not the 'partying' type, the organisations had regular Christmas parties which he joined in because he saw the value and need for them. John was concerned equally for getting results and for maintaining the relationships that make them possible. Separate departments were encouraged to carry out team building activities. Money was spent to make the offices and facilities attractive and inviting workplaces. In business we were encouraged to work hard and play hard.

Balance

John Wimber further demonstrated an ability to balance his roles as pastor, boss, friend and family man. His staff knew that they served someone who had different roles in their lives. Sometimes he addressed us in a direct and uncompromising manner. It was to challenge us and help us learn, grow and succeed. At other times he showed an extraordinary compassion for our personal needs. He was genuinely interested in our families, background, health and home life. He cared for single people, married couples, young and old equally.

Many of his staff played golf with him at one time or another (and more often than not were beaten!). We spent many hours eating at restaurants – and he always paid the bill.

He took time out to foster replenishing relationships with his close friends – particularly Dick Heying. He also demonstrated an admirable balance in seeking to live his own life in balance. He was a good boss and enjoyed his work. But more than that he loved the times at home with his wife, children and grandchildren. He would regularly take different family members on speaking engagements and ministry trips, and delighted in 'showing off' his latest grandchild.

Generosity of spirit

Many attendees of Vineyard conferences have asked what happened to the profits. Let me go on record and say that not one cent went to John Wimber. He took no honorarium or payment from the conferences. Yet at the same time he gave honorariums – some very generous ones – to the other speakers and worship leaders. He was an enormously generous person. He saw ministry as a life of giving. Hundreds of thousands of dollars went to the poor and missions. But it did not stop there. He constantly looked for ways to give away those things that God had blessed him with. Pastor after pastor, church leader after church leader went through our warehouses to get as many tape series, books, manuals and music tapes as they could carry. 'Take it all,' John would say, 'and use it in any way that will be beneficial to the Kingdom.'

John had no time for empire building, power struggles or greed. There were no enormous salaries or company Mercedes in any of the Vineyard's organisations. John drove modest secondhand cars. He lived in a modest house. At the age of fifty-five he took pleasure in letting us know he'd finally paid off his mortgage. Soon after his last son got married, he downsized his living arrangements. 'After all,' he said, 'you can only sleep in one bedroom or use one bathroom at a time!' He gave away the excess.

Conclusion

How good a businessman was he? Well if success is measured in qualitative or quantitative gains, John succeeded. The Anaheim church began as a small group in someone's living room. It grew to over 5,000 members;

gave over a million meals to the poor each year; ministered in fourteen prisons; did numerous mission trips; won thousands to Christ and discipled as many more. Vineyard Ministries International began with two other employees (only one was paid!). It grew into two organisations (Vineyard Music Group was split off in the late 1980s) employing over forty-five staff; carried out hundreds of conferences all over the world; ministered to hundreds of thousands of people and massively impacted the church. The Association of Vineyard Churches began with a small collection of loosely affiliated churches in the mid 1980s. Now there are over 750 churches in fifty-two countries. But, however strategically brilliant he was, the truth is he didn't ask for any of it. He just lived his life before an audience of one – Jesus Christ. He did the best he could with what he had.

Where do we go from here?

When I arrived at 2:30 p.m. on the day of John Wimber's funeral (which was due to begin at 5:00 p.m.) I was powerfully moved by the sight of several hundred people from all over the world standing in line to pay tribute to someone who had impacted their lives. Eventually several thousand were in attendance to honour John Wimber. In the main, people will thank God for someone who challenged their commitment to Christ, his church and his cause. His impact on the international church of Jesus Christ has been immense. But John Wimber, the businessman, will also leave his mark on the church and many individuals who came into contact with him. He challenged our attitudes and reasoning and focused our direction. We will seek to emulate his visionary thinking and inquiring mind. We will seek to build a church that will be as attractive as Jesus to the unchurched. We will live our lives in the unassuming, self-effacing style John lived his life never again to return to a place of faked superspirituality. We will treat others the way he treated others.

Equally the church has been internationally impacted by the results of the businesses he headed. Vineyard worship music, with its intimate style and quality of production has had an international impact. Vineyard songs are sung all over the world in our churches and the impact continues. Much of the approach and methodology that we established through Vineyard conferences has now been copied. The strategy John employed to evangelise through planting churches not only continues throughout the Association of Vineyard Churches but has been emulated by many other groups.

John Wimber did not leave any of the organisations leaderless when he died. He had had the foresight to replace himself in each of the three organisations. In particular his decision to de-centralise the Association of Vineyard Churches betrayed his characteristic desire to 'release' and not 'hold on'. In so many pioneering church groups the churches suffer after their 'charismatic' leader dies. Because John did not want history to repeat itself he set up a different structure for AVC. Each region is headed by National Co-ordinators and boards and is not centralised in Anaheim or run by Americans. (AVC's structure shares many similarities with large corporations.)

John Wimber was once asked, 'What would you like to be remembered for in 100 years from now?' His response sums up his character. 'I don't want to be remembered for anything! It's not about me. It is about Jesus. He should be remembered. He should be honoured – not me.' I know John Wimber would want us to learn from anything God allowed him to teach us, not to glory in John, but in order that we might glory in Jesus and be better equipped to serve in the Kingdom. So what is it that the Spirit of God has used to change your life through John Wimber? Let us use it and pass it on. There is no better way we can honour him.

In conclusion, I would like to pay tribute to a father; a pastor; an international leader; a godly man who has impacted my life more than any other I have encountered – John Wimber. Like hundreds of thousands of others, I shall be eternally grateful to him.

14

THE LEADER
TODD HUNTER

Involved in church planting, church growth and leadership development for 19 years, Todd Hunter is now the National Director for the Association of Vineyard Churches. He is also the executive publisher of the Voice of the Vineyard *magazine and has contributed to Fuller's* Pastor's Update *tape series. He and his wife, Debbie, and 2 young children, live in Yorba Linda.*

'John was a leader who had
a passionate desire to follow God, and
a strong desire to experience all of the Scriptures.'

One of John Wimber's more oft-quoted sayings is, 'I'm just a fat man on my way to heaven'. People chuckled when they heard John say that, but he was totally serious.

The fact that John wasn't perfect nor ever pretended to be should shape our perspective as we explore what caused some of the difficulties in John's life and how he handled them.

One man – many hats
I'll be the first to confess that John was an enigmatic person, hard to understand or explain at times. He was like a puzzle, and depending on which piece of the puzzle you were looking at, you came to one conclusion or another about him. And his critics have not been shy to

point out his apparent contradictions and inconsistencies. But any examination of the occasional tensions and troubles John found himself in, as he sought to walk out his multifaceted call from God, will suffer from a skewed perspective unless we understand that John lived on a continuum of responsibilities and wore different hats along this continuum. In fact, for many years, in his office he used to keep a shelf full of different colored hats representing his various responsibilities. One said VCF, standing for Vineyard Christian Fellowship, Anaheim. Another said VMI, denoting Vineyard Ministries International. Another said VMG, emblematic of Vineyard Music Group. Another one said AVC, representing the Association of Vineyard Churches.

Perhaps looking at the continuum I mentioned will help (see the diagram on the following page).

Because he lived and worked under this continuum of sometimes conflicting responsibilities, John could not be pigeonholed easily, even by his friends. It helps when attempting to understand this complex man to determine which hat he was wearing or where he was on the continuum of responsibilities at any given moment. He adapted his behavior, and indeed his words, to fit each area of responsibility. For instance, many people who attended one of John's renewal conferences assumed that he would use that same leadership style and persona when he pastored his local church, the Anaheim VCF, only to be disappointed when they visited there and saw how differently he acted at home. When he wore the VCF Anaheim hat, he was acting as the pastor of a local church, not as an international renewal agent.

Because he ministered on this continuum and had to adjust himself to the differing demands and responsibilities of each area, it often appeared as if John was

Placing the Hats John Wimber Wore on a Continuum

Conservative and Cautious	More Moderate and Balanced	Aggressive 'Go For It'

Presiding Leader of a Movement	Pastor of a Local Church	Renewal Agent

John saw this part of his life as the place where he needed to be more responsible, to *police* things	In this aspect of his ministry John saw himself as a guest. He never felt called to correct others; he felt open to experiment and adjust to the Word as he went along

Evangelical	Pentecostal

Outreach Oriented Churches	Blended Churches	Renewal/Revival Oriented Churches

In the Vineyard movement, all of the facets and phases of John's ministry are extant along a similar continuum.

inconsistent. Staying consistent was for him a challenge precisely because he had so many hats to wear.

Handling the authority represented by these hats put John into some interesting dilemmas. There were times where he had to make very difficult choices between two equally unattractive options. For instance,

John 'the renewal agent' made promises in some countries that the Vineyard would not plant churches there. But when he took off the hat of renewal and put on the hat of evangelist and apostolic leader of a church planting movement, he had to go back to those leaders and say, 'I'm sorry. Will you let me out of my promise? Can we renegotiate?'

This tension also played out in John's preaching. Often John used the pulpit in Anaheim to speak to the movement and not primarily to the church.

John was also torn between his renewal travel and discipling his own staff and key lay leaders at home.

Most striking of all, John was a pragmatist who wanted a Christianity with true mystery in it; that's a hard line to walk perfectly straight!

In this chapter I want to help make sense of this complex man and his extraordinarily full life by unpacking this sentence:

John was a leader who had
a passionate hunger to follow God, and
a strong desire to experience all of the Scriptures.

John was a leader
Being an only child prepared John uniquely for 'the loneliness that exists at the top', as the saying goes. This loneliness, I think, is due mostly to having to make tough, unpopular decisions which upset others.

In my judgment, John started out with a remarkably pure vision. Not many leaders see the preferable future they are trying to bring about as clearly as John did. He wanted to experience all of God that he possibly could. He really didn't care about numbers of followers. He often said, 'Look, I'm just driving a bus. If you want to go where I'm going, get on and let's go! If you don't want to go where I'm going, it's okay.' He simply didn't care about the usual scorekeeping. What he cared about were his ideas and getting them across to others for the sake of helping the church.

John knew that as a leader he was called by God to be a change agent. In fact, where maintaining the status quo is the goal, he knew a leader isn't needed but a manager. Groups who desire the status quo reject leaders. 'You can always tell who the pioneers are,' it is said. 'They're the ones with the knives in the back.' Even firmly rejected, with knives in his back, John refused to be flattened by conformity.

Some critics have said that John took the church and turned it into a laboratory and turned church members into laboratory rats. In my view, this is a cynical and unnecessarily harsh view of John. John deeply loved the church, the whole church. And he trusted the Holy Spirit, the Word of God and the church itself through the discernment of its members to sort things out.

He was always very patient with the inevitable mixture of humanity and the Holy Spirit in any given meeting. John may have seemed reckless to those who observed from the outside, but as someone who knew him deeply, John was never intentionally reckless, and would never have treated somebody like a laboratory rat.

John lived like somebody who didn't have a rear view mirror in his car. He was always looking forward. He would learn from his mistakes while they were happening, and then he moved on. John had a way of making failure his friend. He realized that to make any progress in the Kingdom he had to jump into the game of life.

Towards the end of his life John began to change his style of leadership in the church and in the Association of Vineyard Churches. He shifted from almost an entirely autocratic style of leadership to one that was more collegiate and participatory.

In some people's minds, this was a change for the

worse. Critics judged John to be giving in to pressure from some of his colleagues. Some surmised that this might be the reason for some of his apparent waffling on issues, his seeming inconsistencies, or his enthusiastic endorsing of something at the beginning, and then pulling his endorsement later on. In my judgment this is a mistaken view of John. John, as I said, was an only child and was incredibly stubborn. It was almost impossible for anyone to get him to do something he didn't want to do.

John rightly saw the limitations of an autocratic style of leadership once the Vineyard reached a certain size and visibility. I believe the choices John made both at the beginning and at the end were correct. We needed a certain kind of guidance system to get the rocket off the ground. We needed his incredible power. We needed his focus and his sense of autonomy to get the Vineyard started. Once it was off the ground, I believe he rightly shifted to different kinds of guidance systems.

John was a very strong leader, and very much took his own counsel. But there are some who suggest that if John had an Achilles heel as a leader, it was that at rare times he could be manipulated. Typically this might have to do with John feeling inadequate because of his lack of a graduate education. People with letters after their names could sometimes make John feel unintelligent and ill-equipped to sort through the complex issues he often grappled with. Or he could occasionally be manipulated over guilt in his personal life, such as perceived failings with family or being overweight. A third way he could be manipulated was if John really loved somebody who he considered to be down and out or in some need; they could sometimes have sway in John's life that wasn't congruent with his higher rational and thoughtful self.

John had a passionate hunger to follow God and a strong desire to experience all of the Scriptures.

Many in England remember John as the radical renewal/change agent. Though I know *that* John, and have traveled many parts of the world with him, the John I'm more acquainted with is the John who refused to exceed the speed limit on our Southern California freeways, who was frugal with his money and was diligent to help those in need around him. This is one of those examples of John being truly perplexing. He could be so conservative on the one hand and so radical on the other.

For John, his passionate hunger to follow God was always rooted in the Scriptures. He often talked about the Bible being analogous to a menu in a restaurant and not the meal. The menu is something you read; it's not what you eat. So the Bible is something we read, but it's not the living of life. The living of life, the meal of the Kingdom, was for him, doing the things of the Word. 'The name of the game for the Vineyard,' John wrote to the Vineyard pastors, 'is the Kingdom of God. This game has two primary aims: evangelize and equip.'

For all of us, our strength can become our weakness. This may have been true for John. Some would suggest that his openness to the things of the Spirit and to people, his reluctance and gentleness in correcting those he thought were wrong, led on the one hand to really great ministry, but on the other to some excesses and confusion.

John's changing style

One of the explanations for John changing his style of leadership towards the end of his life, as I referred to above, is that he was more tolerant of things close to the line and was rather more holistic than was perhaps good for the movement as a whole. Though John himself had a first-class mind and was able to simultaneously carry many apparently conflicting truths in his mind, this was not always so for his followers. John was always concerned that the Vineyard should not lose its distinctives in the midst of his own experimenting. For instance, he was adamant that the Vineyard be 'naturally supernatural'; that we not 'hype-up' a crowd and that we demystify the things of the Holy Spirit as much as possible in order to make them accessible to all the church. Yet his meetings outside the Vineyard sometimes contrasted with this stated value system as he experimented with new ideas.

John often told me that a key moment for him in recognizing the limitations of his passionate autocratic style came during an Association of Vineyard Churches board meeting in Chicago. The board was debating the pros and cons of a church coming into our movement. At one point John grew impatient with the discussion and said, 'Look, you get into heaven through Jesus; you get into the Vineyard through me.' That church came into the movement, and it took John many years to sort through all the fallout. On the other hand, as the Vineyard was distancing itself from the Toronto church later in 1995, John was far more democratic, and the board had more input in that decision.

John's governmental approach to testing the things of the Spirit is found in his oft-repeated saying that, 'You let a bush grow, you see what it's going to become, and then you trim or prune it so that it can be more effective and fruitful.' Whether one agrees with that approach or not, this certainly explains John's forays into and exits from the prophetic movement and the Toronto blessing.

Parameters and protocols

At the end of any time of experimenting, John would always come back to the Word of God and the values God had given him for the Vineyard. He wanted life in the Vineyard to be far more balanced than a renewal conference. Although he was an experimenter, he knew that all experiments need parameters and protocols. John was never afraid to take clear, decisive measurements. In the midst of the Toronto renewal John related the following in a letter to Vineyard pastors:

> The Lord gave me an extremely vivid open vision. In the picture he showed me a magnificent mountain lake. Beautiful sunshine reflected off the water that was so fresh and inviting. The water of the lake spilled over a dam and cascaded into a river and came down the sides of a mountain into a large plain. In the plain, there were thousands and thousands of acres of vineyards. I saw men working in the fields, digging irrigation ditches. Then the vision ended.
>
> So I said, 'Lord, what does it mean?' In my mind, he gave me, 'The lake is the blessing I'm pouring out. Isn't it beautiful? Isn't it fresh?' I was so touched, I began crying. He then said, 'The cascading stream is the church. I'm pouring it first into the church.' And I wept more. I just thought, 'Oh thank you Lord. Thank you for the blessing on the church.'
>
> Then I saw again how the water came down to the bottom of the mountain into the plain, where the workers were tending the irrigation ditches. I recognized these irrigation ditches as 'Ministry to the poor, ministry to the weak, sick, broken, and lost.' There were different kinds of fruit growing on the vines. Then he said, 'That's my people. This blessing can either stay in the church, with great meetings that eventually end, or we can pull the gates up and let the water begin flowing. If you want, you can direct the water, the blessing, into the fields.'
>
> I got the clear impression of a co-laboring. God was pouring out his blessing. But if we don't dig the channels, if we don't go out into the highways and by-ways, if we don't put evangelism forward, if we

don't do the things God calls us to do, revival won't spread.

The following is a diagram that John used to explain how renewal or revival experiences work in conjunction with the Word of God.

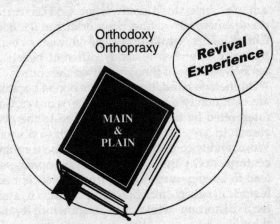

But what if each day of the week there was a different opportunity for newly-revived people to immediately take the water into the fields? Today we're going to package food and take it to the poor. Tomorrow we're going to give out tracts and witness and minister in the streets. The next day we are going to go to all the hospitals and the old age homes.

The diagram is a pictorial way to explain John's concern that sometimes renewal experiences, even those that have some historical precedent, can lead us away from the main and plain things that are illustrated by the Bible in the middle of the picture. John was always concerned that we stay in the realm of classic historical Christian orthodoxy and orthopraxy. He was willing to get near the line, but never wanted to go over it. When he found himself over the line, he was quick to repent, come back and to retreat from any non-biblical position whether in thinking or practice.

This quote from the last leadership letter John wrote before he died sums up his thinking well:

> The Vineyard is a church planting movement that actively seeks to discern what God is currently doing wherever we find His working in the Body of Christ. This philosophy of ministry exposes Vineyard churches to many different beliefs from various streams of thought within the church.
>
> On the one hand, this keeps us honed because we are continually driven back to the Word of God as interpreted by the Spirit of God and to the historic church to ask: 'Is this consistent with God's written Word, and with its historical expression through the centuries?' On the other hand, this openness can lead to a temporary drifting from the anchor of our historical beliefs and practices, and even a short-term distortion while the 'fresh wind' is sorted through.

John's passionate hunger for God married with his concern to follow the Scriptures is what created the main dilemma in his life. He was trying to live in the tension of conservative evangelical theology and the best of Pentecostal practices. It's what we in the Vineyard often refer to as trying to be 'the best of both worlds'.

John loved drawing pictures to communicate a point. Here is one he often used to illustrate what the Vineyard was trying to do.

Trying to live this out, as I said in the first section of this chapter, often led John to making unpopular decisions. He repeatedly made decisions that would make either conservative evangelicals or Pentecostals upset at him. The conservative evangelicals often thought of John as being too wild or too Pentecostal and the

THEOLOGY   EXPERIENCE

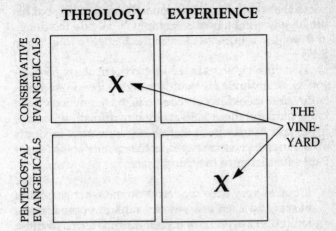

Pentecostals sometimes thought of John as being too cautious and occasionally quenching the Spirit.

Because John was a Quaker and usually pacifistic, he rarely replied to this kind of criticism. However, his attitude evolved over the years. Towards the end of his life he decided that he would reply to anyone sincerely questioning his doctrine. Though he never replied to personal attacks, he did come to believe that he proba-bly should have replied to some of the criticism he received sooner. Not responding caused some unneces-sary confusion in his followers.

Conclusion: a personal tribute

One of the things that I so admired about John was his tremendous spiritual zeal to do what was right, to have a clean conscience. But he always had the humility to know that his own sense of a clear conscience didn't make him innocent. He knew his own conscience could be mistaken, that it was fallen like every other part of his being. In the end, he knew that only God could make the final, authoritative judgment over his life. Only God could say to him, 'You did well.'

That's why John so passionately tried to live out his life by following Christ's example: 'I only do the things and say the things that I hear the Father saying' (John 5:19).

This didn't always make John a particularly fun person to be around. He could be rigid, seemingly autocratic, and incredibly stubborn; just ask anybody who knew him! But these traits made him difficult to manipulate, and it made him therefore trustworthy in God's eyes. Eugene Peterson captures this in his paraphrase of Paul's first letter to the Corinthians:

> It makes very little difference to me what you think of me, and even less where I rank in popular opinion. I don't even rank myself. Comparisons in these matters are pointless. I'm not aware of anything that would disqualify me from being a good guide for you, but that doesn't mean much, it's the Master who makes that judgment.
>
> 1 Cor 4:3 The Message

John held views because he thought they were right, not to be popular. He didn't, like some politicians, use polls to see what to believe. He often wondered what people thought about what he said, not because he wanted to know whether he was liked or not, but because he wanted to know whether or not he was actually making a difference.

One of the things that I learned working with John is this: too much empathy can equal too little authenticity. To be truly authentic means that from time to time you may cause people pain. A leader living his life out before a heavenly audience realizes not everyone will admire him or her.

Henry Kissinger said,

Our age finds it difficult to come to grips with figures like Winston Churchill. The leaders with whom
we are familiar generally aspire to be superstars
rather than heroes, and the distinction is crucial.
Superstars strive for official praise; heroes walk
alone. Superstars crave consensus; heroes define
themselves by the judgment of a future they see as
their task to bring about. Superstars seek success as
a technique for eliciting support; heroes pursue success as the outgrowth of inner values.

John knew the only real praise, the only thing that
would make any difference was not what the public
thought of him but what God would assign at the final
judgment.

If you were to ask me, 'Todd, what's the one thing
you'll take with you from the life and death of John
Wimber? it would be to live my life the way John lived
– before an audience of One.

I have enormous respect in my heart for John. He
not only lived this out himself, but by his steadfastness
and humility, he became a model for us all.

15

VINEYARD MOVEMENT FOUNDER

JOHN MUMFORD

*John Mumford read theology at St Andrew's University,
and after further training and ordination in 1977, he served
in two churches, first in Dorset and then in central London.
He later joined the staff of the Vineyard in Anaheim,
California, working with John Wimber, until in 1987 he
and Eleanor started the SW London Vineyard. He
continues to lead that church, whilst also overseeing the
growing number of Vineyards in the UK and Ireland.*

During one of John Wimber's first conferences in central London in 1984, I went out to lunch with him at an Italian restaurant. That morning he'd been lecturing on church growth and, as we ate, we started to talk about the decline in membership in the mainline denominations and the sudden increase in the charismatic independent churches. (At that stage I regarded the so-called 'house churches' with suspicion if not actually as rivals.) The name of a particular charismatic church and its leader came up, and John asked me what I made of the growth of that church? 'Not a lot,' I thought to myself, but I said nothing, and pretending I had not heard the question, I took another mouthful of spaghetti. After a few moments John came back to the subject. 'Well, let me put it like this,' he said. 'Do you think

what's happening in that church is God or not?' This
time I couldn't avoid the question, I became increasingly uncomfortable and I think I spluttered incoherently.
I couldn't answer. John then leant further across the
table towards me, looked me in the eye and, without a
trace of harshness, said: 'How dare you disdain what
God is doing?' That ruined my lunch but it changed my
life.

This little exchange over lunch showed many of
John's characteristics. He was visionary, he was open,
he was kind, and he saw things that other people didn't
see. He also loved the body of Christ. All of it. John's
love for the whole church, whether the unsophisticated
snake-handling churches in the Appalachian mountains or, at the opposite end of the ecclesiastical spectrum, the liturgy and the drama of high Anglicanism,
humbled me.

At that point in time I had a narrow view of the
church and an ignorance of what God was doing in it.
Clearly John had a very different vision. 'It's all the
church,' he used to say, 'and God loves all of it.'
Conversation over that lunch table revealed another of
his traits: that he cared more for the truth than for what
I thought of him. He didn't mind inducing a little short-
term discomfort for the sake of realising long-term
blessing and benefit. Despite being made to feel so
uncomfortable during this encounter, deep down I had
been amazed at the quality of the man sitting opposite
me. I could have walked away and never spoken to him
again; but I knew that what he had said was true. It was
his unassuming certainty and quiet authority that
struck me. Here was a man who knew his mind, a man
of singular vision, unapologetic, rigorous and challenging.

Over the next few years I came to appreciate these
qualities. It seems that they were essential attributes for
a man who was on course (even if he didn't know it at

the time) to found a movement. What is now known
worldwide as the Vineyard movement began as no
more than a small group meeting in a private home in
Southern California. In fact, the first time John ever visited the group, of which his wife Carol and his sister-in-
law Penny Fulton were a part, he came away smiling to
himself and announcing confidently to Carol, 'That
group ain't going nowhere'. He was to be proved spectacularly wrong. Today, there are some 700 Vineyard
churches in fifty-two different nations, making the
movement one of the fastest-growing Christian denominations.

Looking back now at John's life and ministry, my
own view, and of course I recognise that I am biased, is
that John Wimber was one of the most outstanding
Christian leaders of his generation. Behind the relaxed,
laid-back Californian demeanour there lay a solid, intel-
lectually rigorous theology and conviction. As well as
being an intuitive and pragmatic leader, he had a fine
analytical mind and an excellent grasp of the fundamental tenets of Christianity. For him, the Scriptures
were his bedrock. He would reiterate time and again
that he always saw himself as a conservative evangelical who believed in and tried to operate in the gifts of
the Spirit, as opposed to a conservative evangelical who
didn't.

Despite this, and to my amazement, he often
expressed an insecurity at his lack of a formal theological education, sometimes to the point of feeling intimidated by those seemingly better schooled in such academic matters. I have no doubt that had John's life and
circumstances been different, affording him the opportunity to attend a theological seminary as a fulltime student, he would have excelled for he possessed a
superbly incisive mind. And yet he would often point
out that he was not a theoretician so much as a practitioner. The first time I ever met him, again over a lunch

table, I remember him saying how much his own thinking had been influenced and enriched by British theologians and Bible teachers, whereupon he rattled off a list of household names in the evangelical community: F. F. Bruce, Martyn Lloyd-Jones, J.I. Packer, John Stott, David Watson and Michael Green. 'I have read them all,' he said, 'and theologically I don't think I have anything to add. Maybe the difference is that not only do we believe it, we are also trying to do it.' Wimber certainly believed it, he certainly tried to do it and, I would add, he succeeded in training other ordinary 'lay' (how he hated the term!) men and women to do it. It is perhaps one of John's great legacies to the body of Christ that he was able to bring the ministry of Jesus, hitherto concentrated in the hands of certain gifted individuals on the stage, into the hands of the ordinary believer.

If John had a particular gift or even genius, it was his ability to see things clearly. He had an uncanny knack of seeing straight through to the heart of things, of grasping seemingly complex issues with ease and then an often brilliant ability to communicate them succinctly. It is a gift that I believe has helped the Vineyard grow in the way it has. It's as if God took John, a man of the people with an excellent mind, to communicate to the people. I remember one occasion when, at the end of a long day of meetings with other Vineyard leaders in Houston, Texas, somebody asked him a question about a pastoral problem. He suddenly seemed to come alive and, reaching for a marker pen, he started scribbling on a flip chart. The rest of us – by now wide awake again – wrote furiously, trying to keep up with a flurry of insights and new ideas that were little less than breathtaking. Only afterwards did we stand around and shake our heads, wondering: how on earth does the man do it? John had a gift for seeing things and anticipating issues that at the time no one else had even realised were issues. He possessed a superb blend of worldly canniness and spiritual wisdom – he was, in a way, a kind of streetwise saint, blessed with an ability to see what might lie ahead and act accordingly.

John's leadership was, at heart, confident and assured, based as it was upon a close relationship with the Lord. He was convinced that every good leader must first learn to be a good follower. He himself loved Jesus with a passion, and talked about him naturally, engagingly and often. It was said of John at his funeral by Todd Hunter (the National Director of the Association of the Vineyard Churches in the United States) that 'he lived his life before an audience of One'. It's as if he took as his text 1 Corinthians chapter 4: 'I care very little if I am judged by you or by any human court . . . It is the Lord who judges me.' There was in him a seemingly inhuman independence of the opinion of others. I saw this reality in the restaurant that day, and I was to see evidence of it again many times in the next fifteen years. Here was a man who was guileless enough to stroll onto a stage wearing Reeboks (and sometimes, when it was warm enough, a rather awful Hawaiian shirt) and yet confident enough to challenge people. Many of them had been serving the Lord to the very best of their ability for many years, and yet John was prepared to tell them that 'God wants his church back'. It was almost shocking to us, and yet we knew that what he was saying was true.

How did he do this and get away with it? The answer, I think, lay in John's engaging sense of humour, his complete lack of pretension and his great gift for communicating ideas simply and clearly. All this helped to make him credible. People would laugh at the man who said that he was just a fat saxophone player trying to get to heaven, but no one doubted the serious-ness that lay behind such a statement. The humour was self-deprecating and yet made a profound point. It was an indicator that he never took himself too seriously, for in my opinion he simply did not know how to be pompous. On more than one occasion he was approached by someone who asked him how he prepared himself to minister. No doubt expecting to hear words and phrases like 'fasting', hours of study', nights of prayer' and so on, John simply replied: 'I finish my diet Coke, turn off the TV and go heal the sick.' This reply sometimes offended his critics, who missed the point. Far from decrying the need for a devotional life (in fact, invariably John was up very early praying and studying his Bible), by his seemingly flippant answer he was simply attempting to defuse the false piety, and the tendency towards the hero-worship of leaders so endemic in the Christian world, that he disliked so intensely.

John entitled his own story 'I'm A Fool For Christ', and often he would risk looking foolish even in public. He was quite prepared at a meeting, for example, to stand seemingly for ages in silence (agonising to many of us) while waiting for the Lord to give him directions. Frankly, he couldn't care less what we thought. He was living his life before an audience of One, and his only concern was that he heard clearly from the Lord and spoke honestly to the people. And what you saw of John in public was exactly what you got in private. There was no 'side' to him. There was no sudden change once he came off the platform, whether he was praying for people, or joining in an informal conversation or eating supper. What you saw really was what you got.

One of the things that struck me forcibly when I first met him was John's unusual ability to integrate the natural with the supernatural. Most of us tend to live life on two levels, so when for example conversation takes a spiritual turn, there is usually some grinding of gears. But this was not so with John. The two ran into each other, the transmission was automatic. He was never more natural than when he was spiritual, and vice versa. His life was not departmentalised into the spiritual or the natural – they permeated and infected each other. For example, when a decision had to be made, he really didn't mind where he got his information from, whether it was from his own thinking, analysis and research, from the Lord through the Scriptures, or his or others' prophetic words or dreams in the night. In his perception, there was no need to set up the natural over against the supernatural. He learned to live with both, in a well-integrated way, drawing the best from each of them for the overall benefit of the church. He was a keen advocate, for example, of planning – I found some of his best training material for church leaders was on planning, and for this reason among many others, he loved the Book of Proverbs. He didn't see it as at all incongruous that, on the one hand, you could be thoroughly sensitive to the Lord's leading and direction, and on the other hand, approach decision-making with all the acumen of a shrewd businessman. Wimber's was a refreshing presence in the church. There was the supernatural dimension to him (praying for the sick and seeing them get better), and there was the church consultant. There was the risk-taker for Christ, and the down-to-earth pragmatist.

John was a leader who had the ability to grow a small group into a large church, and multiply churches into a movement, because he understood the crucial importance of training and equipping others. Repeatedly he would teach from Ephesians chapter 4 verse 12 that it was our task 'to equip [NIV: prepare] God's people for works of service, so that the body of Christ may be built up'. Perhaps more than anything else, he will be remembered as an equipper. He would teach the words, and then demonstrate the works of Jesus in a way which was possible to imitate. His lectures or his sermons would be followed by what he called a classroom 'clinic', in which the truths he had taught could be put to the test.

John's intuitive understanding of leadership was one of his most outstanding gifts. He never assumed leadership as his right: 'I'm supposed to be your leader. Now let's see if I can lead you,' he would say. He believed that there was a divine, sovereign, almost mysterious element to leadership. He recognised as a truth that some people are leaders and some people are not, that God causes leaders to emerge in his church, but equally that he shares with us a responsibility to help in the training process. But John also produced a highly pragmatic, functional definition of leadership. 'A leader is someone who has a following. So if you're a leader, then go ahead and lead.' The practical reality for John was that a leader was only a leader if he was leading, and that a leader had to have followers. He also understood the importance of reproducing leaders without which growth – of an individual church or indeed of a whole movement – would be so hampered. And when it came to the question of handing over his own succession, based on a knowledge of church history and his own observations of the contemporary church, dating back to the time when he travelled all over the United States as a Church Growth Consultant on the staff of the School of World Missions at Fuller Theological Seminary in Pasadena, I think one of his enduring legacies will be that he trained and left a group of leaders behind. We will all lead differently, but we will go on.

'The ability to identify, recruit, train, deploy, monitor and nurture a workforce is the principal missing-link in the non-growing church today,' he would say. He knew that it is only God who causes leaders to emerge in his church, but equally that he shares with us a responsibility to recognise and encourage and contribute to that process, by identifying, recruiting and training them. It was always John's instinct to equip others to lead, rather than to shine himself. It was part of his humility, I think, that he was willing to delegate. I often felt he gave some of us much more responsibility than we were ready to assume. There were many occasions when, having been invited to lead a conference in some part of the world, he would arrive as usual with a team of younger leaders 'in training'. It was by no means infrequently that he would say to one of his colleagues, usually in a very casual way over breakfast, 'Oh, by the way, I'd like you to teach at the main session of the conference this morning.' To him this was an essential means of training young leaders on the job, tossing them in at the 'deep end' with a minimum of warning, though it has to be said that on occasions his hosts were surprised and sometimes initially disappointed not to hear the main speaker. But John was never intimidated by the opinion of others, especially since he placed a very high value on providing opportunities for training younger leaders.

John's understanding of Christianity, and the application of that understanding, was essentially high in risk. He himself said that faith is spelt R-I-S-K, yet he was quick to recognise and acknowledge we would all (himself included) make mistakes. There were instances when he mis-read people's motives or character or intentions, and would later freely admit that he had been wrong about them. But he refused to be deflected from his task, being realistic enough to know that mistakes were part of the package. In fact, he believed that if you were not making mistakes, you were not doing enough, not putting enough new ideas into practice, not taking enough calculated risks. Perhaps for this reason some people assumed that he had a thick skin, or was insensitive to their particular view or situation. But this was not the case, for he was frequently pained by errors he made and hurt by criticisms he received because of them.

I think it was true that he was, in many respects, a shy man without very much in the way of small talk. But all of us who had him to stay in our homes were invariably struck by his unfailing courtesy, his unforced but irresistible charm and his appreciation of home-cooked food. He was hard working and yet at the same time managed to remain relaxed. He never seemed to be in a hurry nor too busy to laugh at a good joke, enjoy a new story or join you for a meal (which he usually ended up paying for). But were there no warts on this remarkable, this unique man? Yes, I suppose there were. His realism, an almost ruthless ability to see things as they really are, rather than how we might wish that they were. There was little place in his thinking for sentiment, convention or prejudice.

Such realism proved to be unpopular at times, for it was disconcerting, and meant that he was not always the easiest person to work with. There were times when he could be tiresome, even exasperating. But looking back, I have the feeling that what we were tempted to describe as faults were more often than not the flip side of his strengths. At times he was inclined to be a little ruthless, even intolerant. He was prone to exaggeration, but this was merely the overflow of his enthusiasm, I think, rather than a deliberate attempt to mislead. John could occasionally be stubborn, he could be autocratic, and he would often leave debris in his wake; it usually fell to those working closely with him to try and clear up the mess.

ut for all that, John was a truly great leader, a pioneer and an initiator. He would be content to let an untidy or messy situation continue for a long time, rather than intervene too early. His own personality allowed him to tolerate a high level of 'orderly chaos' and to live with ambiguity and unresolved situations in the belief that, given time and God's influence, things would resolve. Where others might have become over-anxious or over-directive, he would be content to wait and let people work things out for themselves. He would always resist being rushed into a decision either by circumstances or the expectations of other people. In the words of a wise maxim he would offer to new leaders or young church planters, 'Let the bush grow'. By this he meant that it is often wiser to wait and let things develop, and then at a later date by all means trim them back.

I loved the way John defined success. I remember hearing him say once: 'Success is simply rendering humble service. It is finding out what the Lord wants and then doing it. Whether it is to five, fifty, five hundred or five thousand.' But given his track record, I later asked him in private, 'How do you stay humble?' He answered with disarming honesty, 'God gives me enough failure, difficulty, criticism and misunderstanding to keep me humble.' Bob Fulton, his brother-in-law and long-standing friend and colleague, once said to John 'The reason I follow you is that when you are wrong, you are quick to repent.' Such humility explains to me why so many different men and women across various denominations and cultures, and in different nations of the world, were able to hear and to receive what he was saying.

For all his risk-taking, John was essentially conservative, even cautious, by temperament. The radicalism only came out of his conviction that obedience to God's prompting was all that mattered. So for him, John's Gospel chapter 5 verse 19 was a cardinal text: 'The Son can do nothing by himself, he can do only what he sees the Father doing.' This was fundamental to John's understanding of the Christian life in general, and Christian ministry in particular. He resolutely maintained that it is God's task to initiate, and our task to follow. So, whether speaking to an audience, or planting a church, he was convinced that all we can do is nothing other than respond to God's leading and initiative. If Jesus couldn't operate on his own and independent of his Father, how on earth could we? So, regarding healing, for example, he believed that it's our task to pray and it's God's task to heal. He knew only too well that we can't heal anybody. Only God can. And sometimes God would choose to heal, sometimes he wouldn't. This ambiguity was evident in his own life, plagued as it was with illness and suffering.

Greatness often consists in the harmony of opposites. I've read countless biographies where the person under scrutiny appeared to exhibit a number of apparent contradictions or paradoxes, and one was left with the distinct impression that their greatness lay not in a compromise between opposites, but in their collision. John Wimber was no exception.

The way in which John taught and then demonstrated broke through people's unwillingness to trust God. He made the supernatural power of God seem normal. His style was accessible to everyone and his own confidence in God was infectious. Much as he did to me that day over lunch, he challenged people's perceptions of the ways in which God works today, and put them in the context that God had always intended. Those who knew John well, and those who worked closely with him, never expect to see his like again, for rarely can anyone have meant so much to so many as did this man.

16

PLANTING A LOCAL VINEYARD CHRISTIAN FELLOWSHIP

JOHN WRIGHT

John Wright (b. 1960) was university trained as a designer jeweller. For several years he served both at home and abroad in the 'Faith sharing' team from St Andrew's, Chorleywood. Following his second 'team' visit to New Zealand, he joined the Vineyard Christian Fellowship at Anaheim for 9 months as an 'intern pastor' at John Wimber's invitation. He then studied at the London Bible College and worked as an associate pastor with John Mumford who founded the first UK Vineyard in W London. After 9 years he moved to plant the new Trent Vineyard in Nottingham. He is married to Debby and has 2 sons.

I first met John Wimber in 1982. I grew up in a wonderful Christian home, involved for most of my youth in St Andrew's, Chorleywood, but through peer pressure and my own foolishness I drifted in my commitment to the Lord in my late teens. Then, following three years as a student I started work in Banbury as a jeweller. Having heard of the impact of John Wimber's visit to St Andrew's a few months previously, I returned when I heard that he was visiting once again. Even as I was preparing to come into the tangible presence of the Spirit of God, I found myself repenting for the direction

my life had been headed, and committing the rest of it
to God's will.

I do not recall much of what happened at that meeting, but I remember standing with my arms raised,
shaking all over. I can only say that the Lord *arrested* me
that night and drew me back to himself.

Following that day, my wife Debby and I spent
increasing amounts of our spare time ministering to the
sick, the emotionally broken and the demonised, seeing
some remarkable healings both among Christians and
unbelievers. Whenever John Wimber came back to the
UK for public meetings and conferences we were there.

The call to full-time ministry

As 1985 drew to its close, Debby and I sensed increasingly the call to church leadership. At the time there
seemed very little likelihood to us of the Vineyard
planting churches in the UK so we assumed that the call
must be to ministry in the Anglican Church since that
was our background. There followed an eleven-month
process culminating in a weekend away before a selection committee, and finishing with a letter to explain
that I would not be recommended for training. Since we
were due to go with Barry Kissell (on the staff of St
Andrew's) on an extended ministry trip to New
Zealand a month later, we asked John Wimber whether
we could visit the Vineyard in Anaheim for a couple of
days on our way back. John replied by inviting us to be
his guests for two months.

We both quit our jobs, and by January 1987 we were
living in what had been the Anaheim Vineyard offices,
initially duplicating tapes by day and getting involved
in the life of the church in every other waking hour.
During that two-month period, a definite decision to
plant Vineyards in the UK was made, and it became
clear to us that that was where our future involvement
was to be. In the event we stayed on for nine months in

all, training as intern pastors before returning to the UK to help start the first British Vineyard led by John and Eleanor Mumford.

Our nine years with them, two whilst pursuing further Biblical studies at the London Bible College in Northwood, and seven on the pastoral staff of SW London Vineyard, proved to be invaluable experience. There we began working out, in the growing local church context, so much of what John Wimber had taught us, under the mentoring and leadership of John and Eleanor.

My family and I finally moved to Nottingham in the summer of 1996 to plant the Trent Vineyard. To begin with I worked as a self-employed painter and decorator just to keep food on the table, and we were joined by three other couples from SW London Vineyard. They had sacrificially resigned from their jobs and sold their houses to come to Nottingham where they found new jobs and new homes, and helped us to build a new church plant.

Over the past nineteen months we have seen the Lord establishing a church with the 'genetic code' of a Vineyard. We have built up a fellowship, based on John Wimber's teaching, example and practice, 'working it out at ground level' as it were and where I am now supported full-time. The church has developed in a number of specific areas, the most significant of which I discuss in the rest of the chapter.

Worship

Worship is our highest priority. Much of our worship involves the congregation in singing which we often loosely call 'the worship time'. Following the Anaheim model we have extended times of singing using words that are more usually directed to the Lord – than to each other about him. The words which are projected onto a screen are mostly intimate and tender though we also include some more up-beat songs of praise. Most of these come from within the Vineyard movement, though some of the songs and the occasional hymn come from the wider church. We also include songs that our own members have written, and even if some of the songs we sing may not have the creedal content of others, we would avoid any that communicated anything unbiblical. An increasing number of Vineyard songs do express more precise biblical teaching to reinforce a particular central doctrine, such as the cross, and more may be on the way, but for us a song is mainly to express the heart of worship – to connect the participator with the presence of God – to seek to touch God's heart with our love. The more songs that are taken literally from Scripture the better.

We have a worship band using contemporary instruments, with creative arrangements and new songs which are constantly coming to the fore. At the risk of being considered too subjective, the bottom line is, I believe, that we must guard the intimacy in 'touching the Father's heart' from being deflected or diluted. And as long as that is the case, the musical style, instruments used and lyrical content can change and develop freely.

We have found that 'Vineyard worship' is a major attraction to the younger generation who clearly experience a meaningful level of intimacy through its music and style.

Compassion – works of mercy and care for the poor

During the months of my involvement in the Church of England's selection process I suddenly had to face the challenge of increasing investment in my career as a self-employed jeweller in Nottingham or getting out of my working premises – within two weeks! Knowing I was called into full-time Christian ministry, I closed the shop, and spent the next six months working with homeless young people, an experience which became foundational and formative in my understanding of the kind of church I wanted to be involved with.

When I arrived at the Anaheim Vineyard in Los Angeles, I expected the major focus to be on 'signs and wonders' which is what John had been asked to teach on at those conferences in the UK that I had attended. Great was my surprise and delight to find a church so highly committed to the poor. Many thousands of square feet in their building were taken up with the storage of food and clothing that was regularly distributed to those in need. Amongst other things, during our time there we took hot meals out on the streets and helped to build an orphanage across the border in Mexico. One of my duties was to dedicate two whole days a week to being available for anyone who came to the church needing help, food, clothing or counsel, and to furnish them accordingly.

John's consistent teaching and example on the church's responsibility to minister to the poor has reinforced my thinking and raised my vision to a level never previously considered. This was no occasional optional extra for the church – it was a major ongoing ministry and major part of the life of the church. Recently the Anaheim Vineyard had an urgent collection to raise $500,000 to refinance the loan on their buildings. It was announced up front that the first $250,000 would be given away to the poor. They raised the whole $750,000 in one week!

The previous Sunday, Carol Wimber had addressed the congregation with the words: 'We will never be a church that can spend the outpouring on ourselves . . . This is the heart of Jesus. We will never again be able to pretend to ourselves that we are not surrounded by poor and needy and oppressed and hungry and naked.'

John was about the most generous person I've

known. He loved quoting Jesus' words 'Freely you've received, freely give'. As a young church plant we have tried to follow that example and have given significant amounts of our time, energy and money to blessing our community. This has taken the form of serving people by cutting their hedges, sweeping up their autumn leaves and washing their cars as simple demonstrations of God's love for them – with no strings attached.

House groups are regularly encouraged to come up with ideas, and many of those projects are focused on blessing the poor and needy, such as visiting the elderly, those who are hospitalised or in sheltered accommodation taking cards, flowers and gifts. The church has provided Christmas dinner and presents for battered wives and their children, turned a single mother's overgrown backyard into a garden again and decorated a drop-in-centre for prostitutes. There is usually some project going on each month whereby those who have share with those who have not.

Ministry to the sick

Another area of the expression of Christ's compassion was the demonstration of his power in healing, and this was something which John was often asked to teach about in the UK – especially so in the eighties. John was committed to equipping the saints for the work of ministry, and part of this was the work of ministering healing. He made it perfectly clear that we could not heal people ourselves – it was God's work and was wrought through the power of the Holy Spirit. He taught and modelled this ministry in a very low-key way that enabled us all to get involved – something we have certainly continued at our local church level. John saw this 'power ministry' biblically as an adjunct to every other kind of evangelistic ministry rather than an alternative 'p' to add to what are called 'presence', 'proclamation' and 'persuasion' evangelism. The signs cause people to wonder and make them more open to the other forms of evangelism.

We have experienced power evangelism as *one* of the factors involved in people coming to Christ. When still in London we led a number of public healing seminars which we advertised widely in the community. At those gatherings the gospel was explained and the sick prayed for. We saw a number of people both healed and converted who subsequently integrated into the life of our church. We have also seen others healed who never became Christians. But we would not claim to have seen the full results John envisaged, mainly because we have not prayed for healing to a great extent outside the church environment, and according to John's understanding 'the meat is in the street'.

However Debby and I have seen scores of people apparently healed over the years both in our local church and beyond. I can recall a dozen significant healings in recent months with problems like chronic back pain, severe stomach ulcers and arthritic conditions, which have been very painful in the months or years prior to receiving prayer and where there has been no pain or symptoms since. It seems that we tend to see more healings when attention is drawn back to the subject in our teaching. When people are reminded of Jesus' commission to heal they become increasingly focused on ministering healing as needs arise. John once said to those who did not think that God would want to use them to heal, that they should pray for 200 sick people first before making up their minds! As far as I know those who took John seriously have kept going.

Only last week Andrew McNeil, a Vineyard pastor in the Midlands, related a healing he had received the week before. He had been to see his doctor on the 19th of March with severe shoulder pain and greatly restricted movement. The doctor diagnosed him as having a dropped shoulder, having torn one of the muscles. The shoulder was two inches lower than the other and she said it was the worst case she had ever seen, even by comparison with the photographs in her medical text book. His physiotherapist recommended immediate treatment which might have to continue for up to a year. He was prayed for in church two days later on the Sunday and within seconds knew he was healed, and felt complete freedom to move the arm and shoulder without pain. The following day he told his physiotherapist. She re-examined his shoulder thoroughly and said: 'Something quite wonderful has happened to you, I can't understand it but your shoulder is 95 per cent improved.' She discharged him saying, 'There is nothing else I can do for you.' A week later Andrew returned for a final check-up and the therapist reported that the shoulder was now in perfect working order.

We have seen healings we would never have expected God to do and would never, humanly speaking, have been involved in, had John Wimber not first shown us the way.

John taught leaders how to lead

One of the distinctive features of John's work was his focus on *multiplying ministry* not developing a *mega ministry for himself.* John was endued with giftings from God that could have drawn a great deal of focus upon himself and made him a kind of spiritual superstar. But no! Sometimes he would deliberately refrain from ministry in a public setting so as not to intimidate others there from operating in their gifts. I can also remember conferences when God would be moving in great power during the ministry time and John would quietly slip away, leaving the rest of us to carry on.

John stressed the priority of releasing others to fulfil their potential in the life of the church. He showed us that leadership is not about doing it all oneself, but developing and delegating to others to share the load.

In our church fellowship far more has been achieved this way than could ever have been accomplished by myself single-handedly. When people get to do what God has called them to do (which incidentally is actually what they like doing best), the body of Christ is built up in a healthy way. John used to talk about the church as being an army not an audience. Following his counsel I have taught and encouraged our members to find an active role in the church, and as a result the majority of our people serve regularly in one or more areas of ministry – both within and outside the church. As an army committed to extending the Kingdom of God, we believe that every time a sick person gets healed, a lonely person is embraced, a hungry person is fed and clothed, an outcast is loved, someone is led to Christ, or an oppressed captive is released, so the Kingdom of God is advanced.

The ministry of the Holy Spirit

Some of the manifestations of the Holy Spirit at the meetings I attended in the 1980s were incredible. There was no 'hype'. John stressed that God's work could be 'naturally supernatural'. Somehow, by his self-disclosures and illustrations of his own vulnerability, he made the environment a safe place for us all. I was excited to see a leader so relaxed and 'laid back', and I'm sure that this was a major factor in John's appeal to the British culture. As John quietly invited the Holy Spirit to come in increasing measure upon the people there, that was apparently what was happening. The Holy Spirit was active in healing, refreshing, anointing, blessing, convicting and delivering the oppressed from demons. When I later had opportunity to lead meetings I wondered if the Lord would 'show up' in the same way if *I* asked him to come. It was then that I knew for certain that this was not a ministry peculiar to John, or any other 'charismatic personality' for that matter. I discovered for myself that the Lord would manifestly confirm the message of the Kingdom, and I realised how much better and more effective the Lord's ministry was than anything I could ever have hoped to achieve.

In our church we deliberately make room in every service and in house groups for the Holy Spirit to do whatever he wants. Occasionally someone has initially felt nervous, wondering if we could really trust God. What if we let some other spirit into our midst this way? How could we be sure it would be the Holy Spirit? I think Jesus was foreseeing and forestalling such doubts when he reminded his disciples that it would be unnatural – indeed unthinkable – for human fathers to respond to their children's requests for a fish by giving them a snake, or an egg by giving them a scorpion. 'How much more will your Father in heaven give the Holy Spirit to those who ask him!' (Luke 11:12). There is also the gift of discerning of spirits, and we need to watch and lead with discernment.

I liked what John Wimber once replied when asked if it was the Holy Spirit causing a man to manifest so extravagantly before their eyes. John replied, 'I'm not saying that that is the Holy Spirit but I believe it is that man's response to the Holy Spirit.' In the end it comes down to the fruit. What are the fruits of it? This is not always immediately apparent – sometimes it takes time to ripen, but those of us who have been privileged to observe, over a length of time now, the lives of people who have been touched in this way by the Holy Spirit can testify to seeing some truly impressive fruit.

Spirit-led and pragmatic

John was widely seen as a leader who functioned in a 'ministry' context, but he also helped us greatly with his wisdom and commonsense. He was used by God to enable leaders across the denominations to build healthy churches. He had a good understanding not only of church leadership, but also of church infrastructure. He taught us (and this we have sought to reproduce), that the body of Christ was like a human body. It did not need simply a head to lead it but a bone structure to support it. With the right leaders in place, carrying the weight of different ministries and small groups the body could be much more than an amorphous jellyfish; it could become active and effective for the Kingdom of God.

In our local church context the Lord has given us people with significant leadership potential, and by developing this through training and deploying them, trusting them with responsibility, we are seeing a promising infrastructure develop. This has enabled the establishing of a loving community of believers which is able to achieve a fair amount, and is also pastorally supportive and relationally cohesive.

John's approach to planning and evaluation gave us understanding and tools for the task of training leaders. He showed us how to marry the two extremes of 'head in the clouds' (the spiritual) and 'feet on the ground' (pragmatic). He believed that the Lord could speak to us in the planning process, that specific goals could be set, so that we would know what we were aiming for, and yet be free to change plans if at any point we sensed the prompting of the Holy Spirit to do so.

Love for the whole church

John was widely criticised (in North America mainly) for embracing the whole church in its various forms, refusing to use his platform to criticise anyone in the body of Christ. He taught that *unity* didn't have to imply *uniformity*, and whilst he might not necessarily have agreed with their different theologies and practices, he loved and respected sincere believers across the board. John believed that Jesus wanted to return for a '*big bride*' and that much of her beauty would be seen

in the colourful variety of the believers of which the
'bride' was made up.

As a new church plant, we have sought from the
beginning to follow John's example, doing whatever we
can to foster unity in our city. Debby and I, and any
who follow our example, never invite members of other
churches to join us or even to visit, because we have no
desire to entice people to move away from their churches. If people have come from other churches earnestly
desiring to join us we have encouraged them to go back
and talk things over with their leaders, asking them for
their blessing. We endeavour to speak well of other
churches, quashing negative talk whenever we come
across it. We have also had the privilege of visiting
churches of other denominations to share with them
something of what the Lord has given to us, and we
regularly take teams out to teach on a variety of areas of
church life.

John had a significant impact on my life, and I was
privileged to be numbered among his many friends. I
will certainly miss him. But I think the greatest lesson
he taught us is that we no longer need him to teach and
model for us. He pointed us to Jesus, not to himself.
And Jesus showed his disciples how vital it was to discern what the Father was doing (John 5:19), and constantly to do just that.

Many of the newer people in our church have never
heard of John Wimber – never got to meet him or listen
to him. But they have seen something of the values he
stood for being modelled and grounded in their local
church situation, and this has become as much a part of
their lives as it has for many of us who knew him well.

17

A CATHOLIC EVALUATION
CHARLES WHITEHEAD

Born in 1942, Charles Whitehead is President of ICCRS (International Catholic Charismatic Renewal Services), a leader in Charismatic Renewal since 1976, a regular contributor to Good News *magazine and to many Christian publications around the world. He is author of* Pentecost is for Living *(DLT, 1993) which has been published in 6 languages. Charles is married to Sue and has 4 children. He combines Christian ministry with a business career, and is managing director of a sales and marketing company in the paper industry.*

He came as a witness

How good and pleasant it is
   when brothers live together in unity!
It is like precious oil poured on the head,
   running down on the beard,
running down on Aaron's beard,
   down upon the collar of his robes.
It is as if the dew of Hermon
   were falling on Mount Zion.
For there the LORD bestows his blessing,
   even life forevermore.

                                        Psalm 133

I am absolutely certain that unity among Christians is high on God's agenda as we enter the third millennium.

The scandal of our divisions constantly undermines our Christian witness, and this stands in dramatic contrast to the positive response we find on those occasions when we work together to present the gospel with one voice. In my experience God honours the statement made in Psalm 133, and there's a particular blessing on us and on what we are doing when we accept and trust one another enough to proclaim Christ together, and give witness to our shared inheritance side by side.

In this move towards greater unity, God chooses and uses certain men and women. Some of those he chooses work in theological and pastoral commissions, examining doctrines and language to seek greater understanding and common ground. Others have a more public profile, and to such men and women God gives a burning desire for unity, and equips them with a special gift enabling them to cross denominational boundaries. It's a matter of grace building on nature – God often takes someone with a warm, engaging personality, and gives them a heart for unity. When such a person is also a powerful leader with a superb gift of communication, we can expect to see things happen. John Wimber was just such a man, chosen and equipped by God for many things, one of which was his commitment to praying, preaching and working for unity in his Lord's fragmented body. He practised what he preached and came as a witness, so that through him we might believe in the importance of unity among Christians.

For me, John Wimber so often created the psalmist's 'good and pleasant' feeling when men and women from many Christian traditions came together under his ministry. He even had the beard down which the precious oil of unity could run! But standing for God's truth is usually costly, and I know that there were those who ostracised Wimber because of his commitment to working with all the members of God's family. It was a price he accepted without criticising anyone, because he knew where God was calling him. In his own words 'I try to take personal criticism without response. I never write back. I don't respond in any way. But I try to take criticism of doctrine with an appropriate balance of teaching. I've spent days answering questions that I thought were fair-minded.'

One of the many interesting things about John Wimber and his ministry was that he was accepted by so many different kinds of Christians. Pentecostals and charismatics accepted him because of his commitment to the exercise of the spiritual gifts in the healing ministry. Many, but not all, evangelicals accepted his teaching on the supernatural because he always sought a scriptural base for what he said and did. Protestant denominational Christians accepted him because although he was a New Church leader and founder of the Vineyard, he respected the history and place of the denominations and made no attempt to steal their sheep. Catholics accepted him because of his openness to the mystical, his desire for dialogue and greater understanding, and because we knew he was prepared to pay the price for relationship with us.

So what was John Wimber's contribution to the cause of Christian unity? What gifts did he bring to this troublesome area of Christian life? It is my task to address these questions from a Roman Catholic perspective, leaving others to speak from their own particular view-points.

In the Roman Catholic Church, John Wimber's influence was almost exclusively among charismatics. During the early 1970s the charismatic renewal had spread throughout the worldwide Catholic Church, and millions of men and women had experienced their faith coming alive in new ways as a result of being baptised in the Holy Spirit. There was vibrant praise and worship, the charisms were being used, new communities were being founded, and people were experiencing new fellowship with their Protestant and Pentecostal brothers and sisters. Towards the end of the decade things began to change. In North America and Europe the increase in numbers began to slow down, the early excitement was passing, and new problems started to emerge. We began to slip back into the safety of structure and ritual, even trying once again to reform ourselves and society by our natural energy and not by the power of God. One area in which difficulties appeared was in ecumenical relationships as we discovered that in spite of our new enthusiasm the old problems remained. We also learned that to try to bring the message of new life in the Holy Spirit to our Catholic people, together with a call to unity with our newly discovered Protestant and Pentecostal brethren was too difficult. The results were foreseeable – the first steps in a return to the security of the known and predictable.

Into this situation in Britain came John Wimber, and whenever I read the early part of John's Gospel I believe that the following words could equally be said of our John, John Wimber: 'There came a man who was sent from God; his name was John. He came as a witness to testify concerning that light, so that through him all men might believe' (John 1:6–7)

Amazing mix of Christian leaders

John Wimber's teaching in the early 1980s in Britain related to the gifts of the Holy Spirit and their use in evangelism. The major thrust of his ministry was to teach, encourage, model and equip. But running alongside this vision for his work among us was his commitment to unity. He provided a setting in which everyone was welcome, in which we all sat on equal terms at his feet as he taught us. At the first Wimber conference I attended I was struck by the amazing mix of Christian leaders who were present from every church and fellowship. No one knew the Vineyard worship songs, so we struggled to learn them together; no one had heard such thorough teaching on the gifts of the Spirit; no one was expecting to see ministry modelled for us on the platform, nor for the team of new, young Christians to be released to move among us and pray for us. We were united as we received from this man and his team. In a real sense, Wimber's meetings were neutral ground for all of us, and no group ever felt promoted or put down. John Wimber provided a setting in which all Christians could come together in the unity he created, without the need to feel protective of their own position or defensive of their teachings. He challenged us all with what he said and did, but never in the area of our identities as Anglicans, Baptists, Methodists, Catholics, Pentecostals or New Church leaders. He offered a 'safe' environment in which we could all learn. For me this was Wimber's greatest gift to us, and particularly important for the Catholic charismatic leaders.

As we learned together we began to form friendships. From friendship grew trust and recognition, so although we did not agree about some things, we accepted and respected one another. On such a foundation were many enduring Christian friendships built, and our fellowship is the richer for it. What Catholics learned from John Wimber was mainly about the gifts of the Holy Spirit and how to use them, but although it seemed less spectacular we also learned that in the eyes of at least one charismatic evangelical Protestant leader it was OK to be Catholic! His teaching about the gifts of the Spirit came at a vital moment – we were in danger of slipping away from depending on God's power – and Wimber highlighted and demonstrated the importance of the charisms in all that we do. He also raised the profile of genuine ecumenism, and demonstrated the importance of his commitment to unity in the church. Without knowing it, he strengthened my conviction that it's always worth paying the price for unity.

I am certain that John Wimber's impact on Catholic charismatic renewal was timely, godly and effective, reaching far beyond the relatively small number who actually attended his meetings and experienced his teaching firsthand. Because of his faithfulness in answering God's call to minister regularly in Britain, new life has flowed into all our groups, fellowships and churches. For that we all owe him a debt of gratitude which I am happy to acknowledge. But above all he was a warm, open, engaging, courageous, humorous and tremendously gifted man of God. I liked him enormously, and although we only met from time to time, I really miss him and will always be grateful to him. For me and for many others he was truly a man sent by God into our lives, and we are much the better for knowing him.

18

AN ANGLICAN EVALUATION

JOHN GUNSTONE

John Gunstone (b. 1927) has been a vicar in London-Over-the-Border, a chaplain of Whatcombe House in Dorset, and a county ecumenical officer of Greater Manchester. He is a canon emeritus of Manchester Cathedral, a founder-trustee of Anglican Renewal Ministries and a consultant editor of Healing and Wholeness. *He is the author of 18 books on worship, congregational life and the ministry of healing.*

How do we assess the influence of someone like John Wimber on the Church of England? And what are the criteria for making such an assessment? Do we calculate the proportion of the clergy who are incorporating his jargon into their vocabulary ('power healing', 'power evangelism', even 'doin' the stuff')? Or count the number of churches using his music in their services? Or make a list of the parishes that claim to have been 'Wimberised'?

Whatever is the answer to those questions, research like this is beyond my capacity. For this essay I have had to rely on my personal impressions. I've been to three Wimber-led conferences. I've read nearly everything by him published in England. I've even written a book about him, and edited another.[1] And during the Wimber era I've been an honorary curate in a parish which has attempted cautiously to apply some of his lessons to its pastoral and liturgical practices. These experiences, plus conversations with a few friends, are the data for this assessment. So here goes.

In general terms, Wimber's influence made its impact mostly on those Anglicans who had been touched by the charismatic renewal. But, because he never aligned himself completely with the renewal scene, some Anglican evangelicals and others have listened to him as well. However, to many folk in the Church of England John Wimber is little more than a name, linked in their minds with alarming slogans such as 'signs and wonders' or with controversies about the Toronto Blessing. Others, rejecting what they regarded as his fundamentalism, dismissed him as just another American preacher marketing his wares on this side of the Atlantic. The rest – and they are probably the majority – have never heard of him at all. My guesstimate is that Wimber probably influenced to a greater or lesser extent around fifteen per cent of Church of England parishes, though a higher proportion of the clergy, especially the younger ones (Wimber and the Vineyard Christian Fellowship has been a favourite topic for student dissertations in Anglican theological colleges for years).

To appreciate his ministry, you had to go to one of Wimber's meetings. For it was his particular charisma – his style of leadership in public and his interest in you when you met him privately – which most attracted us at first. In front of an audience of thousands he had the most laid-back of laid-back attitudes. His informality became legendary. He nearly always appeared wearing a checked shirt, jeans and trainers. He spoke with a slow Southern drawl which fascinated English ears. He was a superb teacher, mixing scriptural doctrine with humorous reminiscences in a manner that held the attention of any listener. He could also laugh at himself and admit his mistakes – a refreshing change from many such speakers I've heard. The effect of this was that as his audience we felt we could relax and trust ourselves to him. For he had extraordinary personal authority. If anything went wrong in a meeting, it was immediately obvious Wimber was in charge. What would he have been like, we wondered – and the thought made many of our hearts leap – if the Lord had called him to be a Church of England bishop?

It's a basic principle of teaching that, having explained something to people, you then get them to try it out for themselves. Wimber applied this principle to a remarkable degree. For example, after teaching about the ministry of healing, he would invite those who wished to receive prayer to come to the front. There he would either minister to them himself, at the same time explaining to his audience what he was doing step by step, or he would get his team to minister to them while he gave a running commentary on the proceedings. Then he would invite his audience to invoke the Holy Spirit to show to them individually through words of knowledge or inspired pictures who sitting near them needed ministry, and to get up out of their seats and go and pray with them – much to the consternation of those who had never done that sort of thing before. He wanted us to discover that such ministries are ministries in the body of Christ, and that the Spirit could use any member through his gifts. The *Come Together* meetings of the seventies used a similar technique, but not to the same extent. Amazingly, this often seemed to work: some claimed that they had been blessed, a few that they had been healed.

Undergirding Wimber's teaching was his belief that God's resources are available to us here and now in a far greater measure than most of us ever dare imagine. Our Western scientific mindset, he claimed, obscures from us the truth that God can act in and through us in ways far beyond what we expect. We read about the Kingdom of God in our Bibles and we teach a theology of the Kingdom in our sermons and lectures, but we do not allow the power of the Kingdom to operate fully in our Christian lives. While the Kingdom will not be manifested in all its glory until Christ's second advent, supernatural manifestations of it can break through if God is given room to act. In Jesus' ministry, and especially in his death on the cross, the Kingdom of God was engaged in a battle against Satan. This conflict ended with the victory of Christ, proclaimed in his resurrection and ascension. Faithful Christians, as they engage in that same struggle in obedience to that divine commission, Wimber affirmed, can also experience something of that victory as the New Testament church did after Pentecost. Where the gospel is preached, signs and wonders will follow in healings, deliverances, convictions of sin, conversions to new life in Christ. This was an aspect of the apostolic succession of the church's ministry which, as Anglicans, many of us had not recognised before.

Those of us who had been practising the ministry of healing with prayer, the laying on of hands and anointing were much heartened by this. The healing ministry has had a long history in the Church of England. Since the beginning of this century groups like the Guild of St Raphael and individuals like Dorothy Kerin have led the way to a recovery of faith in this ministry, and the charismatic renewal enlightened us so that we understood better and had more faith in its scriptural and traditional foundations. But Wimber gave a fresh impulse to that ministry. We suddenly saw that it was part of the church's evangelistic outreach as well as part of its pastoral care. Some years ago I led two parish missions – one in England and one in Canada – during each of which an individual who received prayer for healing was told by their doctors that – in one case she, in the other he – had been amazingly cured. The news gave a boost to both missions. At the time I just regarded it as a gracious coincidence bestowed on us by God. Not any more.

So we adapted what we learned from him to our own circumstances. Like him, we didn't just talk about the ministry of healing to sceptical and fearful congregations; we copied his teaching methods and demonstrated it for them. Those who specialise in teaching the ministry of healing are now more aware of the evangelistic opportunities their meetings might offer, and those who specialise in the ministry of evangelism are now more aware that gifts of healing may suddenly appear on their agenda. There has been a shift in some Anglicans' perception of and faith in what the Lord might do.

Wimber's theology of the Kingdom was often expressed in terms of power – the power of God the Holy Spirit. 'More power, Lord!' he used to cry, as he was ministering to individuals. Initially this was off-putting. Anglicans have become so used to the decline in numbers of churchgoers and the apparent ineffectiveness of the Church of England in the nation that we have taken refuge in those scriptural texts which seem to show that weakness is a sign of God's strength, and that the new Israel is called to be a shrinking remnant. I think that Wimber's power theology, however much it is criticised by our contemporary theologians (and by those Anglicans who find it painful to admit that God might act in a supernaturally powerful manner), has helped some of us to recover our faith that the church can be a body so filled with the Spirit, and revealing to others an authority not its own but that of the reigning Saviour. I've noticed how the term 'power' has crept into our ecclesiastical vocabulary recently. We are more likely to talk of 'empowering' (the laity, the clergy, the youth) than 'enabling', the word which came with the charismatic renewal in the sixties and seventies.

After years as an evangelist and teacher, Wimber

became a Church Growth consultant at Fuller University and travelled extensively in the'seventies across North America, visiting different kinds of churches. Through seminars and consultations he taught the principles of church growth and became an expert in helping congregations to apply these principles to their own situations. Later, when he became chief pastor of the Vineyard Christian Fellowship, he began practising what he had preached and in his lifetime some 700 churches were planted by the Fellowship, two thirds of them in North America, the remaining third in over forty different nations in the world, including nearly fifty in Britain.

During these years Wimber supervised the production of a great deal of teaching material on strategies for church growth and church plants, including the oversight of new congregations and the training of lay and ordained leadership. Anglicans have adapted this material in planning and supporting the church plants which have been initiated in the last two decades. It is now recognised that the creation of new Christian cells and congregations is a necessary strategy in any attempts at evangelism and church growth, and much of the credit for the way in which some in the Church of England have accepted this should go to Wimber's teaching.

Before he was converted, Wimber was a highly successful musician in what is known as 'the West Coast soft rock' school, and it is in the use of music in worship that the Wimber influence has been most marked on Anglicans (as well as others, of course, especially in the New Churches) who have attended his conferences.

For most of us, the hymns in a church service, led by the choir and the organ, are items which comment on or express devotion to the gospel truths being celebrated in the liturgy. These hymns are not primarily intended to stir up our emotions deeply, though of course they

may often do that. Compositions such as R.F.
Littledales's translation of Bianco da Siena's 'Come
down, O Love divine', sung to Vaughan Williams'
beautifully flowing tune (a composer, incidentally, who
remained an agnostic all his life), usually brings a tear
to my eye because I associate it with the service at
which I was ordained. Other hymns move different
worshippers similarly. The charismatic renewal loos-
ened up the formal atmosphere which normally accom-
panies Anglican worship by introducing simple choruses led by a guitar group, with the congregation (or,
at least, some of them) shyly clapping, swaying and lift-
ing their hands in the air.

Wimber took us further. He made music the major
component in the liturgy. Those attending Vineyard
conferences or churches are left in no doubt that it is the
singing that matters above all else. At the beginning of
a meeting the choruses flow without break for half-an-
hour or so. The repertoire is not extensive: the idea is
that worshippers should be able to sing without the
intrusion of books or overhead projectors. People stand
or sit with eyes closed and hands outstretched, centring
their attention and their feelings on Jesus. This often
promotes an emotional response which deeply affects
many of them. A few are so moved that they weep or
cry out. Into this corporate sense of Christ's presence
prayers and prophecies are offered, the sermon is
preached, and an invitation is given to those who are
seeking to be ministered to.

Among other things, this style of worship has the
effect of focusing attention on Jesus, not on the one
leading the service, or the preacher, or the musicians, or
even those who are being ministered to. For Wimber
and the Vineyard 'worship' equals songs that are often
exclusively addressed to Christ or that comment lov-
ingly on who he is and what he has done for us. One of
Wimber's own compositions, 'Isn't He beautiful', is typ-

ical. Singing those words over and over again to a simple rocking tune helps the worshipper to express his or
her love of Jesus and to be carried gently into an attitude of adoration for his or her Saviour. Our minds are
involved only to the extent that we are thinking of
Christ's presence among us through the indwelling
Holy Spirit. Such experiences can lead those who participate in them to the threshold of what is called con-
templation in traditional Christian spirituality – the
prayer in which the believer is caught up by the Holy
Spirit in loving, wordless, wondering attention to Jesus
without any concern for himself or herself

This kind of worship evolved in Wimber's first
Vineyard congregation which met in a Californian
warehouse. Most had no kind of Christian background
whatever, so anything like a formal liturgy would have
been totally foreign to them, and many needed rescuing
from messed-up lives. The singing was designed to
help them to begin to open up psychologically and spiritually to the forgiving and transfiguring power of God.
That is why the words of the songs focused on Jesus.
Critics have dismissed such songs as being too individ-
ualistic, but that is precisely what they are intended to
be – and originally for good reasons.

It's very different from the stand-up, sing-up and
sit-down pattern we are familiar with in Anglican services. However, worship in the Church of England has
become more relaxed and spontaneous during the thirty years since *Series Two* and *Series Three* were launched
upon us. Cultural changes have made certain features
of ecclesiastic ceremonial look stuffy or comical. We are
not so shocked as we used to be when the vicar leads
our services from his stall in a suit – or even, like
Wimber, in an open-neck shirt and jeans. We sometimes
see small groups praying for one another after the final
hymn. Wimber's kind of worship has invaded our
churches alongside these developments. As a result,

some have abandoned Evensong and adopted the Vineyard pattern completely, so that their evening services are just songs, sermon and ministry. Others have introduced a period of continuous choruses at the beginning or at some part of their services (calling it – oddly – 'a time of worship'! What else do they think they are doing during the rest of the time they are in church?) Many have used two or three songs together in place of a hymn (particularly appropriate during the administration of Communion at a Eucharist.)

While these innovations to Anglican worship have their value, they are not always introduced wisely; and at this point in this essay I should list briefly what I see as some of the downside of Wimber's influence on the Church of England, and especially on its clergy.

While a reaffirmation of the power for the body of Christ is to be welcomed, some clergy and lay leaders are too insensitive towards others, or too insecure in themselves, to handle such teaching in a godly fashion. They can easily employ the fantasy that they are being endowed with authority from on high to compensate for their own sense of worthlessness and inadequacy. Human power masquerading as divine power corrupts horribly. Fortunately the checks and balances within the Church of England as an institution can act as a brake on such tendencies, but there have still been scandals and malpractices associated with ministries and techniques introduced by Wimber, one or two of which have been publicised in recent years through the court cases which followed.

Another downside is the difficulties that arise in any public meeting where healings are claimed without reliable medical confirmation. At one of Wimber's early meetings in Sheffield, three individuals who came forward for ministry declared that God had healed them, though the doctor sitting beside me whispered she could see no signs of the cures from where she was. She may have been mistaken, of course, but the dangers of such a high-wire ministry are apparent. And when you have preached the gospel in such a way as to lead your audience to expect that they are going to see signs and wonders there and then, you are subjected to enormous inner pressure to produce the goods to convince them. Under the leadership of less discerning leaders than Wimber, who was always open to the frank criticism of the team which accompanied him, the dangers of manipulation and of deceit draw closer.

Finally, the kind of Vineyard worship I have described, while opening up a new way of corporate prayer for Anglicans, has had a less than welcome effect in some quarters. Stress on an individual's emotional response to God in worship can reinforce the idea that what matters above all is what we feel when we come to church, and that liturgical traditions are of little or no importance. We can be seduced by the current popular philosophy which assumes that if you do not have emotional experiences about someone or something, then he, she or it, are not real. Now, while emotion certainly has its place in prayer and worship, our faith is fragile if we depend so much on our feelings when we are in church. Prayer and worship, like the whole of our Christian life, depends on the truth that is in Jesus which remains whatever our feelings happen to be. For stretches – maybe long stretches – we often don't feel God's presence with us, or see his power working through us. Everything then depends on our accepting a personal discipline – what used to be called a rule of life – which helps us forward on our pilgrimage towards the Kingdom during these desert seasons where there isn't any emotional back-up. Formal liturgies can be a stable support during such times.

Whatever its other weakness, Anglican service books take their inspiration from the Scriptures and the church's responses on those Scriptures over the

Christian centuries, so that however spontaneous we
may want to be, and whatever novelties those who lead
worship want to introduce, at least part of each act of
worship is gospel-rooted. Those who abandon all liturgical forms are cutting themselves from this anchor of
our Christian hope. And they are also cutting us off
from sources that can enrich our worship if discerning-
ly used: the liturgical movement in its various ecumenical manifestations, the ancient sacramental rites of
the Roman Catholic and Orthodox Churches, the Taizé
prayer gatherings, the Celtic devotional heritage, the
praise meetings of the black churches, and the liturgical
experimentation now being undertaken by the Church
of England and the rest of the Anglican Communion.
These can offer us so much. Indeed, some Anglicans
who initially adopted the Vineyard pattern
often turn back to the Church of England's liturgy with
a newly realised thankfulness for what they find there.

I must add, however, that the downside of Wimber's
influence is not due to the man himself He declared his
purpose was to help Christians to grow spiritually so
that they can be more effective servants of God in their
homes, in their lives and in the congregations to which
they belong. He urged them to respect the pastoral
leadership of their churches and to esteem the traditions they had received within their fellowships. I never
heard him make any suggestion that Anglicans should
leave the Church of England and join the Vineyard, or
that parishes should adopt Vineyard strategies and cus-
toms. His overriding desire was that we should be fully
equipped for the purposes of the Kingdom, including
social concerns as well as evangelistic opportunities.

I asked at the beginning of this essay how we can
assess the influence of Wimber on the Church of
England. Perhaps it will be impossible ever to answer
that question adequately. Maybe the influence of one
man and his team in such circumstances is too elusive

to pin down. But at least I can mention individual Anglicans and a few parishes I know who have benefited from his missions. David Watson introduced Wimber to the churches in this country – most tragically of all through the American's ministry to Watson as he was dying. David Pytches, the former vicar of St Andrew's, Chorleywood, sponsored Wimber's visits and still does much to help us understand his teaching. The Chorleywood parish has also provided a base for Barry Kissell's worldwide evangelistic missions. Bob and Mary Hopkins' interest in Anglican church planting began in Chorleywood, leading him to found 'The anglican Church Planting Initiatives' and it was from St Andrew's congregation that the annual New Wine family holiday camp in Somerset, the two Soul Survivor youth conferences and the Soul Survivor youth congregation in Watford were started.

Holy Trinity Brompton has planted churches elsewhere in London and launched the amazingly successful Alpha course. St Thomas Crookes, Sheffield, pioneered the Nine O'Clock Service and (in spite of the scandal associated with it at one stage in its development) showed the Church of England how to reach out in alternative forms of worship to unchurched youth. St James, Parr Mount, St Helens, a parish in one of the poorest urban priority areas in the Liverpool diocese, grew to become a centre for spiritual renewal and social concern.

Wimber was not the sole inspiration behind these individuals, groups and congregations. As I have indicated, God has been moving in the Church of England to revive our ministries of teaching, healing, evangelism, church growth and worship through different streams before and during the Wimber era. But the gifted American was a great encourager to those involved in these initiatives, and there are many other clergy and laity whose ministry came alive in new ways through their contact with him.

I am conscious that it is as easy to claim too much for Wimber as it is to claim too little. But I guess that when in the next millennium the history of the Church of England in the last quarter of the twentieth century comes to be written, he will be recognised as one of God's gifts to us for our times. He came, not to teach us anything new, but to be an encourager and to remind us of what is always true in the gospel of the Kingdom. As much as anyone in those years, and a good deal more than most, he did what Jesus Christ charged St Peter to do: he 'strengthened his brothers' (Luke 22:32).

Notes
1. *Signs and Wonders: The Wimber Phenomenon* (London: Darton, Longman and Todd, 1989), and *Meeting John Wimber* (Crowborough: Monarch Books, 1996).

19

A House Church Evaluation
Terry Virgo

*Terry Virgo leads the Church of Christ the King, Brighton,
England. He is a well-known Bible teacher and has written
several books, including* A People Prepared (Kingsway).
*He heads up the New Frontiers International team, planting
and serving churches in the UK and worldwide. He also
hosts the Stoneleigh International Bible Week.*

David Watson was the first person to mention John
Wimber's name in my hearing. Later, when I was in
South Africa in 1984, I heard others speak of him with
such enthusiasm that I wanted to meet him too. The day
before I left Cape Town a zealous pastor gave me a box
of John's teaching tapes and urged me at all costs to listen to them.

Over the next six weeks I soaked myself in the excellent material and was profoundly impacted. To my
delight I subsequently received a phone call saying that
John had invited me to meet him in his hotel in London
prior to a memorable series of meetings at Westminster
Central Hall. We enjoyed a wonderful day together.
This led to my first visit to Anaheim and to his coming
to the Brighton Centre for a series of outstanding conferences. It was a great privilege to know him as a personal friend.

What a man! What a great servant of God! What a
wonderful ambassador of Christ's love and power.

At the Brighton NFI offices we heard about his death

just before a weekly morning prayer meeting. I broke
the news to the fifty or so present and then asked them
to share their memories of John – either his preaching or
maybe more personal experiences. A flood of stories
poured out varying from incredibly powerful moments
in meetings to tender accounts of his personal loving
care for individuals and amazing things he had done to
help them. At the end, there were few dry eyes in the
room. Here are just some of the things we remembered.

Doin' the stuff!

John will forever be identified with this famous phrase.
He loved relating the story of his first encounter with
formal church life. Following the service he enquired in
bewilderment. 'When do we get to do the stuff?' At that
early stage in his Christian life he knew little, but he
was aware that Jesus healed the sick, cast out demons
and all that stuff! The church service didn't excite him
too much. He was not impressed with mere talk about
what Jesus and the early disciples did. His approach
was simple but revolutionary. When were they going to
do the stuff?

Openness and humility

He was unique in his honesty about his early attempts
at healing the sick. I had never heard any other preacher with a healing emphasis admit to so many mistakes
and disappointments. He had the ability to draw us all
into his early battles. His stories of frustration were
hilariously funny yet very challenging. He was so
accessible. This was clearly a man not impressed with
himself – and everybody loved him for it.

Theological satisfaction

He continually appealed to Scripture to vindicate his
stance on signs and wonders. Greatly influenced by the
writings of George Eldon Ladd, he loved to expound

the gospel of the Kingdom – the now and the not yet. Healing was not seen as an isolated subject, but part of Christ's advancing Kingdom. He was not just a 'faith preacher' or a 'healing evangelist'. In the past I had often heard 'healing evangelists' who taught a package of verses which implied that healing was available and virtually automatic. If you were not healed it was your fault for not having enough faith. By contrast, John never bullied anybody or harshly demanded more faith from his hearers. Although he always exhorted us to believe, he never condemned anyone for their unbelief.

Robust faith

What he did demonstrate was his own childlike confidence in God. He would amaze us at his conferences in Brighton. In front of 5,000 people he would first inspire our faith then kill the 'atmosphere' stone dead by having a coffee break! Then he would courageously lead the re-gathered congregation to a level of expectation where if God did not vindicate him he would look an absolute fool. But again and again God came in power. Amazing words of knowledge about people's needs were given and the sick were healed.

His laid-back and almost casual approach meant that he did not depend on the meeting being at a certain 'pitch'. Often it was noisy and chaotic, with people walking around. Nevertheless most of us had never experienced God so powerfully in a meeting. When John prayed 'Come Holy Spirit' we became aware of a new dimension of God's presence. John was, of course, fully acquainted with the Holy Spirit's omnipresence but he also knew the scriptural prayer 'O that you would rend the heavens and come down'.

Intimacy in worship

How John loved God's presence! Worship in his conferences was unique, with a great concentration on intimacy. At first we were disappointed that there were no songs with any prophetic content. Also the question arose. 'Does the Vineyard have any up-tempo songs?' But gradually we came to enjoy the intimacy. Song after song expressed personal love, appreciation and adoration toward the Lord Jesus.

On one rare occasion I remember sitting next to him when he was not at the keyboard on the platform. Tears were pouring down his face as he expressed his love to Jesus. John was a devoted worshipper and led thousands into a new experience of personal encounter with God. He did not 'use worship' to achieve another goal. No worship leader ever exhorted the congregation in order to stir them up. John taught his worship leaders to worship God simply because he was worthy of worship and was there to be enjoyed and loved. You almost felt that they could not care less if nobody else joined in. They were going to sing their love songs to Jesus. But if you got into the worship currents you were lifted to heaven with them.

Love in practice

For John, love was not in word only, nor was it just for meetings. He knew nothing of Christian professionalism. What you saw was what you got. He loved God in worship, but he also loved God in action and demonstrated that by expressing loving concern. The Anaheim Vineyard, which he led, had a massive social action programme, feeding and clothing hundreds of local underprivileged in Los Angeles. Also, his acts of personal kindness to his friends were amazing – as my own family can testify.

Personal leadership skills

His love for people always lifted them into greater levels of Christian activity. His passion was training others to do the stuff. He had no desire to hog the limelight, but derived enormous pleasure from giving away to others what God had taught him. Ordinary believers suddenly felt that God could use them to do signs and wonders and heal the sick – things that had previously seemed way out of their reach. He reminded us that Jesus did what he saw the Father doing. Then he taught us to watch for God's activity and follow it. He taught us to be alert to see where the Holy Spirit was active and then become involved as channels of his power.

An excellent communicator, John was totally free from religious clichés, loved humour and created a totally relaxed atmosphere. His laid-back style often concealed the burning passion that kept him going on an incredibly demanding programme of international travel and multiplied conferences. At heart, he was an evangelist. He led thousands to Christ and longed for the whole church to rediscover the call to get out among the lost and win them for Christ. Winning the lost was one of his mainspring motivations. His longing for more spiritual power in the church was rooted in his desire to see vast numbers saved.

Love for the church

Though so much of his time was spent at conferences, his zeal for the church shone through. He was the pastor of the large Vineyard church in Anaheim, but he loved the whole church. He worked across the denominations and made a huge contribution towards unity among the churches. Although he was happy to work with Christians from diverse denominations, including the most formal and structured (such as the Roman Catholics), nevertheless he had a passionate longing for the church to recover her early freedom and devotion.

At Westminster Central Hall, he thundered out that God was saying. 'Give me back my church!' Although he truly loved all of God's children, he also hated the structures that locked them up and locked God out.

He believed in the success of the church. As a former church growth consultant, he believed that healthy churches should grow and showed very practical and helpful skills in training pastors to handle that growth.

His love for the local church was also wonderfully displayed in his willingness to become involved in the difficulties encountered by Mike Bickle's church in Kansas City when it came under unjust attack. His painstaking appraisal of the situation was deeply impressive. Unafraid to get his hands dirty, he got in among the trouble and did exemplary work in unravelling a highly complicated situation.

Handling pain

John certainly had no easy path. He was the subject of controversy almost from beginning to end. His commitment to the message that God gave him was costly and he had to endure a lot of persecution. In addition, he had frequent bouts of serious illness, yet battled on in a magnificent way. He fought cancer and heart disease. When I heard that his death was caused by an accidental fall, it occurred to me that ultimately none of his sicknesses beat him!

A loving father

All who knew him, and the church at large who never actually met him, will miss this great father in God. He was a unique gift to the body of Christ. Indeed, I would say that in this century only Billy Graham has surpassed his influence as an American visiting our shores. Many English churches have been unrecogisably transformed because of him.

The church around the world will miss a great hero and a true friend. Our responsibility is to make sure that we are living in the good of all that he taught and showed us. Jesus challenged his own contemporaries about their personal response to the life and ministry of another 'man who was sent from God whose name was John'. How they received the Baptist was important to Jesus. No doubt we shall one day give account for how we lived in the light of John Wimber's amazing contribution to our lives.

20

A BAPTIST EVALUATION

NIGEL WRIGHT

*Dr Nigel G. Wright is the senior pastor of Altrincham
Baptist Church, Cheshire. Born in 1949, he was ordained in
1973 and has been pastor of Ansdell Baptist Church,
Lytham St Annes (1973–86) and lecturer in Christian
Doctrine at Spurgeon's College, London. Nigel is married
to Judy and they have two grown children. His most
recent book is* The Radical Evangelical: Seeking a Place
to Stand *(SPCK).*

The evaluation offered in this chapter is inevitably personal, both in the sense that it takes account of John
Wimber's total presence, as a human being, a minister
of the gospel, a musician, a thinker and a pioneer, and
in the sense that it reveals my own perspective. For
these reasons it must relate in the first instance to the
church in Britain and to the British experience of John's
ministry. If those in other places and cultures are able to
make connections with what is here set down, well and
good. But there is no pretence here to magisterial, sociological or theological objectivity, even if such things
exist. Instead this chapter speaks out of the particularity of specific encounters with John within a clearly
defined social context.

It is worth staying with the 'particularity' theme.
John's contribution to the contemporary church, the
church movement he headed, his writings, music and
tape legacy, is already the stuff of academic investiga-

tion. Theses have been written and published trying to quantify what has been going on in the Vineyard movement. The Vineyard is a modern religious phenomenon and so is grist to somebody's analytical mill, all the more so now that John has died, and rightly so. This has been no insignificant episode in the late twentieth-century experience of the church. There are things worth the saying and there is knowledge worth the gaining.

However, words of caution are worth noting also. Academics, like journalists, need their 'angle' on whatever they investigate, except that they usually call it 'propounding a thesis'. In religion as in other areas of study the temptation is to develop a generalised understanding about how the world is and then to show how this is true of a particular case study. The case study is subjected to analysis and everything that would support the thesis, some of it persuasively, other parts merely plausibly, are displayed and laid bare for this end. And yet always the danger is that the model of understanding originates primarily from the mind of the researcher rather from the way things are, and that the researcher is determined by a desire to reproduce the conventional wisdom of contemporary sociology or theology. The resultant 'evaluation' resembles more the Procrustean bed of Greek mythology and simply cuts off the parts of the story that its thesis finds inconvenient or incomprehensible.

Predictably, then, John will be taken as an example of modern American fundamentalism (a term defined in this instance neither by the theologians nor the historians but by the sociologists) and no doubt will be used to validate all manner of claims. Yet grand theories need to come up hard against particularity. John Wimber fits no iron bed of academic theory and those who knew him personally will often wonder, I predict, how some of the theories that will be developed about him can gain acceptance. The evaluation I enter into here is one that is directly born of personal experience and observation.

I count myself fortunate to have come into contact with John in the early days of his ministry in the United Kingdom, in 1982. At the time I was the pastoral leader of a growing Baptist church in Lytham St Annes on the north-west coast. It was an unlikely, pleasant but uncosmopolitan place for John and Carol, Bob and Penny Fulton, Lonnie Frisbee and their party of culture-shocked Californians to come to. Yet it worked wonderfully. The church was just at the right place to receive what they had to give and they gave it. On a friendship level the entire group fitted in fine. The church experienced a visitation with spiritual power such as it had never known and yet ministered with great gentleness and wisdom. The effects lasted for many years. Here it is possible to identify some of the significant areas.

The first impact to be felt was in the intimacy of worship which the group brought with them. As a church we were into a mixture of hymns which stated reasonably objectively the great acts of God for our salvation, and high praise, newer worship songs mainly culled from the Bible Weeks which were then at a zenith. It was virtually obligatory to stand in worship. The Californians brought with them a different approach which was instantly attractive. This both rubbed home the point that there was no 'politically correct' way to worship and that gentle intimacy with God was a supreme goal in worship. An evaluation of John Wimber must reckon significantly with this dimension since the Vineyard style has become a major strand in contemporary praise. Time, of course, allows us to see its inadequacies. Intimacy can become an over-subjectivity. If songs and hymns are there to state the objective, saving acts of God despite whatever I might feel about them at any point in time, then the majority of

John's and Vineyard's songs fall short in this area. They may be strong in intimacy, but are liable to be weak in intellectual content. It might be true to say that when originated, this style was a reaction against over-objectivity, but once established as the norm the style invites a reaction back in the opposite direction. The criticism that the Wimber style acts hypnotically, drawing the worshipper into a certain state of mind and brain prior to the 'manifestation' of the Spirit is not without validity even if it is never the whole of what is going on. Of course, this applies to all other forms of worship as well in diverse ways and degrees.

British charismatic Christianity in 1982 was being simultaneously influenced and threatened by the onset of Restorationism. I put it in these stark terms because it is now observably true that Restorationism has positively influenced the wider church. Yet its style in the early 1980s was both aggressive and threatening towards what it perceived as the 'denominations'. Its rhetoric suggested that the new wine of renewal required the new wineskins of the 'restored' churches and that the historic churches were incapable of achieving this unless they came under the 'apostolic authority' of the leading Restorationists. Of course, all of this language has now been moderated and relativised to the point of acceptability. At the time in the church I was leading we were being rocked by the claims of Restorationism, some of our people taking it on board unreservedly, others cautiously and some not at all. Most of all, the claims of Restorationism made us feel that we were not 'proper' church. Whatever we had going for us it was not quite kosher or Kingdom enough because we had no apostle, because our worship did not fit the accepted pattern and because our building actually looked like a church (inside and out) rather than the local Co-operative hall.

It was refreshing that John brought with him an

utterly different spirit which taught us a better way and
a great deal more wisdom. The message was that God
loved the whole church with all its quirks and idiosyn-
crasies; the modelling was that we were as important as
anybody else and that, in fact, we were just great as we
were. It is this personal dimension that grand theories
have little way of coping with. Behind this experience
lies something of immense significance, namely John's
ability to accept people and affirm them without regard
to the boundaries and barriers of their religious affiliation. In this regard he has contributed to the reshaping
of the British church in the last two decades of the century. He was a living example to the Restorationist
churches of an alternative spiritual pathway which was
as Spirit-filled and 'anointed' as their own, and probably more so, and yet which had no truck with the sectarian mind-set that, knowingly or unknowingly, they
had more or less fallen into. At the same time, John's
friendship with people like David Watson, and his close
connections with Holy Trinity, Brompton, in some
ways so unlikely, has added to the growing confidence
of some parts of the Anglican Church. John's ability to
relate equally well to a Terry Virgo as to a Sandy Millar
has certainly added to the cohesion of the British church
at a time when it badly needed it. This is godly and it is
good.

A further feature of John's ministry has been to
model a more participative approach to ministry. We
had become used to the charismatic star who would hit
town and hit us for six. The healing ministry was thus
associated with the healing evangelist. John's burden
was to mobilise and to enable, to give people confidence that they too could be used to minister. The characteristic scene in the early Wimber visits was that of
'clinic', people gathering round each other to pray and
to minister with John and others giving helpful instruction as to how to proceed, on what had been found to

'work' in his own experience. Here the proclamation of reliable truth was joined with an experimental methodology, with a Californian pragmatism and the best kind of relativism. By this latter term I mean the willingness to recognise that we are all on a 'learning curve'. A characteristic phrase to enter the vocabulary of many British Christians as this stage was, 'my perception is . . .' In this is the recognition that whatever we see we see from a limited, fallible perspective that is open to improvement with the accumulation of more experience and greater wisdom. At the time this felt like a refreshing freedom to test out one's ideas, to be that bit more honest about what one understood and did not understand. This was a gracious gift.

But here we must come to the central thesis that it was John's concern to propound, that of 'power evangelism'. The claim, now well-rehearsed, was that the most effective way of evangelising was that which was characteristic of the early church: proclamation of the gospel accompanied by the confirmation of signs and wonders. It is historically quite true to say that one main reason why the apostolic and sub-apostolic church grew in the context of the ancient world was because it could demonstrate a spiritual energy and authority that exceeded that of its rivals. This spiritual dynamism took form as healings and exorcisms, encounters with the powers of darkness in which Christ's power would be shown to be victorious. Here is the way to validate the gospel in the contemporary world, to show to a watching world that the gospel is true. To restore this means of evangelism the church needed to break out of its bondage to scientific rationalism and to open up its world view to take account of the interventions of God. If it did so it would grow.

This thesis was forged out of John's own experience and that of his church. Through Lonnie Frisbee the church had experienced a pentecostal visitation with signs and wonders and, as a direct consequence, had grown dramatically. This was John's expectation for our church in Lytham St Annes after, through the same Lonnie Frisbee, it had experienced a visitation of similar proportions to that known in John's home church in Yorba Linda. Yet we did not experience the kind of growth that John had predicted. John's own interpretation of this some months later was that our church had laid down 'discipleship tracks' rather than 'outreach tracks' with the consequence that we were pushed by the visitation of the Spirit along the tracks that we had already laid. This might well have been true. However, other points are worth making about the power evangelism thesis which, for me at least, have made me question its viability.

1. Within a British culture it appears to me to neglect the deep cynicism against which we have to struggle. Research and experience tend to suggest that people when confronted with new experiences do not readily reconceive their world-view. Rather, given time, they interpret the phenomena with which they are confronted in terms of their existing modes of understanding. Faced therefore by the signs and wonders that accompany power evangelism they are much less likely to interpret them as validating the message than Christians might want to believe. They are more likely to search for an alternative interpretation which does not require them to sacrifice their naturalistic framework. They are most likely to regard churches which go in for weird phenomena as dangerous cults.

The possibility of alternative explanations has become much more viable with the growth of interest in stage hypnotism in parallel with the signs and wonders movement. This could indicate that there is a shift in the wider culture of which interest in signs and wonders and hypnotism are but diverse manifestations.

Non-Christians and Christians alike might therefore find it more persuasive to see the phenomena of the signs and wonders movement as being the product of an instinctive ability to tap into whatever human dynamics are taking place when people are hypnotised either singly or within a group context. Such manifestations do not therefore carry the weight that the proponents of the power evangelism thesis might expect.

Certainly my own experience suggests that within our culture, I cannot speak for any other, the 'wonders' of the signs and wonders movement are probably more repellent to the seeker than they are attractive. People are liable to feel fear at the unusual things they observe, or to feel threatened by the possibility that against their will they might be engulfed. It is worth reminding ourselves that the authentic sign of the church is not so much power as love. To say it risks sounding like a cliché, but the fact is that we are in every way on much safer ground when we talk about love. In the church I was pastoring at the time it was the love of the people which was the impetus for growth and the search for the powerful church might be a deflection from the more proper search for the loving one.

2. In the first point I have queried the value of manifestations of power. It might well be objected that in the power evangelism thesis it is signs rather than wonders that are the more powerful component, supremely the power of healing which is surely a true and accurate sign of the wholeness that Christ brings. The point is a valid one but it comes up against the buffer of hard reality. My own experience and my observations of that of others, plus the reading that I have done, suggest to me very clearly that in the signs and wonders movement there has been more evidence of wonders than of signs. In other words, while there has been no shortage of people, myself among them, shaking and trembling

and experiencing the most unusual phenomena, the paucity of credible healings is astonishing.

In this it is worth saying that by far the vast majority of people who experience 'wonders' are able to speak of the enjoyability of the experience. Some unlocking of unconscious energies or tensions is taking place which brings largeness and renewal, at least for a time. Within the context of worship and preaching this is received as blessing and refreshing from God. However, the lack of visible healings must surely make us question the power evangelism thesis. It is not that we are denying that the early church experienced healings as part of its evangelistic growth; it is rather that however much we try and however much we trust God, the same things do not appear to be happening today.

Admittedly this is a complex area. There are many people who can testify, as can I, to apparent healings of disorders of body or of soul and who gratefully attribute this to God and the ministry of healing. But those people who insist that such testimonies are of a different order to *biblical miracles* have a genuine point. To qualify as a sign, a visible pointer to spiritual truth and reality which all may observe and recognise, a work of healing has to be of an order way beyond anything that, after sixteen years contact with signs and wonders, I have personally seen and researchers have come up with. At some point we have to confront the fact that it is not happening in the way that the power evangelism thesis, which predicates itself upon the New Testament, says it should be happening.

We might derive two conclusions from this. One is that our faith is inadequate and our technique needs refinement. So we are led into a hopeless spiral downwards as we attempt out of our own resources to produce the conditions required for a healing. I reject this approach entire. The other conclusion is that God is not doing what we were hoping he would do. And, if he is not doing it it can't be as important or vital as we thought. This calls the thesis into question.

It is customary to object to the evaluation I have just offered by appealing to accounts of healing that have been heard of, often on another continent. However, if the days of power evangelism have helped me see anything, it is the way in which anecdotes are embellished in their re-telling and become estranged from their point of origin. They may end up as good stories to be retold from platforms hundreds of miles away but they do not thereby tell what actually happened and glorify God.

3. In evaluating the power evangelism thesis which has been at the centre of John's contribution to the church, I have asked myself whether there is here the rediscovery of something vital or whether it is a temporary flirtation with religious and psychic energies similar to other such episodes in the church's history. If so, does it greatly matter or does it simply belong to the diverse religious experience of the church throughout history? It has always intrigued me that John's conversion led him into the Evangelical Friends, a branch of American Quakerism, and so into a stream of experience reaching back to the ministry of George Fox.

English Quakerism was the charismatic movement of its day. They knew a great deal about ecstatic religious experiences and the power of the Spirit as the nickname 'Quaker' indicates, much to the embarrassment of present-day British Quakers. In George Fox was a marriage of evangelical faith and ardent spiritual experience which could reach, in some of his followers if not in himself, disruptive proportions. The Quaker connection is a valuable one since it places John Wimber in a tradition of Christian experience which has been tested by time and which has shown its worth.

It has equally intrigued me that the prime mover in

the impartation of power into the Vineyard movement was the mysterious Lonnie Frisbee, now also dead. Lonnie represents one of the keys to understanding the nature of the spiritual experience that has characterised the Vineyard. I recall Lonnie saying in my presence that even before he was converted to Christ he had the power to make dramatic things happen to people. Could it possibly be that in Lonnie Frisbee we are confronted with one of those human beings who is naturally gifted with great psychic energy (I suggest nothing sinister by this, believing that psychically as well as psychologically people are variously endowed with gifts and energies)? And if so, is the kind of experience generated by him merely a natural experience, benign and enjoyable in its own way, but of no great spiritual or Christian or anti-Christian significance? Or, as explanations are not mutually exclusive, was God using him and his gifts empowered by the Spirit to do again what he has done at other times, to release the power of the Spirit among us? Or could it be that it was a merely natural human experience, characteristic of the diversity of human religious experience, which was given meaning because it took place within the context of Christian worship and belief? Or is there some other interpretation? (I deliberately exclude the category of the demonic because it seems quite evident to me that the hallmarks of concern for the love and glory of Christ are strongly evident in everything the Vineyard has stood for.)

It is difficult to ask these analytical questions for fear that they might be misunderstood or that they might be construed as saying that experiences which have been very significant to people are of no value. This is not the intention. They are questions we must ask in order to provide sufficient understanding of what is taking place to evaluate experiences properly. I would be amazed if John did not ask them himself, frequently.

Out of them a fruitful open debate is waiting to happen which could enrich the understanding of us all.

4. In considering power evangelism and the place within it of signs and wonders there are also questions of social context to be raised. I accept that in the ministry of Jesus and the early church signs and wonders, especially healings and exorcisms had great significance and contributed to the growth of the church. Does this therefore mean that this fact can be transposed into a different social context and still have the same meaning? There is a world of difference between works of healing, for instance, in the social context in which Jesus ministered and that in which we are set. To be physically sick in Israel often meant to be excluded from the community, as with skin disease, and from the worship of the temple. When Jesus healed the sick he was not just healing them but restoring them to the community and this has overtones of salvation and justification which are close to the heart of the gospel.

Once transposed into a privileged, prosperous Western culture the sign-value of healing undergoes a profound change. We are shaped, particularly so in the United States, by the 'culture of entitlement', the belief that we have a fundamental right to life, liberty and the pursuit of happiness. Within this context prayer for the already wealthy and privileged, although entirely right, assumes a considerably different meaning from that we see in the New Testament. It is no longer about the inclusion of the excluded but more likely about those who already have being given more. This alone requires us to question whether healing can function as the sign which validates the gospel within our culture. More likely, the people of our generation will be compelled to accept the authenticity of the gospel when they see it producing an authentically self-sacrificial church.

The cumulative effect of the points I have raised is to question the validity of the power evangelism thesis. As this was a central plank of John Wimber's life and contribution this might seem a severe blow to our appreciation of the inheritance he has passed on to us. I do not see it this way. The comments I have made are outweighed by the good things that he has brought us. And even if it is true that the evangelistic mission of the church is more likely to be carried forward in our context as it is accompanied, yes, by spiritual power, but all the more so by the loving self-sacrifice of an authentic Christian community, there is no doubting that John has made more than his fair share in example and in word to the coming to be of just such a church.

21

THE INTELLECTUAL

J.I. PACKER

Dr James I. Packer was born in England in 1926 and educated at Oxford University. He taught theology in a number of British colleges before becoming Principal of Tyndale Hall, Oxford in 1970. He then became Associate Principal of Trinity College, Bristol. In 1979 he became Professor of Systematic and Historical Theology at Regent College, Vancouver. Married with 3 children, he has preached and lectured widely. He is a Senior Editor and Visiting Scholar of Christianity Today. *He has written more than 30 books, perhaps the best known being* Knowing God.

My assigned title came to me, to be honest, as a surprise. John Wimber – an intellectual? The idea did not at first sink in.

Had Wimber himself been told that one day he would be classed as an intellectual, he might have frowned, though I think it likelier that he would have laughed. The frown would have reflected the fact that among Bible-believing activists like himself 'intellectual' is something of a dirty word, suggesting an owlish egghead with pet theories who looks down with elitist contempt on un-self-critical people who get on with life's jobs in the usual way. Indeed, the image can be worse than that; as W.H. Auden waspishly wrote, thinking no doubt of the sort of secularists profiled in Paul Johnson's *Intellectuals:*[1]

To the man-in-the-street, who, I'm sorry to say,
  Is a keen observer of life,
The word 'intellectual' suggests straight away
  A man who's untrue to his wife.

Wimber would not have been willing to be tagged with
such associations, any more than you or I would be.

But as I said, I think the idea that he was an intellectual would have made him laugh, since intellectuals are
thought of as brainy folk who are unpractical, unrealis-
tic and doctrinaire, while Wimber saw himself as just a
saved pop-jazz musician with a Bible-based ministry
that God was blessing. He was neither arrogant nor
argumentative, and did not regard himself as learned,
and to call him an intellectual would have seemed to
him ridiculous.

Yet, for all that he led meetings dressed like a cow-
boy on vacation, and doubled as a piano strummer to
start services off, he was in truth a clear-headed, well-
focused, thrustful thinker, with his own quota of theories about evangelism, church growth and church life:
so that calling him an intellectual is not really wide of
the mark. It would, after all, be very odd if one who
served so successfully as a church planting and church
growth consultant, and as a pastor of two large congregations, both recruited virtually from scratch, and as a
seminary teacher of embarrassing effectiveness, and as
a leader of electrifying conferences all round the world
on renewal themes, and as the creator of a new fellowship of some 700 congregations ('we grew more than
1,000 per cent in our first decade'[2]), did not have a first-
class mind as well as energy and an ardent heart. In
fact, Wimber had such a mind, entrepreneurial indeed
rather than academic in its cast, but probing, discerning
and reassessing constantly. Anyone inclined to dismiss
Wimber as a mere noisemaker should think again.

John Wimber was essentially a Bible student and

Bible teacher, and the theology that held his heart was biblical theology in the modern sense of that phrase – the Bible, that is, understood directly in its own terms. But he knew the value of systematic theology as an orienting, stabilising and mind-opening resource for exposition and application of Scripture, and so when asked which writers had done most to shape his thinking he began with Charles Hodge. 'My first thology was Hodge. I read it for years. I still have it. It's all worn out, falling apart, but I loved it.'[3] After that he named Carl Henry, F.F. Bruce and D. Martyn Lloyd-Jones, even indeed myself, as authors he read frequently, and in the same context he showed knowledge of the Puritans and Jonathan Edwards. Among biblical theologians his chief debt, it seems, was to George Ladd on the Kingdom of God, and among missiologists he learned especially from Paul Hiebert and C. Peter Wagner. Generally, in matters biblical and evangelical he knew his way around, as we say, without seriously interacting with other versions of the faith.

Dr D. Martin Lloyd Jones used to say that Christians were the greatest thinkers in the world, both because they have to re-process in terms of God all that our fallen and upside-down culture tells them, and because their own regenerate hearts drive them to work hard at doing precisely that. This was certainly true of Wimber. As a latter-day prophet in the areas of evangelism, pastoral care and church renewal he may well be compared with Francis Schaeffer; the difference being that while Schaeffer re-thought the world critically and correctively in light of the evangelical heritage that he had embraced, Wimber re-thought that heritage itself critically and creatively in light of what seemed to him (though I do not think he ever put it this way) Spirit-quenching worldliness of thought in the churches. The aim of this present chapter is to review the fruits of Wimber's re-thinking.

All human beings are shaped to some extent by their surroundings and impact-making experiences and Wimber was no exception. To get a proper fix on his ideas, therefore, we need to bear in mind some background factors. First, there was the conditioning effect of Southern Californian culture, where hype abounds, the fantastic flourishes, urban restlessness obtrudes, inhibitions melt away and a great deal of personal life gets dramatically paraded in best Hollywood style. Second, there was the conditioning effect of Western entertainment culture, which requires public figures to have some novel, attention-getting 'thing' constantly going, lest the public come to ignore them as old hat. Third, there was the conditioning effect of church growth theory, which, whatever its initial motivation, tends to come across as so much sociological pragmatism for achieving numerical expansion, as if big is always beautiful and quantity always matters more than quality.

Fourth, there was the conditioning effect of the Pentecostal and charismatic streams of Christian community life, both highlighting spiritual gifts of a kind that all dispensationalists and most Calvinists thought had been withdrawn. And, fifth, there was the conditioning effect of personal experience of trouble and triumph both before and after conversion. It would be strange indeed if none of these realities were reflected in his theorising, and it is not to his discredit that to some extent they all were. The truth is that everyone gets marked by local and personal factors of this sort, so that we are all more provincial than we know; and to say that this was true of Wimber is only to say that he too belonged to the human race.

To his theories, then. Though he did not come to them all at once, when put together they form a coherent body of thought, and I shall set them out as such, in the form of a logically and theologically connected series of affirmations.

First, and foundationally, *the Triune God continues:* as the hymn puts it, 'God endures unchanging on'. Basic to all Wimber's theories was his certainty that God's will, work and ways have not altered since New Testament times. If we believe this (and who does not?), it makes perfect sense, with Wimber, to ask evangelicals, who habitually insist that they alone do full biblical justice to the second person of the Godhead, Jesus Christ our Lord: are you also doing full biblical justice to the third peson, the Holy Spirit? We labour to go all the way in trusting, loving, honouring and obeying the Son of God; do we equally seek to go all the way in trusting, loving, honouring and obeying the Spirit of God? Wimber came to think that the true answer to that question was no, and that an upgrade was needed here. To a Reformed theologian he said: 'I believe everything you believe. I just believe a little more in terms of pneumatology [the doctrine of the Holy Spirit]. I've got some ideas that, yes, are foreign; but they're not unprecedented in church history; nor are they nonbiblical.'[4] Thus he positioned himself in relation to his evangelical critics. To honour the Holy Spirit by expecting more, and attempting more, than was usual, was from one standpoint the whole thrust of his ministry. His public expectations and demeanour modelled for all to see the upgrade he thought necessary.

Second, *God's kingdom continues.* Here we come to Wimber's main theme, which we may state as follows. The long-promised Kingdom of God, which became reality through the post-baptismal ministry of Jesus and the post-ascension outpouring of the Holy Spirit, is not geographical but relational: it exists wherever human lives are put under Christ's sway. All believers are in the Kingdom; all churches and Christian gatherings are modes of the Kingdom's expression; and as a sphere of faith, worship, obedience and empowering, the

Kingdom is on earth to stay till Christ returns. The Kingdom is manifested in the supernatural life of believers, which brings Christlikeness of character; in the supernatural fellowship within churches, in which the King's spiritual gifts are identified and used for mutual blessing; in the supernatural 'power encounters' (demonstrations of Jesus' domination) that go with evangelism, whether in the form of exorcisms or of healings; and in corporate renewal experiences, where spiritual battles against evil in the inner life constantly recur. Wimber had a lively belief in Satan and demons, and spiritual warfare, offensive and defensive, was integral to his idea of how the Kingdom stands and advances.

As the Association of Vineyard Churches grew, Wimber stressed increasingly that in Kingdom ministry the focus must ever be on evangelism and edification – renewing and equipping the saints and extending the Kingdom by multiform outreach and church planting. 'Signs and wonders' (which for Wimber meant supernatural healings) and 'phenomena' (which for him meant the whole range of vocal utterances, bodily convulsions and physical prostrations in meetings) only belong within this frame; their value is as means to Kingdom ends, and they should never become a focus of interest in themselves. Labouring to sustain an authentic Kingdom ministry in what he called a 'naturally supernatural' style, and knowing that phenomena, so-called, are more psychologically conditioned responses to what is felt as divine pressure than a manifesting of God in any way, Wimber walked a fine line here, alternately emphasising and downplaying the strange and striking things that happened when he invited congregations deliberately to open themselves to the Holy Spirit's ministry; and when in 1995 he and his Vineyard fellow-leaders disfellowshipped the Toronto Airport Vineyard for letting phenomena be so central in their gatherings as to obscure the Kingdom perspective, not everyone saw on what principle he was acting. Some, indeed, thought he was going back on his own earlier teaching and career. But the clarifying fact is that Wimber was always a Kingdom man, judging and dealing with everything according to whether he saw it furthering or frustrating the advance of the Kingdom of God.

Third, *miracles continue:* healing miracles in particular. So the church should pray for its sick regularly, and expect that from time to time healings will occur that are truly supernatural – medically inexplicable, that is – as were, apparently, the healings performed by Jesus and the apostles. The crypto-Deist habit, widespread in the West, of not expecting supernatural healings ever to take place must be broken, and positive expectations of God intervening to heal, as we already expect him to intervene and have known him to intervene, in other ways should be cultivated. So far, surely, Wimber was right.

But he went further, stepping out onto very thin ice. That the church should regularly pray for the sick, and involve such prayer in its regular evangelistic outreach is, I think, true;[5] that from time to time supernatural healing happens in answer to prayer is, I think, certain; but Wimber seemed to say that the church could command God to heal sick persons in order to give credibility to the gospel, and that this practice constituted 'power evangelism', which was much more biblical, and would be much more fruitful in soul-winning, than any form of programmatic, proclammatory, or persuasive evangelism, bereft of healings, could ever be. To speak so was surely to go far too far, for (1) no biblical passage warrants the idea that we can command and control God in this way; (2) the credibility of the gospel depends on the evidence of the apostolic witness to Jesus, and is brought home to us by the illuminating of the Holy Spirit accompanying that witness, and nowhere in Scripture is it said to depend on observing or experiencing healing; (3) New Testament theology tells us that those recorded as having become followers of Jesus after he had healed them would not have done so without renewal of heart by the Spirit; and (4) it is apparent that most of those Jesus healed never became his disciples – a fact that may alert us to what we might expect today. This theory, therefore, seems to me to be a failure.

Wimber himself was thoughtful to the end, and the year before he died, three years after he was diagnosed with a nasal cancer, that went into remission after months of horrendously painful radiation treatment, he wrote about healing as follows:

> Sometimes our experiences don't fit with our under-standing of what the Bible teaches. On the one hand, we know that God is sovereign and that he sent Jesus to pray for and heal the sick. On the other hand, we know from experience that healing does not always occur . . . Our part is to obey his com-mands, and his part is to execute his will. We know his will; it is given in the Bible. Still, the Bible doesn't tell us which people God will heal or not heal, and God has the sovereign choice concerning each person for whom we pray. Will he heal, or will he extend grace for suffering instead? Or will he grant healing at a later time? Is there another factor hindering the healing, such as demonic oppression or the lack of unity in the church? These very real issues leave us where we began: trusting God to make the sovereign choices for our lives.[6]

He then spoke of 'two wonderful men' who died of can-cer at the time he was being treated for it.

We earnestly prayed in faith for their healings over

the course of weeks and months . . . Yet, in God's sovereign choice, he took each of them home to be with him. He chose to let me remain. I can't explain that. It's impossible to explain. The mystery of God's sovereignty is the only answer.[6]

However one relates these words to what Wimber was urging a decade before, they are very wise words in their own right.

Fourth, *the revelatory work of the Holy Spirit continues.* Here again, as it seems to me, Wimber grasps a truth and then pushes it too far. The truth is that the Holy Spirit, who through some forty penmen gave us Holy Scripture, the written revelation of God, God's own witness to himself in the form of human testimony to him, now operates through the Word as the divine communicator, enabling us to see not only what Scripture tells us objectively about God and godliness, but also how its teaching applies to each of us personally as individual believers. Through his quickening of our consciences he impresses on us whatever God has to say to us by way of rebuke, or correction, or direction, or encouragement, or warning. Wimber knew this, and was himself an applicatory preacher of some skill.

But he went further. He identified Paul's 'word of knowledge' (1 Cor 12:8; the phrase probably means didactic instruction in general) with informational disclosures about and for other people, to be delivered by the recipient to those people as a gesture of fellowship and goodwill. Also, Wimber affirmed the ongoing reality of admonitory and predictive prophecy, as a ministry in the church to the church and to individuals comprising the church; and on this basis he took the Kansas City prophets into the Vineyard. Careful thought is needed here. That God in Bible times occasionally sent personal messages in these ways is clear. That he has on occasion done so in the present church age is undeniable. That we must remember this might happen again and to any of us is obvious too. But whether there is wisdom in expecting regular ministry of this kind, when theologically it is the Spirit speaking beyond the Word and psychologically it is a matter of impressions, a notoriously murky area of human mental life, is another question altogether. Bushels of mistakes are virtually certain if such ministry is institutionalised. Wimber's enthusiasm for it is understandable, since he had experienced 'words of knowledge' and received prophecies that turned out to be true; nonetheless, his belief that beyond-the-Bible utterances of this kind were specially significant, and therefore to be encouraged, seems to me to be one more unsuccessful theory.

The Kansas City prophets left the Vineyard in the end, and it is worth quoting Wimber's final words about them:

> Their entrance into the Vineyard was entirely my fault, and I take full responsibility for that. I turned my brain off for a couple of years. My son Sean went through years of alcohol and drug addiction and some prophetic people came and said, 'God is offering you a grace package. If you'll do thus and so, God will retrieve your son.' This man prophesied when and how. And it came to pass exactly as he had said . . .
>
> I loved the gifts the prophets exercised; I didn't like the package. The package involved the presupposition that a gift in itself authenticates you. I don't care if you're the finest communicator around, the finest expositor, the most brilliant theologue – if you can't come under the church . . . if you can't commit yourself to the leadership of others, if you can't commit yourself to collegiality and relationship, if you can't be inspected as well as teach, I don't want to play.[7]

Whatever our explanation of informational institutions and veridical predictions, Wimber's initial idea that this is key ministry for today and tomorrow can hardly be endorsed, however great its romantic or occult appeal. 'The Spirit through the Word' is the safe and scriptural formula of ongoing revelation; 'the Spirit beyond the Word' is a sure-fire recipe for recurring bewilderment, uncertainty, confusion and delusion. It is affirmation of Wimber to say, what I think is clearly true, that with half his mind he knew this all along.

We have now reviewed the three distinctive thrusts of Wimber's theorising: signs and wonders are marking the reality of the Kingdom of God; a continued flow of healing miracles, making possible power evangelism; and words of knowledge and prediction as a basic form of ongoing revelation from the Holy Spirit. We have seen that in each case Wimber took a truth and pushed it further than sober reflection can justify. Wimber's emphases, strong-minded and enterprising as they are, give the Vineyard the image of a cutting-edge confraternity that sees more, knows more, expects more and receives more than other evangelical bodies, but there is not as much reality in these emphases as Wimber thought, so that some quiet adjustments in Vineyard thinking over the next few years are inevitable.

Meanwhile, however, there is a Wimber legacy of contemplative worship, openness to God, 'naturally supernatural' ministry, high expectations and practical neighbour-love (Wimber's Anaheim Vineyard has a major prison ministry and serves about a million meals to the destitute each year), that can and should benefit all of us, shaming our comfortable conventionality and shaking us out of it. D.L. Moody was once goaded into saying to a critic of his evangelistic methods, 'I must tell you, sir, I prefer the way I do it to the way you don't do it,' and some who doubt Wimber's theories will remain grateful for the way he 'did' church worship and mutual ministry, pioneering patterns of spiritual reality that they had not met before. 'Expect great things from God,' said William Carey, 'and attempt great things for God.' Wimber's ministry helped many to get a little nearer to fulfilling Carey's formula than once they were. For the life-enhancing impact of this flawed but fascinating evangelical intellectual we do well to thank God.

Notes

1. Paul Johnson, *Intellectuals* (London: Weidenfeld and Nicholson, 1988).
2. 'God's Wonder Worker', *Christianity Today*, July 14, 1997, 47.
3. Ibid, 46.
4. Ibid.
5. See my Foreword to Don Dunkerley, *Healing Evangelism: Strengthen your Witnessing with Effective Prayer for the Sick* (Grand Rapids: Chosen Books (Baker), 1995) pp 9–13.
6. John Wimber, 'Signs, Wonders and Cancer,' *Christianity Today*, October 7, 1996, 50.
7. 'God's Wonder Worker,' op. cit. 47.

22

A FRIEND'S RECOLLECTIONS
SANDY MILLAR

*Sandy Millar practised for ten years as a barrister before
being ordained into the Church of England. He joined the
staff of Holy Trinity Brompton in central London as curate
in 1976 and became vicar in 1985.HTB is closely associated
with charismatic renewal, and well known as the impetus
behind the successful Alpha training programme. He is
married to Annette and they have four children.*

We first met John Wimber in the spring of 1982 when he
came to a meeting in the crypt here in Holy Trinity
Brompton. We had never heard of him, but David
Watson had said that we ought to invite him.

We collected together all the home-group leaders of
the church – about eighty of us. John came with a little
team and gave a talk about healing. When he had finished his talk, he said in his characteristic way, 'OK.
Now we'll have a break and then we will come back
and do some healing.'

My heart stopped because I didn't know what
'doing healing' meant. None of us knew really. We had
that same sort of frisson when you think that the Spirit
of God might appear: supernatural things might happen. And the flesh hates the supernatural.

So we had the longest coffee break we have ever had
in this church. I was rushing around saying, 'Have
some coffee!'

'We've had some.'
'Have some more.'
'We've had some more.'
'Well, there's lots there.'

Watching from the back row

I had sat in the front row for the talk on healing and I thought it would be selfish to sit in the front row again, so I went right to the back of the room and watched.

John, as you may know, operated with words of knowledge and he had a number on this occasion. He said he believed there was somebody there with a 'congenital back defect', to which Jeremy Jennings (now Pastoral Director of HTB) responded. At the end of praying for him, he looked at Jeremy and said, 'That will be 2p!'

We didn't know whether or not to laugh because we didn't know that John often had these flashes of self-deprecating humour. That was his way of relieving tension because he hated religiosity.

Then he had a word of knowledge for a girl who was 'trying to conceive' and he asked if she would like to come forward so that he could pray for her.

I didn't know where to look or what to do, I was so embarrassed by the whole thing. There were five or six married women in the room at that time and I knew them all. I also knew that not one of them was trying to conceive. They were all young couples getting going in life with mortgages, etc.

I was also embarrassed because in this part of London we don't talk about conception. We take part in the process, but we don't talk about it. I presumed he didn't know that because he came from California where I imagined they talked of nothing else!

I felt the whole thing was going wrong and I felt responsible in some way. Then, one of our leaders, Sarah Wright, got to her feet and said, 'I think that must be me.'

The moment our fellowship grew up

I have often said that I think that was the moment at which our fellowship grew up. Because it suddenly became possible for a beautiful girl in a beautiful congregation in a beautiful part of London to confess that all was not well, that something was wrong in her life.

John prayed for her with huge love – intensely and simply. He just put his hand on her head and *commanded* healing.

At theological college I had been taught that God doesn't do that sort of thing today. Yet here was a man from America who seemed to think that God *does* do that sort of thing today.

Nine months later, Sarah Wright gave birth to a beautiful little boy. In our Anglican tradition, as you know, we baptise babies of believing families. I had the privilege of baptising this little baby and it was one of the most moving things that I have done. Since then Sarah and her husband have gone on to have four more children. They don't know how to stop!

We caught it from John

John prayed for all of us – all in different ways. He opened our eyes to all sorts of things. He showed us that night what healing might mean.

I remember saying to my wife Annette on the way home, 'If that is New Testament we have got to go for it,' because I saw already what a blessing it was to Sarah, to us and to the community.

Any tribute to John is a tribute to Jesus. What John taught us first and foremost was intimacy with Jesus. So many things flow from that, including the style of worship which we now use at many services at Holy Trinity.

There was none of that in this country before the Vineyard took it up. We caught it, as it were, from John.

The secret of the worship is a hunger for that intimacy with God which is the secret of the Christian life. It isn't rules and regulations. It isn't what you say in liturgy. It is seeking the favour of God – and the favour of God comes through Jesus.

John taught us the principal values of the Vineyard: 'intimacy with God' and 'intimacy with one another'. Everything else followed from that in his own inimitable style, which included a terrific sense of integrity, honesty and simplicity. He never tried to make things work when they weren't working. He just asked the Spirit of God.

On one occasion when everything was hyped up – not through him – and everybody was 'getting religious', he broke off for coffee.

He wanted God to have the glory. He wasn't going to use the emotionalism of human beings. There was a total lack of pretentiousness that we loved. It felt like what Jesus would do if Jesus were here and Jesus is here.

Did what was right in the eyes of the Lord

One of the things that Carol said about him was that he reminded her of Josiah and Hezekiah in this. They did what was right in the eyes of the Lord and they tore down the high places. I think that, for me, this was the most precious thing, in a sense.

I went for a number of years to International Vineyard Pastors meetings. I was neither international nor a pastor. None of us was. But he invited us and just said, 'Come, if you would like to.' He had a generosity of spirit that was immensely attractive. He got it from Jesus. He never said, 'What are you doing here? You are not an international pastor. You are not Vineyard.'

He just said, 'Come.'

At those conferences I saw the freedom for which I longed. Annette used to say when I got back I was particularly difficult to live with because I had tasted freedom. And what we were then dealing with seemed so dull and boring, hypocritical, pretentious and unattractive. But in those days we had nothing else to put in its place.

These conferences enabled us to feed our spirits and to respond in the Spirit to the love of God and the sense of God's favour and friendship.

It gave us the confidence to move in the direction that we have moved. It has enabled us to worship as we worship. John had a balance between the spiritual and the practical that was immensely attractive. He seemed to know how things worked and he also knew who God is; the two went together. At the heart of all that was obedience to the Lord.

I think of John with a Bible in his hand – but not just reading it. Reading the Bible wasn't enough for him. He was determined to read it and to do it. One of his great expressions was, 'Everybody gets to play!'

Released

We are all the ministers of Jesus. 'We get out on the street and we do this stuff,' he would say. We don't just read about Jesus healing. We don't just read about Jesus speaking to the poor and the lost and the underprivileged. We get to do it. John released everybody. He said the Christian church 'is an army, not an audience'.

One of the high places that he tore down was exclusiveness – any attempt by any particular group of Christians to dominate or monopolise the Spirit of God.

He told the story of when he was in prayer one day and asking God about some of these other denominations.

'What about the Baptists?' he asked God.

And the Lord said to him, 'I love the Baptists.'

He said, 'Really? All that simplicity . . .?'

'I love them.'

'What about the Catholics?'

And the Lord said to him, 'I love the Catholics.'

'Really? You mean all that smoke and smells?'

'I love it,' God said.

John went through the various denominations, and then he asked, 'Is there any part of the church that you don't like . . .?

'Your part.'

It struck him in the heart and from that moment, if not before, he had that openness and generosity that embraced every denomination: Church of England, Catholic, Salvation Army, Methodist, Free Church, house church, New Church, Restoration church.

For him, the Vineyard was but one vegetable in the stew, as it were, to give flavour. I would want to add that it was a very strong flavour and a wonderful flavour, but it was just one part of God's church. Jesus loves the *whole* church. If we want to honour him, we must remember that.

It is an extraordinary thing to think of the effect that John Wimber has had. There is now hardly any part of the world that hasn't been touched by the Vineyard.

From our point of view, John didn't just touch the Church of England but the church *in* England. He came year after year and did conference after conference. I think the whole church owes him a tremendous amount. He gave us the confidence to change.

Intensely simple

At heart he was intensely simple and just loved his family. He was always wanting to get back to them. At his funeral his grandson Evan read out a little quotation from John Wesley that John Wimber kept in his Bible.

'Do all the good you can, by all the means you can, in all the ways you can, in all the places you can, at all the times you can, to all the people you can, as long as ever you can.'

I think that is what he tried to do.

He always felt he didn't teach as well as other people, didn't pray as much as other people and didn't speak as refinedly as other people. One of his most famous expressions reflects his intense humility: 'I am just a fat man trying to get to heaven.'

The wonderful thing is that we are now in a position to say, 'He made it!'

I often think about the graciousness with which John put up with the criticism from so many people snapping at his heels – men (and possibly women) who had no understanding of what is involved in running a church, just yapping, criticising, carping, willing to wound and yet afraid to strike.

At one conference he did here, a man asked two rude questions, with real hostility. I was so embarrassed. I took John over to tea afterwards and said to him, 'I do hope you didn't mind the tone of those questions.'

His reply was characteristic.

'Mind?' he said. 'I've been there. I know what they feel.'

Keeping going

I remember expression after expression that he used. Perhaps you remember the one on commitment? 'Commitment is spelt M-O-N-E-Y!'

And, again, 'Faith is spelt R-I-S-K!'

They go round and round in one's mind. It is the Spirit of Jesus bringing to memory a simplicity, a love for God, a passion for obedience to him, a ministry for prayer, for the poor, for the lost, for getting the gospel out, the 'main and the plain' things of Scripture.

Our resolve in our turn is to do exactly what St Paul said to the Corinthians: 'Keep going!'

Because one day (and who knows how soon?) it will be our turn to rest.

So we don't dwell on these thoughts; we dwell on Jesus. We take courage and comfort from all the saints that we have known and we press on to stay close to Jesus.

Jesus says every time a sinner comes to Christ there is a party in heaven so let us do what Jesus wants us to do with the short life that we have, so that we may be partying in heaven.

The importance of having intimate times with God

The first time I heard the Vineyard style of worship was in autumn 1982 when I went with about twenty-six people from HTB to the Vineyard church in Anaheim.

John had invited us to the conference and, of course, I couldn't wait. It was in the Sheridan Hotel in Palm Springs, which was so liberating. When we weren't in the sessions we were in the jacuzzi outside. It was just enormous fun.

Bear in mind that our Sunday morning worship at that time was 1662 Sung Matins with a robed choir. We had the Venite, a Psalm, an anthem and hymns.

What I think I noticed in the Wimber worship was the unconscious activity of the Spirit during the worship time, with songs addressed to God, such as: 'Lord, we love you'. It was very different from the songs we had then.

We learned that worship leaders need to give us ten to fifteen minutes of real intimacy with God, without loss and additions and eccentric repetitions that bring us back from heaven. The band's function is the same as the organ's function: to lead us but not to interrupt us. We need time to tell God we love him.

It is worth saying that, with the possible exception of the Romford Christian Fellowship, there was nowhere in Britain where we had worship of that kind, worship of twenty-five minutes, song after song. If there were churches who sang such songs, they were nearly always interrupted by the vicar's commentary.

He provided the theology

John's strength was that he provided the theology. I use
it all over the world now, if it is not too pretentious to
say. If there is anything new in the church, he used to
say, you will need a theology for it, a model for it and a
practice for it. That is to say, you need to do it. He provided a theology for the song 'Isn't He beautiful,
Beautiful, isn't He?'. Otherwise we would have thought
it was wet.

At Anaheim, while intimacy with God was their
number one value, their second value was intimacy
with one another. All this was a formative time for me.

The rest of the conference was pure sociology. It was
about groups and groupings – but once again it was key
for us here at Holy Trinity because we were going
through all the things to which that conference was the
answer.

People had been saying, 'This church is too big, we
want a small church where we can know everybody.'

I didn't know what the answer was. None of us did
because there was no literature written on church
growth in English. There was only a little in American.

Now we know why they were beginning to say, 'We
don't like this church any more.' It was because nobody
noticed whether they came or not. Nobody asked how
they were. This conference took us all the way through
groups: kinship groups, homegroups etc.

Because the Vineyard's priority was intimacy with
God and their engine for intimacy with God primarily
was worship, what we began to understand (and I felt
instinctively) was that the key to releasing worship in
the church was finding a smaller group in which it was
possible to worship.

Pastorate grouping proved vital

What we had at HTB at that time was a whole lot of
Bible studies of around twelve people which were not

ideal for worship because they were too small. We learned that the pastorate grouping of thirty upwards-people was key to releasing giftings and ministries and worship which the small group finds more difficult. We put together four or five Bible study groups under a pastor, and said, 'Let's meet up every month as a pastorate.' I came back from the conference and thought, 'We've got to do this.'

And things began to change.

John took us through the Scriptures and showed us where Jesus taught the Twelve, then the seventy, sending them out to heal the sick and announce that the Kingdom of God is near.

That is what they did and that is what Jesus did. He was always doing it himself and he taught his disciples. He took Peter, James and John when raising Jairus's daughter from the dead and modelled it for them. Just before he left to go back to heaven, in the Great Commission, he said to them. 'Go and make disciples of all nations, teaching them to do all that I have commanded you to do.'

What had he commanded them to do? *Heal the sick and tell them that the Kingdom of God is here.*

Proclamation follows demonstration

John Wimber often said, 'Proclamation followed by demonstration' or, in some cases in Acts, 'Demonstration followed by proclamation – but always the two going together.'

Before John's arrival with us, there hadn't been that emphasis. Charismatic things were all based around the spiritual gifts found in the epistles.

What this did, of course, was to open up the *Gospels* once again. People weren't preaching so much from the Gospels in those days because they didn't expect these things to happen.

All we were dealing with was what *Jesus* had done.

Most people had no difficulty in believing that *Jesus* did those things. What they hadn't realised was that Jesus did them and that he expected that *we* should do them.

Jesus wasn't just showing them how wonderful he was: he was *modelling it for us*, and intended that the Kingdom should continue with that emphasis and agenda.

What God gave John was particular favour with us.

Other Americans had in the past presented different models of church life which, although perfectly good, were things which we simply couldn't do, either because of our cultural setting (or our Anglican background), or because of the architecturally traditional setting of the church.

We didn't like shouting. And John did not shout. He spoke peacefully.

We weren't keen on models which appeared eccentric and odd.

But John provided a model that showed us the day of the 'expert' was over. The model was simply that you put your hand on people's heads and prayed. And we thought, 'Well, we can do that.'

We didn't know that there was a certain amount of prayer and fasting beforehand, but the model we took to straight away because it was not eccentric.

It has become second nature to us now but we have to keep an eye on the whole issue of simplicity.

Even now, there doesn't seem to be a conference in this country where people don't come back with some new oddity, some eccentricity, that makes people say. 'That is weird. I don't want that.'

Model

The manifestations can happen with any model. The model that we are after is the model that draws people on to the playing field rather than sending them off it.

John's theology was unimpeachable. Once you see

it, you see it. There are very strong reasons why theological colleges up and down the country prevented us seeing it because we were taught that these things didn't happen any more. We read the New Testament with that filter.

We had prayed for and expected gifts before. That was what the charismatic movement was. We prayed mainly for tongues, although we believed also in gifts of healing.

On one occasion, John preached at a Sunday evening service at HTB and the place was absolutely packed. He spoke on the paralysed man who was let down through the roof. Jesus said to him, 'Your sins are forgiven. Rise, take up your bed and walk.' And the problem that the Pharisees had at that time with Jesus was him saying, 'Your sins are forgiven'. They had no problem with him saying, 'Arise and walk'!

The point that John made was how strange it is that nowadays it is the other way round. We are pretty clear that Jesus had the authority to say, 'Your sins are forgiven.' But we get in a frightful fuss if anybody says. 'In his name, rise and walk'!

Both were an integral part of the ministry of Jesus.

It is so obvious when you see it, although theologically speaking John covered himself and I admire him for that. He was always very clear in trying to make it easy for people who want to think theologically.

For instance, he made clear that in one vital respect there was a difference between the two statements: while the forgiveness of sins is an integral part of the atonement, he wouldn't say that healing was part of the atonement. That, of course, is very precious. It means that if you die unhealed, you are nonetheless forgiven.

Then he did the ministry. He had no hype, no pretensions and never tried to make anything happen.

The point was: 'If it isn't happening, it isn't happening and it is no good trying to make it happen.'

'Come, Holy Spirit', was always his prayer. 'Let it come.'

By saying 'Let it come,' he meant that our response should be. 'Lord, thank you,' rather than 'I don't want this!' The Lord looks for an open and hungry heart.

Fear

Sometimes if John felt there was a spirit of fear about, he would raise his voice, but he didn't do that for effect. He did it because he was conscious that there was a spirit of fear which needed breaking. He had a very clear view, like Smith Wigglesworth, that when the demonic was involved, he never felt the need to identify it or express it as such, but he dealt with it in the same way that Jesus stilled the storm – by shouting, 'Shut up! Be quiet.' On one occasion he summoned me over to him and introduced me to a girl who was suffering from asthma. He said to me, 'Speak to the asthma and command it to go!'

I felt rather like Ezekiel in the valley of the dry bones. I don't know how to speak to asthma any more than I know how to speak to dry bones. But I had seen what John did, so I said. 'I command you, asthma, in the name of Jesus. GO!'

That was the first time I saw somebody healed before my very eyes. She was totally changed and she knew it. He explained afterwards that asthma is sometimes just physical and sometimes demonic, but that this time it was a spirit.

Once you have the confidence to bear those possibilities in mind, I think you can still see those things today.

He taught us to look for signs of the Spirit on people. He would say, 'You can see the Spirit.'

John preferred not to have keyboards clattering away while he was leading ministry. He wouldn't interfere if he was in a place where they started doing it (because the alternative is to say to the worship leader. 'Would you mind stopping that noise?' and you can't do that) but he didn't like to have any musical 'hype', no emotionalism. That was what we loved about him.

Church growth analyst
John Wimber's great strength was that he was a church growth analyst. That was his job. By the early 1980s he had visited about 600 to 700 churches throughout the United States. His job was to go round, analyse the churches and help them to understand why some things worked and others didn't.

It is so hard in church life to get reality. You are deemed to be unspiritual if you ask practical questions. It was from him that we got the expression, 'You can tell what you are committed to by looking at those things to which you give your time, energy and money'.

He used to go to all these churches and ask, 'What do you really value?'

'We really value foreign missions.'

So he said, 'How much money do you give to foreign mission?'

'Oh well. We haven't given much this year because we have been doing x, y and z.'

And he would reply, 'Well that tells me how much foreign mission is precious to you.'

It was the reality of it that was so attractive.

I went to those conferences in California in 1982, 1983, 1984 and 1985: four key years. They covered aspects of church growth, spiritual warfare; prayer and healing. In all these conferences there was ministry and worship.

Drunk
At the second conference in California I remember first experiencing being 'drunk' in the Spirit. I couldn't

stand. I couldn't get into bed. I couldn't get into the elevator. I hadn't had anything to drink at all, but I was staggering around the passage in the hotel where I was staying. I was roaring with laughter. I thought it was so funny.

I was sharing a room with a rather dour Texan who had already gone to sleep. I came into the bedroom but I couldn't get undressed. It was just like being helplessly drunk. I couldn't get my coat and jersey off, or my shirt. So I thought, 'I will go out for a walk so that I can recover.'

I walked along the seafront for mile after mile. That was when I said, 'Lord, I will do anything you want me to do.'

I think I heard him say clearly, 'All I want is you.'

When I first came back from these conferences and started talking about intimacy with God, I came in for some criticism. I was taken to one side by a woman who said, 'Please don't use the word "intimacy" because we don't use it in that context.'

So I started talking about the 'closest possible relationship with God'. Then I gave up because it was such a mouthful and what I meant was *intimacy*.

Most can't handle intimacy

Because that is what God means by intimacy. It is there in the Bible. We rarely preach on the Song of Solomon because we don't know how to handle it. Most of us as married men in our culture do not know how to handle intimacy within marriage. We have to stumble our way forward because it is not part of our culture if you come from a background of stiff upper lip and two World Wars.

That had to be re-learnt and of course there is a danger, as one person who expressed a reservation about the way it was going said, 'It is all too chummy. You don't seem to realise that this is the God who created the universe.'

If we *are* getting too 'chummy' then we must stop because we must be respectful and reverent. But we can remember that it is God who has invited us into this relationship with him as sons and daughters.

But the model John gave us wasn't soppy; it was responsible and responsive and obedient. It is the same with children: if intimacy with children means that a child can do what he likes, then we have misunderstood the word intimacy.

Having seen the model in California, it gave me the confidence to know that it could work.

After I was appointed Vicar in 1985, we changed the 11 a.m. service from 1662 Matins to ASB (*Alternative Service Book*) Morning Prayer.

We tried that for about three months and it was a disaster.

People who liked 1662 Matins knew that it was not 1662 and those who didn't like 1662 thought it was!

So we moved to ASB Communion, which was too long. It is a terrible thing to say in a Eucharistic community but there simply wasn't time for prayer ministry at the end of the Sunday morning service. So now we have Communion once a month at 11 a.m., apart from our regular 9 a.m. Communion Service.

The evening service had already moved into having this extended time of worship. But then those attending the evening service got married, had babies, and wanted to come in the mornings – but to enjoy the style of worship which they could find in the evenings.

And these experiences of ours were being multiplied at churches all over the country which I think was the Spirit of God.

This was what was wanted
John started doing his conferences in London, Brighton, Sheffield (and soon other venues) and thousands of

people came. He then went to Manchester. We did some here in HTB of course. Every time he did them, a whole lot more people were filled with the Spirit; the conferences were oversubscribed time and again. In latter years, numbers went down a bit and one of the main reasons was that John released the stage to more and more other speakers who weren't quite up to it. We couldn't hear them in the same way as we heard him. But he did that because he was so characteristically generous.

There were a lot of clergy of a younger generation at that time who said 'This is what we want.' The momentum for change in the denominations came from them because they saw that the skies didn't fall in if you moved in that direction – and that it grew the church!

So it grew and grew and grew. And nothing can stop it if it is the truth.

I know John Wimber loved what we were doing at HTB. I think he felt that we had embraced all that he stood for. And in a way – like St Paul with his churches – he felt that he had done what he could and we had taken it on and he was thrilled.

His generosity of spirit was a model for us. I don't think we had fully appreciated the concept that what God gives you is to be given away.

'You get to give to get – to give to get – to give,' John said.

He is the only person that I ever heard of who, on the last morning of one of his conferences, arranged for a copy of one of his books to be on each of our seats because the conference had sold out. They had budgeted for less than a complete sell out and so had made a lot of money. He wanted to give it back. His generosity of spirit showed itself in offers of help, and a complete absence of proprietary rights in this and that.

The meat is on the street

When I was first asked to go to a conference in Norway I happened to mention it to John. I said, 'I have got to go to Norway and I have no idea what to say.'

He said, 'Well, you tell them what I say!'

Which is pretty well what we do to this day!

The teaching on healing is what he brought to life for us from the Scriptures. He used to say, referring to the Bible, 'You don't eat the menu. You eat the meal.'

There were times when members of his congregation would ask him for more 'heavy' Bible teaching. 'Could we have more meat?' they would ask.

In my presence somebody said to him that they didn't think much of his evening talk because it 'lacked meat'.

He said, 'Were you there in the morning?'

The man replied, 'Yes.'

He said, 'Well you don't need more than one big meal a day, do you?'

At other times when they were complaining about the lack of 'meat', John's response was, 'The meat is on the street. Get out and do it.'

John was devoted to ecumenism. 'Your brother is your brother. He is never your enemy,' he would say.

Manifestations

John always played down manifestations of the Spirit by making people laugh when they were going on. It was a way of releasing tension in order to get genuine spirituality rather than religiosity which was always his enemy.

He often spoke of 'good news and bad news'.

On many occasions he said, 'The good news is that Jesus is interceding for you. The bad news is you are *going to need it.*'

At other times he said, 'The good news is that we are

all on our way to heaven. The bad news is that we have got to get there poor.'

He was a very warm-hearted and generous, encouraging man. There was no side to him. And we miss him.

23

COPING WITH CONTROVERSY
AND SUFFERING
CAROL WIMBER

*Carol Wimber married John in 1955, was for many years
an elder and board member of a Quaker church in Orange
County, California, until soon after her 'charismatic'
experience in September 1976 when she was ejected. She
had helped to develop an effective Vacation Bible School
programme and had an extended ministry teaching
women's Bible studies around Orange County. Her
priority for prayer and her resources for practical wisdom
and spiritual insight were a constructive 'behind the scenes'
influence on John. The creative tension of spirit, heart and
mind in their life together provided the major human factor
in the birth and nurture of a movement of the Holy Spirit.*

*'If you are reviled for the name of Christ, you are blessed'
because the Spirit of Glory and
of God rests upon you.' 1 Peter 4:14:*

You know, we didn't walk into this thing blind, twenty-
two years ago when God started this. We knew too well
the mind-set of the conservative evangelical church
. . . having had it ourselves most of our Christian life.
Therefore it was no surprise to us when the uproar
began. John, being farsighted by nature and wise
because of his education in Church Growth knew exact-

ly the reaction there would be. I, on the other hand, knew because I had been such a rabid persecutor of charismatics myself. I knew firsthand the unreasoning fear of well-meaning Christians, of encounters with God that they themselves had not experienced . . . knowing that most of us judge the authenticity, the validity of Christian experience by whether we can relate and understand the encounter. Somehow we become the plumb line.

We had been warned, as well, by a prophetic woman using the text out of Luke 21:12,13: 'But before all this, they will lay hands on you and persecute you. They will deliver you to synagogues and prisons, and you will be brought before kings and governors, and all on account of my name. This will result in your being witnesses to them. But make up your mind not to worry beforehand how you will defend yourselves.' That was the text, but she added; 'Don't defend yourselves. God will raise up others to defend you.'

At the time we didn't have an enemy in the world, but just a few weeks after this event all heaven broke loose in our lovely, conservative, evangelical church with the predictable reaction from hell. We had expected the devil to do his job so we weren't terribly surprised.

Working against time

Personally, I felt from the beginning that we were working against time. It was my understanding (from God) that we would have enough grace to do the job God gave us to do, and no more. Therefore, if we stopped to defend ourselves or fight back, we wouldn't have enough grace to finish the race. We would get bogged down forever explaining and defending. Consequently, there was the sense of fixing our eyes on Jesus . . . with blinders on so that we wouldn't get distracted and stop because of all the hassle we were caus-

ing the church. A setting our faces like flint, straight forward and just cutting through the brush. A sort of
machete-like action, hewing out a path that we knew
others would be able to walk on if we didn't get caught
and stopped by the fierce undergrowth.

Controversy was a 'thorn in the flesh' that would
always be with us and we expected it though we didn't
like it. It helped that we understood that the very issues
that made people so mad were not caused by us, but by
God himself. As a result, we didn't take the attacks personally. In fact, the myriad of articles, books, theses,
pamphlets, etc. that were published against John we
never read, feeling they were none of our business.
However, he did read and answer the honest criticisms
when they came and often changed or modified his
thinking because of it.

We would never have left the Quakers
John's sermon, the first time we met after our beloved
Quaker church asked us to leave, was on Mary and how
all of her life she would be accused of fornication and
her child be called a bastard. He said it would be like
that for us. We also had been born of the Holy Spirit, the
fruit of the 'overshadowing' of the Spirit of God, and
judged illegitimate by those around us. It was part of it
and would always be our reputation. We could not
have the relationship with God that we wanted, where
he was free to do things his way, and expect to escape
criticism and misunderstanding. He said it would
always be this way. We'd already experienced some
rejection and misunderstanding from our Quaker
church, so it wasn't too hard to believe. Everybody in
that church, except the elders, believed that we had just
coldly left them to start our own church. The elders
knew the truth, of course, because they had asked us to
leave in an effort to stop what was the beginning of the
fire from heaven that for years we, along with them,

had cried out to God for. The truth was we would never have left that church; it was our home, where we were born. But since they weren't talking, so to speak, we didn't want to divide the church by telling everyone that it was not our choice; that we had been invited to leave. We loved those Quakers and they loved us, but they did not want an outbreak of 'tongues', and so they asked us for our resignation. Our futile attempts to convince them that this was not about 'tongues' ended with them agreeing to give us their blessing if we would just leave. We did and they did. I'm always reminded of Jacob wrestling with the Angel of the Lord until daybreak to get the Blessing.

Beggars can't be choosers

No legitimate church in town would have anything to do with us when we asked about renting a place to meet, and after exhausting all other possibilities, we ended up in the Masonic Temple, under the hanging G that stands for God and Geometry. Not at all what we had hoped for, 'but beggars can't be choosers'. It was a new, unpleasant sort of feeling, being 'outcasts'. We had always been so respectable, but no longer, apparently. Those days were over and that unpleasant feeling became as familiar to me as my own face and I got used to it. Even to the degree that when it wasn't there for any length of time I wondered if we had lost our first love or compromised in some way.

It was odd. The Masons were kind to us and charged us only $25 a week to rent their building, at the same time that the Baptist minister in the next town printed pamphlets saying John was thrown out of the Quaker church for adultery. 'Adulteries', I think he said. Plural. Well, that was the beginning of it, and it hasn't let up much since. Possibly, that caused some controversy, but among ourselves we were puzzled by how a Christian man could become so full of hate that he would print lies. We aren't puzzled any more. We accept the reality without trying to understand it.

Threats on John's life

To put it simply, we expected controversy. There is always controversy where Jesus is ministering. Frankly, I've been happily surprised that we escaped with our lives! Most of the time there was someone, somewhere threatening to shoot John. On one occasion in a local restaurant, a man just returning from a Dave Hunt seminar, went beserk and came screaming at John calling him the antichrist. It was embarrassing rather than frightening. I don't know whether it was grace or stupidity but we simply didn't have anxiety over those things . . . most of the time.

Trying to understand why

The things that did cause anxiety and suffering for John and therefore for me, were the too-frequent occasions when a trusted friend and co-laborer would betray John and then blame him for the resulting breach in relationship. He would search his heart trying to understand why. Strangely, it was always someone that John loved and had been extremely generous with. Because he didn't understand it, he didn't know how to fix it and so he suffered.

Those were the sort of things that did real damage to John, not the controversy caused by his teaching and ministry. I wish I could make you understand how he saw his own ministry. John had a detachment that was quite extraordinary and unusual in that he would take no credit at all for any of the things God did through him. The last few months of his life, when he finally had time to think about himself, he would ponder over the way he had lived out his life, the choices he had made, what kind of a father he had been, what sort of husband, or friend. He was thinking ahead to the time he would see Jesus and wondering if there would be any

shame. When I would point out the wonderful ministry
he had or the marvelous healings and deliverances
from his hand, the way God had used him all over the
world . . . he would look at me in that quizzical way he
had, as if I had missed the point of his concern. 'But that
was God, I had nothing to do with that.' He would con-
cede that he did have to make the choice to let God be
God. He did have to decide to obey or not, but that was
about all he would let me credit him with.

The other side of that coin is that he also didn't take
responsibility for God's ministry. If someone was not
healed that he prayed for he did not feel responsible.
He felt bad for them, but no more so than any of the rest
of us standing there watching would have done. He
said it often over the years; 'I'm just coins in his pocket,
he can spend me any way he wants.' He loved what he
did, and hoped to do it until he died, but he would have
been just as satisfied to teach a Bible study. In fact, after
his heart surgery he would talk to me about starting a
little neighborhood evangelistic Bible study, after Lance
Pitluck got here to pastor the church at Anaheim, and
he would have some free time. He was almost stone
deaf by then from the effects of the radiation, and suffered terrible headaches from the stroke, yet he could
hardly wait to start a 'little' Bible study. He was an
amazing man and so simple in his relationship with
Jesus.

His working theory
Another big issue that caused him to suffer was the
growing doubt that he had been a good leader. His
working theory: 'Let the bush grow, then shape it.'
'Let's see what it is first', didn't seem to be working
very well. For example, the prophetic people. It was in
John's mind that the Vineyard was 'lean' in the area of
prophetic gifting, . . . therefore he would focus and
teach as he had done when healing gifts were the issue.

Focus and teach, show and tell. Iron sharpens iron, so give these gifted men a platform and the result should be a great encouraging of the prophetic gifting in the church. This sounds right and it should have worked, but, like any group, they tended to impart their unique theological leanings. This actually resulted in discouraging ministry by the commonplace variety of Christian rather than encouraging it as we had hoped. All too often when the ordinary Christian heard these extraordinary men, any thoughts they had of being able to minister themselves flew away. Our efforts to 'Shape it' or 'trim it' were probably too little or too late. John had wanted to equip the saints, not entertain them. He took full responsibility and he suffered greatly over that one. Although neither one of us regretted 'taking the trip', both of us were sorry we hadn't been wiser, smarter and more mature, but it was just us, John and Carol, doing things the way we did them; . . . trial and error. At the time I asked a good friend of ours, Ed Piorak, how he was doing with the whole prophetic thing and he replied that he felt the Lord had said to him, 'Why don't you sit this one out, Ed?'

There is surely a better way to learn, but 'trial and error' is the path we stumbled along much of our ministry and had some wonderful, glorious times in the process.

For John there was always one question first: 'Is this you, Lord?'. If the answer was 'Yes', the next question was, 'What do you want me to do?' Only after committing himself to do whatever the Lord wanted him to do, did he then ask himself: 'What does this mean to me?' And 'How will this affect the church?'. With John it was always obedience first. I believe he was the most obedient person I have ever known.

Leaders who harmed the church

Extremely painful for him, even until his last breath, was the reality that he had put some leaders in place over the years who had harmed the church. John was such a straight-shooter himself, a deeply moral man, that he couldn't conceive of a Christian taking advantage of the people of God. We were way too slow realizing what was going on and then when we did we were suspicious of our own suspicions, fearing that the devil was trying to cause discord. On one occasion a trusted friend sat across from us at our table and said: 'John, listen to me! Read my lips! The man is a homosexual!' He had known this man for years and was even then counseling a young man that had been seduced by him. So the truth finally penetrated our naiveté and we did what we could to salvage the people involved. But it was us who had allowed that man to minister. We were the ones who had exposed our young people to him.

That was years ago and we dealt with it, confronting the evangelist with his sin; we made him promise to get counseling and he agreed not to minister anywhere until we were satisfied that he was truly repentant and wholly delivered. Of course he agreed, and he was true to his word on about the same level as we should have expected. Since we hadn't dealt with it publicly, no one knew why we weren't allowing this man to minister anymore and we were considered to be quite mean and controlling. When he decided he'd had enough discipline, he left to do his own thing and the church at large was left vulnerable. Next time a similar thing happened, we read the Bible. Suddenly the directions for dealing with sin in elders made a lot of sense. Deal publicly, in the arena of their influence, and it will correct the elder, pre-warn the flock, and cause others to fear. That's how the Vineyard handled sinning elders after that. Some commended us, many criticized us, but we believed we were on solid ground if the Scripture was still our guide. Admittedly, it would have been easier on us as well as the malefactor, to have handled all the dirty Vineyard laundry behind closed doors. Maybe this would have saved our reputation a few blows. But everything we've ever done has been right out there for everybody to see. Years ago we were feeling a little self-conscious about some of the more sensational manifestations of the Holy Spirit, because people would come just to see what new wild thing was going to happen that Sunday night. We just wanted to be left alone while God taught us what we needed to know. That night at church a prophecy came ringing out: 'I have made you a Marketplace! I gave you your reputation, and I can take it away!'

But in all this, John felt as responsible as the guilty one if he had put him in place or given him the visibility that brought his ministry into focus. My 'Oh for crying out loud, John, how could you have known? You can't blame yourself!' had no more comforting effect on him than it would have on a father who had unknowingly invited a child molester to babysit.

We experienced deep pain when the church we had been converted in asked us to leave twenty-one years ago, because of an outpouring of the Holy Spirit. We experienced more pain when the denomination that took us in asked us to change our name for the same reason. There has been lots of pain and we didn't question it because we knew there would be pain and betrayal and rejection. But I guess my point is: it was all worth it! It was worth all the pain and the controversy.

It was all worth it

That's how I remember it most of the time. The controversy going on, but John just ignoring it all and not allowing it to slow us down. But sometimes I remember the ache that went along with the lies written about him, when it was impossible to avoid reading them, the misquotes, the misunderstandings, . . . the constant harangue against John by the 'Bible Answer Man' on his radio program. It was one thing for me to deal with it when he was young and strong, but as the years of illness came with the painful cancer treatments that left him deaf and with a mouth so dry he could never sing again and the debilitating stroke with the 'forever'pain and the loss of his left hand so he couldn't go to the piano and sing songs to Jesus anymore, and the constant dizziness and weakness as his poor used-up body gave out . . . and still the lies, the misquotes, the meanness by the press, the jealousy, the never-ending attacks, were sometimes almost unendurable for me. They were still nipping at his heels when he was too weak to even walk down the hallway without help. I wanted to pick him up in my arms and carry him away to some safe place where he wouldn't hurt anymore. I couldn't do that, of course, but Jesus finally did.

Writing this chapter made me realize just how deeply I have been affected by all these things. Apparently, knowing that controversy was going to be constant in what God was going to do, and determining not to get distracted by it, did not protect us from the suffering.

Good and faithful servant

All life involves suffering though, and the battlefield that we were wounded on had already soaked up the blood of thousands before we ever came along. We were honored to be in the same battle and share in the same suffering, however minor in comparison. I'll never regret the choices we made. Though John came to fear he had not been a good leader, I didn't. On his grave marker I had inscribed the words: 'Well done, thou good and faithful servant. Enter thou into the joy of thy Lord.'

24

A Wife's Tribute

Carol Wimber

*There were a number of fascinating tributes to John's life
and work during the packed funeral service at Anaheim on
Friday 21st November 1997, prior to the internment on the
following morning: possibly the most moving words were
from Carol Wimber. Rarely on such occasions could a
grieving widow be expected to muster both the composure
to speak and the readiness to share such singular reflections
with such delightful feeling and insight. The main thrust
of her tribute is reported below:*

'He did what was right in the sight of the Lord.'
2 Kings 18:3 & 22:2
'And he tore down the High Places.'
2 Kings 18:4 & 23:8

John would never have allowed me to compare him to
a king. He had his sights set on the servant role. That is
what he was looking at. He would tell the story of the
wedding at Cana of Galilee – how nobody knew what
was going on when the water was changed to wine, but
the *servants* knew. That was the role he was after – to be
a servant. Honestly, the only ambition John ever had
was that one day, when he came before the Father, he
might hear him say: 'Well done, thou good and faithful
servant'. And what may have appeared to certain people (who didn't understand him), to be a driving ambi-

tion, was nothing more than a sense of his responsibility before God. He felt that God had given him something for the whole church and he did not want to waste any time, but to fulfil that mission. That is what drove him; it was his sense of responsibility. He had a message that he needed to tell people.

But since John is not here, I can compare him to whoever I want! I have always thought of him (though I never told him this), but I have always thought of him as being like King Hezekiah and King Josiah. The Word says, 'He did what was right in the eyes of the Lord' – 'And he tore down the high places.'

Exclusiveness
Now the first high places which concerned John, were those where religious spirits dwelt and where worship was served, like exclusiveness. John loved the whole church. How did he used to say it? 'From the bare feet to the low church, the casual church' (actually like the Vineyard), to the high church, the liturgical church – the bells and the smells.' He loved the whole church. He loved it! He even liked it when he went to that snake handling church in the hills of Arkansas! I mean he didn't want to get real close to the snakes, but when they asked him to give a message he went up to the pulpit with all those snakes squirming around (though he kept his hands well clear!). But I mean no matter how weird or twisted – if there was an expression of the body of Christ there – he loved it.

He also loved the Catholic Church and you all know he did. Now he never misunderstood what the Vineyard was called to stand for (our part in the body of Christ), but he didn't think of the Vineyard as anything more than one vegetable in the whole stew. And he knew we were obligated and entrusted with something that was needed to provide that flavour, but it was nothing more than that. He had no inflated or

unreal idea about our role in the church. He knew that
we were a vine that God had planted, and John so
appreciated what he believed we were called to do, but
he didn't think we were the only vine or even necessarily the best one. He understood that we had to be true
to what it was we were; and that is what he fought for,
and that is what he stood for, and that is what he was
so unwavering about.

What God had entrusted to him he was true to,
every day of his life. That is why I have never been
apologetic for some of the 'trips' we have taken. To me
it has all been wonderful. Jim Campbell has shared his
appreciation of 'the way we got to experience God,
every new aspect of God; the way we got to be there
and be a part of it'! When things got strained, or a little
twisted, or somebody took it beyond the boundary
lines, then we could lay it down or correct it. But I don't
regret it. How else are we going to learn? Do we think
we are so smart that we can do something and not make
mistakes? So it didn't bother John to have to correct the
movement, and remind us of who we are, and what
God has given the Vineyard to say and do and be. But I
loved the whole ride – the *whole* ride. I was scared, you
know, gritting my teeth most of the time, but he wasn't.
I am so glad I got to go along.

Pretentiousness

Another high place was the hype of theatrics, the pretentiousness, of so much of what purports to be the
church of Jesus Christ. He just would not have anything
to do with that. He took the message of Jesus right out
of these walls, or whatever walls were that we happened to be in at the time; sometimes it was just the
walls of the tent, the canvas, and he made us take it out
on the street. That is what he meant when he said, 'The
meat is in the street!' If anyone complained: 'Oh, I am
tired of hearing the same messages, the milk of the

Word. I want to go somewhere where there is the meat of the Word', John would say, 'The meat is in the street, go out and do it'.

He had no greater delight than to come upon people in a shopping mall or a grocery store or an office, praying for someone. He loved it when a person was healed out in the parking lot, or had the gospel preached to them in a doctor's waiting room. He loved it when a demon was cast out in a restaurant. He didn't mind the big scene and the mess; he loved it. He'd just get that big 'ole smile on his face. It never scared him to hear people screaming and shouting because he knew that they were just moments away from being set free of something that they had wanted to be free of for years. He loved it when the church broke through the walls.

Everybody gets to play

Another high place he tore down (he ended it in our circle at least), was the monopoly of the ministry of the Holy Spirit by the pastor, priest or leader or the 'star' up on the stage. 'Every body gets to play,' he used to say. 'Everybody gets to play!' And to prove the point once, at some conference, in front of a group of academics who were frantically writing notes on how they could heal, he said, 'You don't get it, do you?' Looking down he saw some kids and called them out to him. There was a crippled man there also and he said to the kids, 'You pray for him!' They said: 'Pray for him? What do we say?' John told them: 'Just ask Jesus to do what you think needs to be done.' So the little boys said, 'Jesus, heal this man's legs', or something like that, and the man was healed right there! God taught, with that single event, something that would have taken years for the academics to understand with all their wisdom and scholarship. The ministry of the Holy Spirit is for anyone, any Christian who is willing to take the risk and put their hand to whatever they sense Jesus is doing.

John was always looking for what Jesus was doing. That was the guideline he went by (John 5:19). He never tried to make anything happen; he just kept looking to see what Jesus was doing and he put his hand to that. And that is what he encouraged us all to do.

In Ephesians 11–12 we read, 'He gave some as apostles, prophets, evangelists, pastors, teachers, for the equipping [*not of the stars on the stage but . . .*] the believers.' The equipping of the saints means the equipping of the believers. John's delight was to see us all doing what God had called us to do. We all had a part to play in the ministry of the Holy Spirit – a ministry that for years, it seemed, had been reserved for the special Holy Men.

Once, early on in his Christian life, John tried to get holy, and he tried real hard. He told us, 'I am going up to the mountains to cloister myself away and I am going to fast and pray and seek the Lord's direction for the future.' So I guess he drove up to the mountains. But about 10 o'clock that night the phone rang and it was John. He said he couldn't find a room anywhere up in the mountains, so he was down in San Bernadino eating Big Macs. It was so funny, and I said, 'Oh honey come on home. We have been praying here all day. You don't have to go to the mountains to pray. Come home and get to bed.'

Imparting to others

At the beginning he couldn't grasp why the anointing, the power of the Holy Spirit, only came on him. Everybody he touched at the Bible study got healed. I mean Gigi's leg grew out an inch and a half, or something, and when she went home that night she had to lengthen the leg of all her Levi's. And her grandma got saved, I think because of it! But the anointing still only came on John. He was troubled because people were lining up for him to pray for them. That was not at all

the way he understood it should be, and he kept reading that verse in Ephesians over and over again: 'For the
equipping of the saints for the service of ministry.' So
one night at church (we were in the gymnasium by
then), he called everyone forward after he had been
reading in Leviticus about the consecration of the
priests for ministry; about how they took the blood and
then the oil and anointed the ear lobes. I think it was the
thumb of the right hand and the toe of the right foot.
The blood was for consecration and the oil for ministry.
So he called all of us up and after we had consecrated
ourselves he anointed us with oil. We understood from
this that ministry was for everybody! It was wonderful.
John wouldn't grasp to himself the ministry of the Holy
Spirit.

Later he read of a similar ritual also for the cleansing
and healing of leprosy! But God used it to help us get
the message – *that the ministry was for everybody.*

False piety
And another high place was that of false piety. He
wouldn't have any of it. He wouldn't let anybody
crown him as a king, or put robes on him or call him an
apostle – not that he ever put down the groups that had
that kind of a structure. When I would say, 'Well John,
do you think you are an apostle?' he would answer,
'Carol K [John's nickname for his wife], Nicholas Van
Bew in South Africa, I think it was, planted thousands
and thousands of churches. If there is ever an apostle
walking around today it is him!' John was kind of impatient with all that kind of thing – not irritated, but he
just wanted people to 'get real – I'm just a fat man on
my way to heaven' he would say.

Respect for all
Another thing that I appreciated, was the importance to
him that everyone should be treated with dignity and

respect – especially when the manifest presence of God
was upon them. He believed people are very, very vulnerable when God opens them up that way and he
would never, ever exploit people's emotions to make
anything happen. You know, those of you who have
been to the conferences, how after some of the most
intense times with things building up and up, when
God's presence was so heavy you could hardly stand,
he would have everybody leave for a coffee break. Then
when they all came back, still chewing their cookies, he
would quietly say 'Holy Spirit, come' and God would
break loose.

I mean it was great, no music – cold turkey. Again
he would insist, 'You don't *use* worship for anything
other than to worship God, so you don't *use* emotion.
People are emotional, and that's fine, but you don't use
anything to *cause* the ministry of God. You let God be
God and he will do what he will and he doesn't need
"creaturely activity" – as the Quakers used to call it – to
accomplish that.'

Worship

Which brings me to the last thing. He taught us that
worship is not a vehicle to warm up the congregation
for the preacher, or to soften people up for an offering.
Worship comes from Jesus and goes back to Jesus from
us. Jesus gives us everything, but worship belongs to
him. We do not make stars of the worship leaders.
Worship is not for anything, but just for him: that is
what he gets. He gives everything else to us, and what
he gets back from us is our worship. John taught us
that.

25

QUO VADIS?

NIGEL SCOTLAND

Nigel Scotland has been Lecturer in Religions at the Cheltenham and Gloucester College of Higher Education since 1984 and Field Chair of Religious Studies since 1990. Prior to this he served as rector in Montreal Diocese and as Chaplain and Lecturer at the College of St Paul and St Mary, Cheltenham.

Close to the Appian Way, one of the main routes into ancient Rome, there stands the Chapel of 'Domine Quo Vadis?' Legend has it that Peter, fleeing from Nero's persecution, encountered Jesus approaching the city. Astonished, Peter cried out: 'Lord where are you going?' (*Domine Quo Vadis?*) With a glance that appeared to be one of gentle reproach, Jesus the Lord replied 'To Rome, to be crucified.' Whereupon, Peter about turned. As we reflect on the life and work of one of God's great followers, John Wimber, we all of us, like Peter, need to ask 'Lord, where are you going?' or perhaps to be more specific: 'Where do we go from here?' and how do we take forward the legacy of John Wimber.

When someone dies who has made a significant notable impact in the Christian church, it often happens that one of two reactions result. First, there can be a tendency to idolise them so that the heart of what they achieved is set in concrete, witness certain Anglicans who can't see beyond Cranmer's Prayer Book and

Theodore's parochial system. On the other hand, there can sometimes be a total reaction to what a person stood for with the result that when they die everything is put into reverse gear; witness the seventeenth-century Puritans under Cromwell who overrode the parochial system and threw out the *Book of Common Prayer* altogether and put in its place a *Directory of Christian Worship*. The right way forward in most instances usually proves to be to learn from any mistakes and then to focus and build on what is of primary and significant importance. This of course needs to be done without getting locked into a time-frame, be it Cranmer's, Cromwell's or Wimber's.

As I reflect on John Wimber's contribution to the Christianity of the late twentieth century it seems to me that there are six key areas which he emphasised and on which the worldwide church should be building.

1. Worship that is intimate

Worship is the most fundamental duty enjoined on Christians. Jesus underlined this in his summary of the first great commandment that we're to love God with all our heart, mind, soul and strength. The Westminster Shorter Catechism asks the question: 'What is man's first duty?' To which the answer is 'to love God and enjoy him for ever'. Perhaps more than anything else John Wimber has brought Christians back to the heart of worship. Whilst clearly teaching that worship extends outwards from the sanctuary into every aspect of our work and living he clearly demonstrated that its core is 'intimacy' – a deep personal union with Jesus. In New Testament terms 'we draw near to God and he draws near to us'.[1] Wimber emphasised that *'proskuneo'* the main Greek word used for worship in the New Testament, is a very intimate word meaning to 'kneel down and kiss the hand of' or 'to adore'. Unless we get to this point where we actually connect and engage with God in this way we haven't fully worshipped in the biblical sense.

The problem with the Church of England from which I come and with many of the mainline denominational churches is that their worship in most instances isn't sufficiently long enough to enable the congregation to engage with God. As the late Canon David Watson, a prominent evangelist, wrote in one of his books: 'We stand up to sing one hymn, then sit down to pray; we stand up to sing again, then sit down to read . . . but in this way it is hard to enter any form of intimate worship and that is what worship needs to be.'

In the traditional churches there is often a written liturgy of words, much of it rooted in the early traditions of the undivided early Catholic Church, ancient and beautiful. In some of the newer Protestant denominations there is a liturgy of hymns, readings and responses. A difficulty with both approaches is their tendency to be essentially cerebral, too objective and overly theological. Worship, as Jesus himself taught, is spirit as well as truth. Wimber demonstrated that it's often much easier to achieve intimate worship by singing a series of simple worship songs which are addressed to God rather than about God. These need, he taught, to be sung in an uninterrupted flow without stops for little sermonettes or introductions between them so that the congregation can get their focus and their spirits totally set on Jesus.

Criticisms have been levelled at Wimber's emphasis on worship. The point has often been made that the songs which he advocated lack theological content and that the repetitive way in which they are often sung is mindless. In response to this several things can be said. First, John Wimber didn't write many of the Vineyard songs himself and we can't altogether hold him to ransom for lyrics composed by his associates and other

Vineyard worship leaders. Second, the objective and theological element is often so dominant in the creeds, liturgy and sermons of traditional churches that a group of simple intimate Vineyard worship songs can provide a wholesome balance. Third, repetition enjoys good biblical precedent. Many of the Psalms, the songs of ancient Israel, are strong on repetition. Psalm 107 has a recurring chorus of 'Let them give thanks to the Lord' which occurs six times with minor variations. Psalms 8, 67 and 150 have similar refrains and in Psalm 136 the words 'His love endures for ever' occur twenty-six times in twenty-six verses. The Jewish rabbis, Jesus among them, also used repetition as a teaching method. Incidentally, Anglicans, of all people, should be the last to complain of repetition since they repeat more or less the same service content morning and evening year in, year out and one of their canticles, the Benedicite, contains the words 'praise him and magnify him for ever' thirty-two times in thirty verses. Many have found that once they have accustomed themselves to the repetitive nature in the Vineyard style, like that of Taizé, it becomes a profoundly liberating form of worship in which they can become childlike in the presence of a Heavenly Father.

Large numbers of worshippers have found that the repetition of very simple word forms, many of which are pure unadulterated Scripture, enables God's Word to live in them and become a part of them. On many occasions I have woken in the morning with the words of a simple Christian song ringing in my ears, largely for the reason I suspect, that I have sung it repetitively in corporate worship. Repetition also enables the Holy Spirit to take God's Word and cause it to live in our human spirit. Others are critical of Vineyard music which has little variation in mood, tempo or key. Yet for many, the simplicity of what has been termed Wimber's 'Adult Orientated Rock Songs' (AOR) which resonate with Radio Two's 25–40s culture has been a major drawing point.

The case has also been made by a number of people that a surfeit of subjective intimacy can engender a strong introversionist trait in religious institutions. Significantly, however, the reverse has been the case with the Vineyard movement which has been among the most outgoing of Christian churches in the contemporary Western world.

Indeed, for all their alleged subjectivity, the Vineyard movement is planting new congregations at a steadily increasing rate and at a greater rate than most churches in the Western world.

As we reflect on the present state of declining church attendance in the UK and the campaign launched in April 1998 to try and attract more people to Sunday worship in the run-up to the millennium, there is much to learn from Wimber's insights and teaching. It is the churches which are fostering worship that is personal, intimate and in John Wimber's style which are growing in numbers and drawing in new people.

2. Power evangelism

Of central importance in Wimber's ministry was the concept of 'power evangelism'. John posed the question why were so few people being drawn to make a Christian commitment as a result of traditional evangelistic campaigning? He drew the conclusion that it was because the hearers needed to see something happening which would reinforce what was being proclaimed. In short, they needed to see 'signs' following the preaching as, for instance, in Mark chapter 16 verses 17–18. Such was the norm in the early church – the preaching of the Kingdom was reinforced by healing the sick and exorcisms. This, as Wimber understood it, was basic to Jesus' ministry. As men and women saw the crooked straightened, the lame walk, the deaf hear and the blind made to see, so the preaching would come to them with a more compelling intensity. In the technical jargon this is 'power evangelism'. Wimber set out his argument in his Study *Manual Signs and Wonders and Church Growth*. Analysing the book of Acts in a detailed chart he demonstrated that there are twenty-seven occasions in which church growth was directly related to signs and wonders. Only in one instance did Luke attribute church growth to preaching alone. John's contention was, therefore, that signs and wonders played a vital and integral part in the early spread of the gospel. 'Has this stopped being the case? Surely NOT!' he retorted.[2]

Various criticisms have been levelled at the 'power evangelism' model, notably by Martin Percy in the published version of his PhD thesis *Words, Wonders and Power* (SPCK, 1996). Percy objected that 'power motifs' and 'power stories' and powerful personalities might be alienating to the sick, the poor, the helpless and the handicapped from the church. Yet it has to be said that the focus of Wimber's concern was to impact those beyond the scope of traditional institutional Christianity. The early 1980s were years in which a 'power motif' had a cultural resonance particularly to those outside the confines of the church. The world was dominated by the super powers and power politics. The talk was of nuclear power, girl power and frequent visitors to the American superstores were designated 'power shoppers'.

Effective power evangelism is dependent on power encounters. These included miraculous healings, the expulsion of demons and overcoming of social injustice and poverty. It is undoubtedly true that 'power healings' are very hard to document and that many are not healed and remain in situations of powerlessness. Nevertheless in response to Percy and others, it has to be said that Wimber's theology was never static and in his later years, perhaps through his own illness, he became more sensitive to the problems of sickness and suffering and how this can be reconciled with a God who is powerful. Nevertheless, most of the churches which have set up healing ministry teams à la John Wimber have seen healings such as they have never seen before. In any case, according to John Wimber's teaching, 'the meat is in the street', God's servants are meant to go out into the market place, the highways and byways to preach the Kingdom and minister healing.

The British, in particular, having grown up in a sceptical environment nurtured by lifeless institutional churches and phenomenological Religious Education teaching in schools have shown themselves to be rather more cynical in regards to power evangelism than their American counterparts. Notwithstanding, several things can be said in response. First, it is hard to deny the strong biblical precedent on which Wimber's 'power evangelism' thesis is posited even if the effect of it doesn't seem to be realised in practice. Paul, for example, came to the Corinthians in 'weakness, fear and much trembling'; yet his message 'was in demonstration of the Spirit's power, so that your faith might not rest on men's wisdom, but in God's power'.[3] The same incidentally could be said of John Wimber, namely that for all his rhetoric on power themes, on a personal level he was a loveable, humble and an outgoing man.

Evangelists do not give up their proclamation of the Christian message simply because people don't respond when an appeal for commitment is made. For the same reason, it seems to me, we shouldn't give up praying for healing because not everyone is healed when prayer is offered. I suspect myself that just as most conversions are a gradual process so a great many healings are also gradual and therefore often hard to verify and quantify. But for all this they are still nevertheless occasions of God's saving power. We should be particularly grateful to John Wimber that notwithstanding all his personal suffering and sickness he has kept the need to pray for the sick as well as to evangelise at the forefront of the agenda.

3. Church planting

John Wimber has been able to demonstrate to the wider churches that planting new congregations is a major route to effective evangelism. His conviction was that an intimate relationship or experience with God will ultimately lead to numerical church growth. More than that it will lead to the establishment of new churches or new church plants.[4] By 1997, there were more than 700 Vineyards worldwide and 49 in England.[5]

Already before Wimber had begun visiting England in the early 1980s, the Restoration house churches were busy establishing church plants in schools, halls and community centres. Their thinking was that the new wine of the Holy Spirit demanded 'new wine skins' to contain it. Many parish clergy felt threatened by the new fledgling congregations which hived off some of their more active members. However, because of his love for the whole church and his friendship with leading Anglican charismatics such as David Pytches, Sandy Millar and Robert Warren, John Wimber began to impact the Church of England in particular with the vision of establishing new plants. A fine example of this has been the setting up of the 'Anglican Church Planting Initiatives' by Bob and Mary Hopkins now based in Sheffield. Sadly, because of the rigidity of the Church of England's outdated system of parochial boundaries much of what has taken place has been somewhat muted and restrained either within the confines of existing parishes or, in the case of Holy Trinity Brompton, the reactivating of redundant churches in the South West London Area. David Pytches did succeed in establishing a number of extra parochial plants and forming the FIAC (Fellowship of Independent Anglican Churches) along with Bishop Brian Skinner in 1992. Also emerging from the same network has come Soul Survivor Youth Church in Watford which was formed in 1995. Through a generous gift from John Wimber, David Pytches was able to establish the Kingdom Power Trust in 1989 which generated the annual summer New Wine Family Conference. This, together with the smaller Lakeside Event, drew in some 9,000 people to the Bath & West showground in the summer of 1997. New Wine Conference has also birthed Soul Survivor, a youth conference under Mike Pilavachi's leadership, which now holds two annual gatherings, either side of New Wine, catering for over 11,000 youth between them and now, like New Wine, reproducing itself across the world. Soul Survivor plan to gather a team of 20,000 youth in Manchester in the year 2000 to evangelise their peers. New Wine has a specific vision to encourage churches in evangelism and ministry in the Holy Spirit. The organisation is now in the process of establishing a series of area networks of churches across the country with the aim of providing support, resourcing and encouragement particularly to isolated churches and fellowships.

Clearly church planting is one of the things God is doing and using at the present moment to reach new people groups. John Wimber's enthusiasm for this method of evangelism has done much to encourage some sections of the historic churches, notably the Church of England, the Baptists and the Methodists, to develop a growing vision for it. However, it is salutary to remind ourselves that the decade of evangelism is rapidly drawing to a close as the new millennium approaches. One can only hope that the British church-es will learn from Wimber's input and launch some major new initiatives to establish creative and alternative church plants on widespread and national scale.

In all of this it is clear that John Wimber was a person who invested in people rather than institutions. He was a man of great generosity who constantly gave away money, people, leaders, skills and spiritual resources. In this he is a role model exemplar for the contemporary church who had learned the Pauline truth that 'whoever sows generously will also reap generously'.[6]

4. Concern for the prophetic

Another of Wimber's significant contributions to the contemporary church has been his concern to take the New Testament injunctions concerning the prophetic with seriousness. His concern to put prophecy higher up on the agenda was first prompted by his encounter with the Kansas City prophets in 1988. He wrote in 1990: 'Prophecy is now assuming centre stage in the Vineyard – as we have done in the past with other moves of God – it is almost all that is talked about'.[7]

Some of Wimber's early encounters with the Kansas City prophets proved controversial. In October 1990, he organised the Dockland Conference in response to Paul Cain's prophecy that 'the first shot (of revival) is going to be fired when John (Wimber) comes to England the next time'.[8] A little later another KCF prophet, Bob Jones, had to be removed from his ministry because of 'serious sin'.[9] Shortly after this, the disgraced Chris Brain, whose Nine O'clock Service (NOS) achieved notoriety in 1996 returned from a meeting with some of the Kansas City prophets and then misused a prophecy which had been spoken to him. He had been informed that a swarm of hornets was surrounding his head and that this represented evil. He decided the hornets were his own leaders and told them that unless they 'sorted themselves out', then the sword of Damocles would come down and kill them. Some of his team became

paranoid that unless they conquered their inner problems they would die.[10]

Inevitably in every aspect of church life precious
gifts will be misused in these kinds of ways and mistakes made. True prophets may not always get things
exactly right but they will have the grace and humility
of a John Wimber to admit their mistakes and, where
necessary, apologise for them. John's concern to foster
prophecy has helped many congregations to develop
wise and dependable prophetic ministries. It has
enabled churches to reflect on key issues of culture and
society from God's perspective. It has also facilitated
congregations to develop a vision and produce specific
mission statements. At a more domestic level many
churches have been encouraged by John Wimber's
teaching to use prophecy in very positive and creative
ways to strengthen, encourage and comfort those who
receive prayer (1 Cor 14:3).

5. 'Doing the stuff'

As we reflect back on John Wimber's life, perhaps one
of his greatest legacies will be seen to have been his
encouragement to Christians to change from being
spectators to participators. His emphasis was one in
which he urged all the people of God to be actively
involved in the ministry of the Holy Spirit. His model
for this ministry was always laid back. Rather than
praying lengthy prayers over people, the Wimber pattern was simply to invite the Holy Spirit to come and
minister to the point of need. Those ministering, always
in pairs, were encouraged to wait, to watch and bless
what God was doing. This form of ministry Wimber
termed 'doing the stuff'.

Often when the Holy Spirit's presence was invoked
in a simple 'Come Holy Spirit' prayer at the end of a
large meeting or in more individual contexts, phenomena, often ecstatic phenomena, would follow. John

Wimber always taught that these outward signs whether trembling, shaking or falling were no proof of the Holy Spirit's working. Significantly the same insistence was made by John Arnott at Toronto who constantly emphasised that the ecstatic phenomena were merely human responses to 'the Father's Blessing' which he believed God was bestowing. Without doubt, these phenomena could represent a mixture of the divine, the human and possibly the enemy.

In some cases, particularly following lengthy periods of gentle worship, this may predispose some to enter beneficially into an altered state of consciousness – a similar state could occur following a period of Gregorian chanting in an ancient cathedral, or indeed any truly beautiful experience which caused one to be 'carried away'. Similar phenomena may be observed following an invocation of the Holy Spirit in a public meeting or in a private place where someone is being prayed for in a small group. This has naturally provoked criticism and evoked some off-the-cuff explanations. 'Simple explanations just will not do,' writes Dr Patrick Dixon, who goes on to say: 'What we are seeing are highly complex phenomena of varying kinds caused by a variety of different factors often mixed together in people of different backgrounds with different expectations, different histories and different personalities.'[11] The actual environment could also be significant. People open up to God more readily in a 'safe' place. Such experiences may cause folk to want to 'rest' in the presence of God, whether prostrated or seated. We have never come across anyone who was 'non compus mentis' and with whom we could not talk easily while in this state, though, of course, one was normally very hesitant to intrude other than to quietly bless whatever God was perceived to be doing.

It may be quite misleading to call this state mildly hypnotic but some questions about such possibilities are serious ones and cannot be thoughtlessly dismissed. But even if in any particular instance it could be proved to be a mild form of hypnosis (something which it would actually be extremely difficult to even begin to do – especially when in any case 'there are no satisfactory definitions of these terms in psychiatry'[12]); there are plenty of Christian doctors who practise hypnotherapy who would not consider such an occurence to be at all dysfunctional. We also know of a large number of pastors with long-term responsibility for those having been so 'over-powered' who have been observing these phenomena in their church membership over several years now. They have witnessed the long-term beneficial results from such experiences when people have been enabled to release 'years of tears', emotional trauma and pain whilst receiving various measures of release and physical healing.

Obviously those laity authorised to pray with folk during the ministry times will first normally need some simple basic training when any kind of manipulation will be totally discouraged as John so plainly did. One of John's values was the dignity of the individuals being ministered to. Their autonomy must always be respected, as exemplified by John in his own meetings and personal ministry. He was also insistent that there be no implication that anyone should have to fall (which the positioning of people designated as catchers might suggest) or, worse still, that anyone in a ministry team should ever physically push the persons being prayed for to make them fall.

John Wimber allowed people to be unafraid, to let go, to cry or to give play to their emotions. As a result of these releases there is a catharsis and sense of well-being through which many thousands have professed to receiving degrees of wholeness and healing. Dr David C. Lewis, a trained social anthropologist from the Universities of Cambridge and Manchester, attended two of the early mid-week conferences on healing at Sheffield (1985) and Harrogate (1986). At Harrogate there were 2,470 people registered and 1,890 returned a detailed questionnaire that Dr Lewis had circulated, probing their experiences, not only of healing but of other phenomena as well. One hundred, chosen randomly, were then followed up six months later by personal in-depth interviews. A computerised analytical model was built and Dr Lewis spent over a year in further scrutinising the data. It was the most thorough analysis of a healing conference ever undertaken. According to Dr Lewis, genuine physical healings were taking place and 'the patterns discerned in the results appeared consistent with the character of God as revealed in the Bible'.[13] Clearly this is an important area which needs more thinking than either John Wimber and indeed the wider church has yet devoted to it. We're living in an era when there seems to be more emotional pain, hurt and sickness than at any time previously. The church is indebted to John Wimber for providing an effective model for prayer ministry which needs to be developed and expanded if it is to meet the needs of the growing numbers of walking wounded.

6. Laid back religion

At the point when John Wimber first arrived in England the charismatic movement was in danger of being hijacked by a vibrant house church movement, particularly by those with emphasis on apostolic covering, shepherding and control. A genuinely 'sectarian' spirit was emerging in which the New Churches appeared to be asserting that their separate restored apostolic five-fold ministry was the only way forward. They were the ones who would restore the Kingdom. Somehow John Wimber with his love for all the churches was able at this critical point in time to bring an irenical influence to bear on the situation. Apostolic leaders such as

Gerald Coates of 'Pioneer', Terry Virgo of 'New Frontiers' and Roger Forster of 'Icthus' soon welcomed Wimber's friendship and his less-intensive laid-back style and approach. In him they found someone who dressed down, avoided using 'religious' language and 'hype' and advocated an open-style church without strict membership lists. Many of their churches were able to embrace Vineyard music, ministry and insights and participate in his conferences. All of this had the result of curbing emerging sectarian spirit and drawing a great many in the British charismatic movement together. Wimber has helped the churches to direct their energies to missioning outside the confines of the church into the market place and the wider world among the poor and the marginalised.

Postscript!

In John Wimber, the church worldwide has witnessed the life and work of one of the most influential Christian leaders of the late twentieth century. A post-graduate student researching gospel and culture recently informed me that almost all the churches which are trying to proclaim the Christian message in a relevant idiom in the late twentieth century are influenced in some degree by Wimber's style. John Wimber was a remarkable teacher who read widely and expounded the Bible with many penetrating new insights. He was a great evangelist, church planter and consultant to leaders in many nations. As Bishop David Pytches observed, there are few others who could organise a conference in any part of the world and regularly attract 2,000 or more delegates. Wimber focused the charismatic church on the importance of the central teaching of Jesus about the Kingdom of God and demonstrated that it was good news, through signs and wonders and works of mercy geared to the poor and the oppressed. Wimber was a model of the man of faith.

He was a risk-taker who was always learning new
lessons which he shared readily with any who would
listen. If the Puritan, Richard Baxter, preached as 'a
dying man to dying men', John Wimber preached as a
learning man to learning men and women. He emphasised the importance of the prophetic and perhaps,
above all, brought a great section of the Christian
church back to the heart of worship which is all about
Jesus.

Notes

1. James 4:7.
2. John Wimber, *Signs and Wonders and Church Growth*
   (VMI, 1984) p 14.
3. I Corinthians 2:4–5.
4. John Wimber, *God's Heart for Expansion 1 and 2* (1980)
   p 209.
5. *Daily Telegraph* 25 January, 1998.
6. 2 Corinthians 9:6.
7. *Renewal* No. 167, 1990 p 5.
8. *Renewal* No. 184, September, 1991.
9. *Renewal* No. 190, March,1992.
10. R. Howard, *Charismania* (London: SPCK, 1997) p 47.
11. Dr Patrick Dixon, *Signs of Revival* (Eastbourne:
    Kingsway, 1994) p 247.
12. Ibid. p 259.
13. See D. Lewis, *Healings: Fiction, Fantasy or Fact?*
    (London: Hodder and Stoughton, 1989).